OXFORD READINGS IN PHILOSOPHY

Series Editor G. J. Warnock

POLITICAL PHILOSOPHY

POLITICAL
PHILOSOPHY

Edited by
ANTHONY QUINTON

OXFORD UNIVERSITY PRESS
1967

© Oxford University Press 1967
Library of Congress Catalogue Card Number: 68-75051
Printed in the United States of America

CONTENTS

INTRODUCTION

1. The nature of the subject

The easiest and most uncontroversial way of defining political philosophy is as the common topic of a series of famous books: Plato's *Republic*, Aristotle's *Politics*, Machiavelli's *Prince*, Hobbes's *Leviathan*, Locke's *Treatises on Civil Government*, Rousseau's *Contrat Social*, Hegel's *Philosophy of Right*, *The Communist Manifesto* and Mill's *Liberty*. Such an enumeration, at any rate, defines a major continuing strand in the history of Western thought, a great tradition of large-scale reflection about politics. But a backward-looking list of this kind is really no longer adequate to define political philosophy as a going concern. What has changed the subject is the great increase in methodological self-consciousness among recent philosophers which has led them to accept a more limited conception of their powers and, in consequence, of their responsibilities.

A comparatively definite place has now been marked out for philosophy within the total range of man's intellectual activities. It is generally thought to stand in a very different relation to other modes of thought from that in which they stand to each other. Where they are substantive, concerned with some aspect or region of the world, it is conceptual and critical, concerned with *them* rather than with the reality they investigate. It should be conceived not as just another mode of thought alongside them but rather as superimposed reflectively on them. Very briefly, philosophy has the task of classifying and analysing the terms, statements and arguments of the substantive, first-order disciplines.

In the light of a conceptual interpretation of philosophy the works that make up the great tradition of political thought are methodologically very impure. They are only to a small, though commonly crucial, extent works of philosophy in the strict sense. Besides conceptual reasonings of the approved sort they contain two main kinds of ingredient. First, there are factual or descriptive accounts of political institutions and activities which may be collected under the general heading of *political science*. Secondly, there are recommendations about the ideal ends that political activity should pursue and about the way political institutions should be designed in order to serve these ends which may be called *ideology*.

A good deal of past political science has been somewhat formal or legalistic; taking the rules which are the professed determinants of the working of political institutions, in particular the formal constitutions of sovereign states, at their face value and dealing only as something of an afterthought with the deviations from these rules that occur in actual practice. A further limiting tendency has been the custom of political science of treating the political life of society as comparatively autonomous. Both of these restrictions have been largely removed by the development of political sociology which investigates political behaviour as it actually occurs and seeks to connect it with the general, non-political life of society, with class-stratification, the economy, religious allegiances and so on.

Both the political-science and ideological components of works in the great tradition of political theory were of high generality. The details of local government or the hierarchical arrangement of courts did not figure in them. Nor did the type of very concrete issue to be found in a pamphlet or leading article about the reform of a particular law or the reconstruction of some part of the whole institutional apparatus. But by current standards they are too all-inclusive to count as works of political philosophy, strictly so-called, and their all-inclusiveness has not been much imitated in recent years.

A sign of this change in the way the subject is conceived has been the apparent petering-out of the great tradition. Surveys of the history of political thought either come to an end with Marx and Mill in the mid-nineteenth century or they wind up with apologetic chapters on the major ideological movements of the most recent period and on the highly engaged, rhetorical and practical thinking of the more articulate political leaders. But an occasional magnificent dinosaur stalks on to the scene, such as Hayek's *Constitution of Liberty*, seemingly impervious to the effects of natural selection.

Analytic philosophers have paid little attention to those problems of political theory that do fall within their recognized field of interest. Russell has been an active political ideologist, and, in his book *Power*, something of a political sociologist, but he has been very explicit about the distinction between his work in these capacities and his work as a philosopher proper. It has been widely held, indeed, that there really is no such subject as political philosophy apart from the negative business of revealing the conceptual errors and methodological misunderstandings of those who have addressed themselves in a very general way to political issues. (For an example of this see Weldon's *Vocabulary of Politics*.) A solid testimony to the width of this conviction has been the near-unanimity with which analytic philosophers have, until very recently, avoided the subject altogether. Of course the great tradition of political thought remains an important object of study in its own right. But to study its members is only marginally to continue the work they were doing. Many teachers of political philosophy are in fact students of the history of very general, theoretical, political ideas. But this no more makes them political philosophers than close attendance at the bull-ring makes an aficionado into a bull-fighter.

The application of philosophical analysis to the fundamental concepts and styles of reasoning that occur in political discourse remains an open possibility. But until very recently the only extended example of it has been the excellent but almost unobtainable *Consent, Freedom and Political Obligation* of J. P. Plamenatz, first published in 1938. In the first sentence of the introduction Plamenatz wrote: 'the purpose of this book is to provide definitions of a number of words generally used by political thinkers'. The publication in 1959 of a substantial general survey of political theory from an analytic point of view, *Social Principles and the Democratic State* by S. I. Benn and R. S. Peters, was a sign of renewed interest and the suggestion has been confirmed by the appearance in 1965 of B. M. Barry's *Political Argument*, perhaps the most uncompromisingly analytic treatment of politics yet published.

The first task of an analytic philosophy of politics is to distinguish the two main varieties of substantive political discourse: the factual statements of political science and the evaluative affirmations of ideology. Few would deny that such a distinction can be drawn, however critical they may be of the reasoning associated with it and the irrationalistic conclusions about valuation that have often been derived from it. Within each of these domains there are characteristic concepts of a very general sort whose application is a matter of frequent dispute. Philosophical analysis, it might be hoped, could help the disputants to a better understanding of each other's positions and even, in some cases, of their own.

The central concept of political science is that of the state. Correlative with the state is law. Positive law must have a state or sovereign as its source and it is the first duty of a state to produce and maintain law. A satisfactory account of the nature of law must trace its complicated relations to morality which serves both to supply law with a content and to be a standard for criticism of it. The traditional natural law theory is an attempt to expound this relationship.

The most general concepts of ideology are those of the major political values which are the more or less commonly recognized ends of government: liberty, justice, security, prosperity and, perhaps, democracy. It is by reference to such ends that particular schemes of political institutions are recommended in preference to others. The central problem of traditional political theory has been a kind of generalized limiting case of the problem of justifying a particular institutional scheme. This is the problem of political obligation which is that of why, or under what circumstances, an individual should obey any state at all, acknowledge any obligation to obey those who seek to determine what he shall do, attribute any authority to those who claim to be his rulers.

A theory of political obligation, by giving a rational answer to the question 'why should I obey the state', must inevitably, it might seem, be ideology rather than analysis. But analysis can at least be used to examine the *form* of arguments purporting to justify the state. Equally ideological must be the endorsement of any major political value or ideal as an end which governments ought to pursue. As it turns out analysis and justification are harder to keep apart than formal methodology might suggest, here even more than in other parts of philosophy. Concepts of political ends are what have been called essentially contested concepts (cf. W. B. Gallie in *Proceedings of the Aristotelian Society*, 1955–61, pp. 167–98). The adherents of competing ideologies try to interpret terms such as *liberty* and *justice* in such a way that they apply to the realization of their own ideals. The methodological aim of a strictly neutral analysis of political terms, even of the most general terms of political science, is hard to realize in practice if the results are not to be trivial.

Some have argued, in the spirit of Popper's remark that if the Soviet Union is a democracy then he is against democracy, that the words in which political discussion is carried on do not matter and that a political philosophy which regards the clarification of political terms as its main task must thus be a waste of time and energy. This view is, I think, doubtly mistaken. In the first place disputes that have some ultimately verbal element are extremely influential. Furthermore the verbal element in disputes is not generally so easy to identify and dismiss as the Popperian example might suggest. And even in that example the dispute is not merely verbal. Adherents of both liberal and communist conceptions of democracy would agree that any adequate conception of it must start from the notion of government by the people. They disagree on the extent to which their competing views are better adjusted to this basic and agreed requirement.

The first two selections in this anthology are of the same broadly methodological character as this section of the introduction. Mr Plamenatz defends a moderately traditional view of the nature of political theory which he defines as systematic thinking about the purposes of government. Professor Partridge argues that analysis cannot be kept wholly free from all ideological taint.

2. The state, law and morality

In the second of his *Treatises on Civil Government* Locke introduces something that he calls the executive power of the law of nature. It has three parts: the legislative power of deciding what the correct rules of conduct are, the judicial power of applying these rules to particular pieces of conduct and the penal power of administering sanctions to those who have broken the rules. The function of this moderately complicated idea in his theory is, in effect, to define the concept of the state and, by implication, of the political generally. For it is by the transfer of this executive power from free, natural individuals to a common sovereign that a natural society is turned into a civil, or politically organized, society.

It is not necessary to suppose that the transformation of natural into civil society was brought about by some historically identifiable act of transfer to find Locke's notion a useful one. The executive power of the law of nature can be used to distinguish political societies, as those in which it is formally centralized, from non-political ones, in which it is informally distributed amongst all individuals. There are two significant implications of this use of the idea. The first is that it identifies the essential functions of the state as those of maintaining law and order, the second that it sees them as the responsibility of a state to the extent that they are not left to individuals to exercise for themselves but are remitted to a special person or set of people within the society as a whole. To see the preservation of law and order as the essential function of the state is not to regard it as the state's only function. Nor is it to say that a state could survive in practice if that was all it did. The defence of societies from their external enemies is as ancient and important a function of states as their defence from internal ones. Nor does the requirement of centralization strictly imply that government is, of necessity, oligarchical, though, in fact, no doubt, all governments have been. But even in the most direct and Rousseau-like of democracies there would be a distinction between the weekly meeting during which for an hour or two the citizens were acting in their sovereign capacity as legislators and judges and the remainder of the week during which they would obey, or disobey, the rules they had themselves laid down.

Two more recent definitions presuppose the Lockean concept of the state but significantly extend it. The first of these is Austin's well-known definition of sovereignty. A sovereign, according to Austin, is a determinate human superior, not in a habit of obedience to a like superior, who receives habitual obedience from the bulk of a given society. Austin defines law as the command of a sovereign so conceived. Secondly there is Max Weber's definition of the state. 'A compulsory political association with continuing organization' he says 'will be called a state if and in so far as its administrative staff successfully upholds a claim to the monopoly of the legitimate use of physical force in the enforcement of its order'. Both Austin and Weber hold that a large measure of effectiveness in imposing its rules is necessary to a state. Weber adds that the means by which this effectiveness is secured is wielding the only physical force that is generally recognized as legitimate.

Putting these definitions together we may say that a society is political, or has a state, if it contains a centralized agency for the promulgation, application and enforcement of rules of conduct, if these rules are generally obeyed and if only these rules are generally recognized as legitimately sanctioned by physical force.

One point of these definitions is to distinguish the state conceived as a politically organized society, as when we speak of nation-states, from the state conceived as the rule-enforcing element within such a society. If a society has a state within it in the second sense, then it is a state in the first sense. In colloquial terms a country is one thing, a government another, but what makes a collection of people into a country is the fact that they all have the same government. We can speak of nations that are not politically organized societies. Nationalism is an endeavour to make states and nations coincide, initiated in circumstances where they do not. We tend to think of the government as more particularly the executive or administrative arm of the state as a whole. It remains important to distinguish state from society just because some thinkers have striven energetically to obliterate the difference between them. A society is a collection of people who interact, persistently and in characteristically human ways, cooperating and communicating with each other. A society will persist only if there are generally accepted rules of conduct but these need not be defined and enforced by any centralized agency. At any rate social rules do not logically entail a state even if they practically require one in most circumstances.

Anarchism is not a self-contradiction, but at worst impracticable or intolerable.

Law, in the most ordinary sense of the word, is a product of the sovereign state. Theories of sovereignty can be understood as presenting criteria with which to decide about the rules prevailing in a society which are laws proper, as contrasted with the private regulations of a club, a family or a firm on the one hand and the prescriptions of morality on the other. A familiar tradition in political theory distinguishes law in this sense as positive law from natural law. Many theorists who derive political obligation from a contract, most notably Locke, maintain that what in the end justifies obedience to the state is its protection of the rights possessed by individuals under natural law. Some adherents of natural law have gone further, saying that if a rule is in conflict with natural law it cannot be a positive law at all; but perhaps their point could be less extravagantly made by regarding an enactment contrary to natural law as giving a reason for withholding obedience from the state responsible which may be overridden by reasons for the opposite course.

One origin for the doctrine of natural law is the idea that God stands to mankind at large in the relation of a monarch to his subjects. The same analogy can, however, be turned upside down, as in the doctrine of the divine right of kings, to show that there are no limits to the rights of monarchs. The comparable relation of a father to his children is ambiguous in the same way in its implications. It can be used as a natural model for the right ordering of states but it can also be exploited to argue that fathers, like sovereigns, owe their right to obedience to the services they perform for those who obey them.

In an age like the present, with its apparently irreducible plurality of conflicting moral beliefs, the doctrine of natural law has lost much of its appeal. But there is a minimum interpretation in which only those who take the service of the state to be the highest conceivable duty for man could possibly reject it. It can be taken to say simply that there are moral considerations by which the state's claim to authority must be judged. Unless one holds with Hegel that private morality is a crude, primitive anticipation of the higher morality of positive law or, attaching no meaning to moral discourse, abstains from it altogether, one cannot consistently oppose this position.

A feature of natural law doctrine that has been much objected to, notably by Bentham, is its claim that there are *imprescriptible* natural rights, rights possessed by all men whose infringement by the state strictly entails the forfeiture of the state's authority. Utilitarians deny that any specific moral principle is absolutely and unqualifiedly valid in the way that this kind of natural right is held to be. They would say that to ascribe a right to a man is to say that there is something that he ought to be allowed to do. A right is natural if it is moral and not positively conferred by a state. Now what people ought to be allowed to do varies with the circumstances. It is always possible to conceive circumstances in which it would be morally reasonable, in the best interests of all concerned, to abridge freedom of speech or movement or occupation.

Some analytic philosophers have made curiously heavy weather of the word 'natural' in the phrase 'natural rights', taking it to imply that the possession of these rights is deducible from the nature of man. The nature of man is the set of defining characteristics in virtue of having which things are identified as being men. These characteristics are in fact empirical and so no conclusions about what men ought to be allowed to do can be extricated from the concept itself. This is rather laborious. 'Natural' here means simply 'non-legal'. Natural rights are those which men have by reason of being men and not in virtue of their membership in a particular politically organized society with its prevailing system of legal rights.

In practice there is a good deal of correspondence between the content of positive law and natural law, if this is understood as the broad moral consensus of the citizens. Unless the state in question is very efficiently tyrannous, indeed, there must be, since if a state's positive law is morally repugnant to most of its citizens they will have a reason for disobeying it and in doing so they will remove the effectiveness which is one of the state's essential characteristics.

But there is always some divergence between positive law and the generally accepted hard core of morality. In the first place much of the moral consensus cannot be or need not be or should not be legally enforced. It cannot be enforced if offences are very hard to detect (for example, indulgence in sadistic fantasy). It need not be if the informal sanctions of morality are sufficient to maintain good behaviour (for example, ordinary politeness). It should not be if the type of conduct involved derives most or all of its value from the fact that it is freely undertaken.

Secondly, positive law needs, for a number of reasons, to be very precise, something seldom true of the moral consensus. Thirdly, since positive law needs to be stable it cannot be adjusted to correspond with every apparent shift of the moral consensus. It follows that it will be slow to adjust itself to real shifts. A final point is that the most generally interesting decisions and regulations of modern states concern issues of a broadly economically distributive kind which do not fall clearly within the moral concensus. The main political divisions of a modern industrial society concern the proportion of the national income that shall be taken and spent by the state and the objects on which it should be spent. Complex conflicts of justice and efficiency, of benevolence and personal freedom arise here which are the main topic of everyday political controversy. One virtue of democratic systems is that they provide machinery for the resolution of these conflicts of interest and principle by pacificatory compromise and without resort to violence.

Two items in this anthology deal with subjects discussed in this section. Professor Hart argues that the existence of at least one natural right must be admitted if it is allowed that there are any moral rights at all. Mr Benn conducts a wide survey of the uses to which the concept of sovereignty has been put.

3 . Political obligation

The problem of political obligation—why should I, or anyone, obey the state—has always been the fundamental problem of political philosophy. The question it raises must be distinguished from two others with which it can easily be confused and it is also somewhat ambiguous itself. First, to ask why I *should* obey the state is not to ask why I *do*, though one answer to the latter question (viz. because I think I ought to) raises the former. People obey governments and abide by the law to a very great extent, no doubt, from force of habit and because it does not often occur to them to do anything else. When the possibility of disobedience does occur to them, in cases where there is an obvious clash between the demands of the state and private interests or moral conviction, they are restrained by fear of the probable consequences of disobedience. But people may also be prompted to obey the state by the conviction that they are morally obliged to do so. To inquire into the justification of this belief is to confront the problem of political obligation.

The other question with which that of the justification of obedience is often confused is that of how the state and its laws came into existence in the first place. The two issues look so very different at first glance that it may be hard to understand how they can ever have been run together. One explanation is that many obligations arise from something that has happened in the past: from a positive undertaking, for example, as in a marriage ceremony, or from the coming into existence of a particular state of affairs, as when a man recognizes his responsibility for injuries caused by his carelessness or for children brought into the world by his sexual activities.

A related point, emphasized by Hume, is that people generally regard prescription or customary acceptance as the solidest foundation of a right, though this may be less true now than it was in the eighteenth century. Another consideration is that when the state was created, if there ever was such a moment, the question of whether to obey was a live issue for everyone involved. More generally the confusion between the two questions is assisted by the habit of describing the problem of political obligation as concerned with the *origins* or *foundations* of the state, a mode of expression which can be interpreted historically or justificatorily. At any rate the two questions are entirely distinct. As Hume argued, even if the first states did originate in a contractual agreement between their members this has no bearing on our situation now: we do not inherit our ancestors' promissory obligations, and the states we live under originated for the most part in violent seizure of power.

With the question why I should obey the state extricated from others with which it may be confused, we can go on to consider what precisely it means. It has usually been taken to ask how it is that I am under a *moral obligation* to obey the state. But this is not the only meaning it can have, nor is it the most fruitful one. Morality, strictly so called, has no proprietary hold over the word 'ought'. We can also ask what makes it reasonable, sensible or prudent for me to obey the state. This goes to the opposite extreme from the narrowly moral interpretation of the question and might seem to invite only such obvious and un-illuminating answers as that I am likely to be sent to prison if I do not obey. But between the two extremes there is a third possibility. We may ask: what makes it a generally good or desirable thing for me, or anyone, to obey the state? Here the rationality of political obedience is identified neither with its moral obligatoriness nor with its con-duciveness to strictly personal interest and advantage. A great deal of what we ought to do is reasonable in this sense without being either morally obligatory or immediately advantageous.

There are three main kinds of solution to the problem of political obligation. First, there are what I shall call intrinsic theories, which derive the rationality or obligatoriness of obedience from the intrinsic character of the state. Secondly, at the other extreme, are extrinsic theories, which justify the state by reference, direct or indirect, to the purposes it serves, to the valuable consequences which flow from its possession of effective power. Finally, there are organic theories, which transform the problem by arguing that it implies a mistaken, 'abstract' conception of the relations between the state and the individual citizen.

The simplest of intrinsic theories is *traditionalism*, the view that the state ought to be obeyed because it always has been, Hume's prescription in its most elementary form. A historically important variant is the *divine right* theory which holds that we should obey the state because God has commanded us to do so. The theory of divine right can take a legitimist form, in which the criterion of divine authorization is something other than the possession of effective power, or it can be conformist, enjoining obedience to the powers that be whoever they are and however they acquired their position.

A more intellectually appetizing kind of intrinsic theory is the doctrine of *aristocracy*, which attributes intrinsic authority to the best people, picked out by their wisdom, ancient lineage, heroic qualities (as in fascism) or even wealth. In practice intrinsic theories soon lose their formal purity since any rational argument to justify obedience to traditional rulers, or to the best people, must rest on the pre-eminent capacity of the recommended rulers for realizing ends desired or valued by those called upon to obey them. This fate of intrinsic theories shows their affinity to deontological accounts of morally right action, which are liable to the same loss of identity. According to the deontologist such moral principles of right action as that one should keep promises or tell the truth are self-evident to the moral intelligence. They do not need justification in terms of the valuable results of general adherence to them and are only harmed and enfeebled if such justification is attempted. They do not need it since they retain their validity in cases where good results do not accrue: one should keep a promise even though no-one will be better off for one's doing so. If such principles are made dependent on the production of good consequences, it is argued, morality is degraded into calculating expediency. But few deontologists are brazen enough to insist that a trivial promise should be kept whatever happens, that one should leave someone drowning in a lonely spot to his fate in order to make a promised appearance at a tea-party. A rigidly deontological theory of political obligation, one that holds the principle that one should obey the state to be simply a self-evident truth, is conceivable. But this will not be very plausible unless 'state' is redefined in terms which guarantee that only rulers who rule well qualify for the description.

Extrinsic theories are the political correlates of teleological accounts of morally right action which define a right action as one from which it is reasonable to expect good consequences. In the doctrine of the *social contract*, the most famous of extrinsic theories, the connexion between obligation and good consequences is indirect. According to the contractarian I ought to obey the state because I have somehow promised or undertaken to do so. But the commitment from which my obligation arises is not conceived as arbitrary, purposeless and unconditional. It is entered into for the sake of some ultimate end (for example, security in Hobbes's version, the protection of natural rights in Locke's). Its binding force is conditional on the effectiveness of the state in realizing the end in question. For this reason a contract theory can never be absolutist. It cannot, in the manner of some intrinsic theories, assign unlimited authority to the state. Political obligation may always lapse and the state's authority be forfeited if the conditions of the contract are not satisfied.

Two main objections to the contract theory should be mentioned. First, since most people give no explicit undertaking to obey the state, there is a difficulty about identifying the thing they do which is to be interpreted as their making an implicit promise to obey. There is a dilemma here. If the supposedly contractual act is not voluntary, such as passively benefiting from the protection of the armed forces, it cannot be regarded as a promise. If it is voluntary, such as voting in an election, failure to perform it is not generally recognized as relieving a man from his obligations as a citizen. Secondly, there is Hume's favourite objection that the good ends for which the promise was made are sufficient to justify obedience to the state by themselves and without the intermediary of a highly speculative act of moral commitment. This leads to the conceptually more economical view of *utilitarianism*, that obedience to the state is justified on directly teleological grounds as a necessary condition of the general welfare, the advantage of society at large.

The *organic theory* of political obligation is implied by the doctrine of a general or real will advanced by Rousseau and Hegel. The theories considered so far, intrinsic and extrinsic, conceive the fundamental political situation as one in which some men, the citizens, are seen as quite distinct from and wholly subordinate to others, the state. This, the organic theorist maintains, is at any rate unnecessary and undesirable and perhaps, metaphysically considered, is an illusion. In any properly constituted political system, perhaps in any effectively functioning·one, the state is or represents the better selves of the citizens, their real, general, impersonal, moral will as contrasted with their private, particular, irrationally self-regarding will. In a political system so conceived the citizens in obeying the state are following the promptings of their real or better natures, subjecting their irrational and self-interested passions to the control of their social and moral reason. Rousseau thought that an organic and genuinely obligatory political system was hard to attain, possible only in communities with small populations and directly democratic institutions. Hegel believed that it was approximated to in every effective state, to the extent at least that it was historically possible that it should be. Rousseau's hyperdemocratic ideal seems as impossible of achievement as Hegel's bland redescription of the facts of political life seems unrealistically complacent.

The analytic philosopher of politics does not give the general problem of political obligation so central a place in the subject as his traditional predecessors. It has the merit of raising conceptual questions about arguments designed to establish the rightness of action and of drawing attention to the difference between power, the ability to secure obedience, and authority, the right to expect it. But of more interest than the problem they have in common are the different values which theorists of political obligation, to the extent that their reasoning is teleological, see it as the state's justifying function to serve. The problem of political obligation represents the citizen as confronted by a single absolute choice between obedience and resistance, between conformity and treason. Even in the least democratic societies the scope of an individual's political action is seldom so brutally circumscribed. Whether or not he has the formal right to vote, to organize political associations and to convert others to his way of thinking, he will have many means at his disposal for bringing pressure to bear on the government, its acts, its composition, its institutional form. The values that are relevant to the ultimate choice between submission and rebellion are also relevant to a much more extensive range of political choices. It is more profitable to consider the ends of government on their own, detached from their traditional involvement with a single extreme issue of political action.

The selections in this anthology from Professor Peters and Mr Winch make up a debate about the correct interpretation of the concept of authority which it is the aim of theories of political obligation to explain. The paper by Mr Barry, in defending the concept of the public interest, considers issues raised by Rousseau's notion of the general will.

4. The ends of government

An ideology prescribes ends for government. It lays down certain ends as those to be pursued through political activity and through political institutions. The simplest kind of ideology describes an ideal society or utopia in which the ideologist's values are fully realized. Here the ideological aim is quite explicit. At the other extreme a theory of political obligation can serve an ideological purpose more indirectly. In it the preferred ends will appear as necessary conditions for justifying the state's authority.

There are objections to both procedures. Utopias, concentrating on the long-range goal of political endeavour, neglect the problems that arise about getting to the destination. Not all of these problems are practical. The realization of one part of the ideal may bring unexpected results in its train which obstruct the realization of the remainder. One ideological defect of theories of political obligation was pointed out at the end of the last section. The scope of an individual's political action is not confined to deciding whether or not to obey the state. He can usually bring some influence to bear on its selection of policies, its composition and its institutional form, even in societies that are not formally democratic. Another defect is that the essential conditions of political obligation, though they will be included in one's ideals, are not usually wholly coincident with them. Only if I take the wildly extreme position of refusing to admit an obligation to obey any government but a wholly ideal one will the conditions of political obligation and the principles of political action in general be identical.

The first task of the political philosopher in this field, and on one view his whole responsibility there, is to clarify the concepts of political ends. In the light of such a clarification he can critically examine the arguments that are used to support the choice of political ends. The conflicting conceptions that prevail of the political ends he is concerned with express ideological disagreements and this makes it hard to operate with strict neutrality and detachment. Opposing ideologists try to pre-empt words like *liberty*, *justice* and *democracy* for the type of political arrangement they favour. The political philosopher can keep himself from being embroiled only if he confines himself to articulating the way in which different ideological groups use the terms in which they proclaim their ideals.

A plain example of this kind of ideological competition over a concept is provided by liberty. The negative conception of liberty favoured by liberal individualists is repudiated by collectivists in the interests of positive liberty. Negative liberty is absence of interference by states, groups or individuals with the activities of individual men. For interference to be an infringement of liberty it must be directed against activities those interfered with actually want to carry out, it must be intended to have this effect and it must work through disincentives serious enough to be proper objects of fear. Positive liberty, being commonly defined as the ability to do what I *really* want to do, turns out to be very much like my ability to do what I ideally ought to want to do. The conflict is not resolved by simply giving different names to the two kinds of liberty and recognizing that one party favours the one and its opponents the other. For both parties agree that liberty ultimately consists in being able to do what you want to do. But they disagree as to what this is and about how we are to find out what it is.

There is a similar distinction between competing concepts of democracy. Here, however, it is the positive conception that is the more traditional: the view of Rousseau that a state is democratic to the extent that its acts express the common will of its citizens. The opposite view conceives democracy as a peaceful way of getting rid of governments with which the majority of the citizens are dissatisfied rather than as a means for the direct realization of their political aims. Both parties agree that democracy is in some sense government *by* the people. As for the rest of Lincoln's formula: all government claims to be *for* the people and all government is *of* the people—of whom else could it be?) They disagree about how this agreed purpose is best brought about.

There is some slight analogy between these opposed views of liberty and democracy and two views about the nature of justice. The negative view would be that the state ought not to treat its citizens differently unless there is some relevant difference between them. Its positive opposite number is that the state should seek to eliminate or compensate for the natural inequalities of advantage that there are amongst them. It could be argued that there is no real difference here, since what one side sees as a natural inequality which the state ought to do something about the other side could recognize as a relevant difference justifying difference of treatment.

The most elementary form of justice is the impartial administration of the law. This can be represented as a kind of equality since it involves no account being taken in the judicial treatment of citizens of those differences between them that are not mentioned in the law itself. But laws that are justly administered can still be unjust in themselves if the differences of judicial treatment they prescribe are in some way unreasonable. While few would deny that equality is one principle, perhaps the fundamental principle, of justice, few would maintain that it is the whole of justice. The principle of equal treatment must be qualified by the recognition that people have different needs and, because of the services they have done, different deserts. Justice might seem to be the most comprehensive of political ends, with the possible exception of the common good, but on any definition it can come into collision with other widely shared values. Unequal distribution of income or property may be defended on the ground that it promotes general economic welfare. By according privileges to a naturally well-endowed minority it calls forth specially productive effort. Those who favour the maintenance of some productive inequalities—and there are, as the practice of professedly egalitarian societies suggests, few who would wish to exclude them altogether—are reluctant to say they approve a measure of injustice, But in this they are perhaps as unreasonable as those who find it hard to admit that the penal institutions of society are designed to reduce the liberty of evildoers.

Everyone agrees that it is an essential function of the state to preserve the security of its citizens. Hobbes held its preservation by a sovereign to be the sufficient condition of justified obedience to him, thus placing it above all other political values. Later political theorists have taken a less gloomy view of the costs of achieving it and have been prepared to accept some risk to security for the sake of other political ends. The general agreement there is about it accounts for the fact that it poses no serious conceptual problems.

One political value that has not yet been mentioned has had a very large influence on the course of political history but is seldom emphasized in works of political theory. This is prosperity. In so far as it does occur in theory it is as a slightly embarrassing aspect of the common good. No doubt its somewhat unspiritual character is responsible for this neglect. Until fairly recent times governments have taken no very direct part in its pursuit. They have confined themselves to legal regulation of the conditions of economic activity by controlling the currency, levying customs duties, limiting hours of work, granting monopolies and so forth. Only in the last century have they undertaken the direct management of productive enterprises and, as a result of more extensive economic knowledge, taken up the positive planning of the economy. The explicit ideological motive for much of this extension of the state's control of economic life has been socialistic, and has been based on considerations of justice rather than of prosperity. A major problem here is to determine how large a part of the common good material prosperity is. The ideology of laisser-faire maintains that the common good will be most fully realized in a society with a freely competitive economic system. But the economic theory on which this ideology is based includes the concept of social cost which applies to deprivations inflicted on the community by the competitive pursuit of wealth which the market mechanism does not correct.

The simplest way of recommending a political value is to assert that men have a self-evident natural right that it should be secured to them. The doctrine of axiomatic natural laws drew much of its appeal from its connexion with the idea that the principles of morality are divine commands. With the recession of that idea arguments of a teleological kind have come to be generally relied on. In some cases these arguments are utilitarian in the narrow, traditional sense. Such is the inference that liberty is good because the kind of restraint in whose absence it consists is unpleasant. On the other hand, in his famous defence of liberty John Stuart Mill, a professed utilitarian, recommended it as the indispensable condition for the discovery of new truths and the preservation of old ones, without stopping to consider the bearing of truth on utility in the sense of happiness.

Political theorists have very often fastened on one political end or other as supremely valuable and have argued that everything a reasonable man would consider good will be achieved by its pursuit. In doing so they have been led to extend the concept of their prime value so that it covers things far outside the original field of its application. Socialists have represented poverty as a kind of unfreedom while conservatives have objected to limitations of the privileges of wealth as cases of injustice. But there is no need to assume that all political ends are ultimately identical, that in pursuing any of them to the limit we must in the end realize all the others. It certainly seems that there are direct conflicts between them. Liberty and equality are often at odds with one another, as are liberty and security, or prosperity and justice. If the concepts of political ends are clearly articulated and understood, an effective kind of rational discussion about them is possible which has no real point if they are all so stretched that they run into one another.

Four of the selections of this anthology concern the ends of government. Professor Berlin discusses positive and negative conceptions of liberty, Professor Schumpeter positive and negative conceptions of democracy. Mr Carritt examines the relations, and particularly the tensions, between liberty and equality, as Mr Barry does in the cases of justice and the common good.

I

THE USE OF POLITICAL THEORY[1]

JOHN PLAMENATZ

I

EVEN IN OXFORD, which more perhaps than any other place in the English-speaking world is the home of political theory or philosophy, it is often said that the subject is dead or sadly diminished in importance. I happen to have a professional interest in assuming that it is still alive, and as likely to remain so as any other subject as long as man continues to be a speculative and enterprising animal. I do not think I am biased; I do not think I need to be. The importance of the subject seems to me so obvious, and the reasons for questioning that importance so muddled, that I do not look upon myself as defending a lost or difficult cause. Political philosophy is dead, I have heard men say, killed by the logical positivists and their successors who have shown that many of the problems which exercised the great political thinkers of the past were spurious, resting on confusions of thought and the misuse of language. Apply the solvent of linguistic analysis to these pretentious systems, they say, and when the dross has melted away, little that is valuable remains. I think that this is a mistake, and I want to explain why I think so.

I admit that the great political thinkers have raised many spurious problems, that they have been confused and have misused language. I believe that those who study their theories ought to subject them to close and rigorous criticism. I believe that they made many mistakes; but I do not believe that they were mistaken in trying to do what they did. I do not believe that the progress of science and philosophy has left no room for their kind of activity.

By political theory I do not mean explanations of how governments function; I mean systematic thinking about the purposes of government. Perhaps it would be better to speak of political philosophy rather than of political theory, keeping the second expression for what

From *Political Studies*, Vol. 8 (Clarendon Press, 1960) pp. 37–47. Reprinted by permission of the author and the Clarendon Press.

[1] This article is based on a lecture given at the University of Exeter on 13 March 1959.

purport to be explanations of the facts. If I have not done this, it is because the word philosophy is nowadays used in a narrower sense than it used to be, especially in English-speaking countries. The political theory that I wish to speak about is emphatically not linguistic analysis. It is a form of practical philosophy; it is practical philosophy as it relates to government. I want to argue that it is a serious and difficult intellectual activity, and that the need for it, in modern times, is as great as ever it was—indeed much greater. It is not a need which disappears with the progress of science (and especially of the social sciences), and is in no way weakened by the achievements of contemporary philosophy.

It is not a less urgent need than it was; it is only a need less easily satisfied.

II

The belief that political theory or philosophy is dead rests on several misconceptions.

1. In the past, political theory has often been a mixture of two activities: it has sought to explain how government functions or how it arose or why it is obeyed, and it has also put forward opinions about what government should aim at and how it should be organized to achieve those aims. These two quite different activities have not always been kept distinct. Indeed, the Utilitarians were among the first to insist that they ought to be so kept, though they did not always take their own advice. Both these activities are useful. But, for reasons which are not far to seek, the fact that they have so often been confused has brought discredit on one of them much more than on the other. In this scientific age, the explanation of what actually happens is always respectable. We must have theories about how this or that form of government functions; we must even have theories about government in general, we must take notice of what is common to all forms of government. These are all theories that can be verified; they are attempts, more or less successful, to extend our knowledge. But, it is said, theories about what government should aim at and how it should be organized do not extend our knowledge; they merely express preferences, while pretending to do much more. They vary from age to age, from country to country, from party to party, from person to person. It is conceded that they affect action and that therefore we need to know what they are and how they arise. But it is also taken for granted that what they are matters less than how they affect men's behaviour; that it is more important to inquire into

their origins and consequences than to study them for their own sake. They have to be studied because people have in fact taken them seriously and been influenced by them, but reasonable men can do without them.

There has been in recent times some resentment of, and contempt for, political philosophy. It is said of it that it not only pretends to give us knowledge but also stands in the way of our getting it. Durkheim, in his *Rules of Sociological Method*, argued that political theorists, in order to reach the conclusions they want to reach, define the terms they use in such a way as to make it seem to follow from their definitions of the state or of law or even of human nature that government should aim at this rather than that and should be organized in one way rather than another. Political theorists, it is said, have produced concepts which stand in the way of a scientific explanation of the facts because their real (though unacknowledged) function is to justify what the theorists happen to think desirable.

It is certainly true that political theory or philosophy does not produce the same kind of knowledge as political science, and it is also true that it has stood in the way of political science.[1] But even if political philosophy has stood in the way of political science, that is no reason for dismissing it as fantasy or the mere airing of preferences. It is only a reason for distinguishing it from intellectual activities of other kinds.

2. What has gone by the name of political philosophy in the past has been shown to be remarkably confused. This has caused some people impressed by the confusion to speak as if what the political thinkers of the past attempted were not worth doing, and as if the only useful function of political philosophy were to dissipate confusion. Political philosophy, they say, is properly the analysis of political concepts.

I do not deny the need for this analysis, and though I should wish to use the expression *political philosophy* in a wider sense, I do not quarrel with its being used thus narrowly. But if this is to be called political philosophy, there still remains another intellectual activity, which is neither political science nor political philosophy, which is more important than the second and not less important than the first, and which is likely to endure when political philosophy, in this narrow sense, has lost what importance it now has. I should not wish to

---

[1] I think this second charge exaggerated: I suspect that it was much more ignorance than the failure to distinguish between explanation and advocacy which impeded the progress of political science. But I am not concerned to argue this point.

quarrel about names. If, for instance, Mr. Weldon had wanted to do no more than make a narrow use of the expression *political philosophy*, I should neither have followed his example nor condemned him for trying to set it. But I suspect that he wanted to do more than this; I suspect that he wanted to suggest that, apart from political philosophy, as he understood and practised it, and political science, there was nothing important, difficult, and useful to be done by rigorous and systematic theorists in the field of politics.

Political philosophy, understood in Mr. Weldon's sense, is not likely to remain important for long. At the moment, because political thinkers still use ambiguous concepts, the careful analysis of these concepts is still needed to show that many traditional problems are spurious, arising only because the men who put them have fallen victims to the confusions and intricacies of language. Since these concepts are often borrowed from, or shared with, other studies traditionally known as philosophy, the philosopher is better placed than other people to show how they generate spurious problems. This is an important service which the philosopher, in the narrow sense, can still do for the student of politics. But those who practise this kind of political philosophy should notice their own limitations. When they show us what confusions of thought there are in Rousseau's doctrine of the general will or in Hegel's doctrine of the state, we have cause to be grateful to them. They see the nonsense in these doctrines, and they explain what makes it nonsense. So far their work is useful. If, however, they go further, they risk doing harm. They are too ready to assume that where they have seen nonsense there is no sense which they have not seen. Just as it takes some skill in linguistic analysis to see the nonsense in Rousseau, so perhaps it takes some knowledge of sociology and psychology to see the sense in him.

The philosopher in this narrow sense already does no service to the natural scientist. He studies scientific method as the scientist does not study it; and there is therefore a sense in which he understands what the scientist does better than the scientist himself understands it. He knows better than the natural scientist how science differs from other kinds of intellectual activity. Yet he has nothing to teach the scientist, for what he knows about science that the scientist does not know is not knowledge needed to make a good scientist. The philosopher does not help the natural scientist to either his ideas or his methods. And so it will eventually be with the political scientist; the time will come when he will need no more help from the analytical philosopher. He needs him, even now, only to rescue him from confusions of thought; he does not need him, any more than the natural scientist does, to produce the ideas he uses to explain the events he studies.

3. The great variety of theories about what government should aim at and how it should be organized has discredited these theories. It is said of them that they do no more than expound the preferences of their makers, and that in any case they are socially determined.

I do not see the force of these objections. What does the variety of these theories prove about them? That they are not true? But if they expound preferences, the objection is out of place. It is unreasonable to argue that they are not scientific, and then to object to them that they are not true. They are neither true nor false.

Does the variety of these theories prove them unimportant? In just what sense? Will anyone deny that they have had a large influence on the course of history? The fact that they have not served as blue-prints for the reconstruction of society is no evidence that they have not been important. They have powerfully affected men's images of themselves and of society, and have profoundly influenced their behaviour.

Does the variety of these theories prove that we no longer need them? I do not see that it does. What are we to have in their place? Political science? But its function is not the same. It does not attempt what these theories attempt. Why then should it supersede them? And we can say the same of political philosophy as Mr. Weldon understood it. Its function is different. It does not satisfy the same need. And just as political science and the analysis of political concepts do not satisfy this need, so they do not remove it. It is still there, no matter how active and successful they may be.

Are these theories unimportant because they are socially determined? The production of such theories is an activity of man in society, and is therefore affected by his other social activities. All social activities limit one another. What men can do or even imagine in one direction is limited and affected by what they can do and imagine in other directions. We may agree that a theory like Marxism could not have been produced in the Dark Ages. But then neither could the steam engine have been produced then. The feasible and the imaginable are limited by the actual. This is as true of industry and science as of political theory.

We soon get into difficulties if, like Marx, we treat political theory as of secondary importance. Marx called it a form of ideology or false consciousness, contrasting it with science, which gives us real knowledge; and he looked forward to the day when we should have true social science and be able to dispense with ideology. Yet he could not help attributing great importance to ideology. A class, to be politically effective, must have an ideology; and unless it is politically effective it has no active role to play in history. Ideology is illusion, and yet, unless men had these illusions, the course of social evolution would not be what it is.

We have here an example of a type of simple and false reasoning to which many people—and sometimes even philosophers—are still prone. They show that one kind of theory is mistaken by its producers for another kind, and then conclude that the second kind supersedes the first. Marx's version of it is this: the makers of ideology mistake it for science, and therefore when science shall have come into its own, there will be no room for ideology.

Marx made one kind of mistake, Burke made another. He thought that political theory, except when it justifies the established order is harmful. That, at least, is to admit its importance. Yet Burke, because he did not see clearly the function of political theory, mis- understood the French revolution. He saw the revolution as a disaster caused by people's being misled by the philosophers. Its immediate cause was that the unprivileged classes were making new claims on society, claims which could not be met unless society was greatly changed. The philosophers did not create the conditions that disposed the unprivileged to make these claims; their task was rather to formulate the claims, to expound them systematically, and to condemn the old society which could not meet them. It was useless to rail at the philosophers for disturbing society. It is true that there was no overt demand for the theories they produced. There never is a demand for such theories in advance of their appearance. But there was a readiness to accept them when they appeared. There was, in that sense, a need for them. Burke's mistake was in not understanding this need, and Marx's in speaking as if the need would disappear when the social studies had become scientific.

It may be true that the need is more difficult to satisfy the more the social studies become scientific. It may also be true that, because of the discredit into which traditional political theory has fallen, the need is less widely recognized, especially among intellectuals, than it used to be. The old political theorists did so many things which they ought not to have done that we are tempted to conclude that there is no longer a need to do anything that they did. We may admire their fantasies, and yet say that the time for fantasy is over. We may say: By all means, let us state our preferences if we feel so inclined; let us make explicit the rules of conduct and the ideals which we accept. But this is something altogether more modest than what the old political theorists attempted.

There is some truth in this way of thinking, but it falls so far short of the whole truth as to be profoundly misleading. I want to explain why this is so.

III

In primitive societies, custom and prejudice are perhaps sufficient guides to conduct. And by prejudice I mean here what Burke meant by it; I mean a belief about right conduct which the believer takes on trust. In primitive societies, men can perhaps do without a systematic practical philosophy, just as they can do without a dogmatic religion. In the eyes of a sophisticated student of a primitive society, the customs and beliefs belonging to it may form a coherent whole; he may see how they fit together to make it the peaceful and contented society which it is. But in the eyes of the primitive man, they are not a coherent but only a familiar whole; he does not see how they fit together, he merely lives comfortably with his neighbours and with himself because in fact they do fit together.

The sophisticated man needs more than a set of customs and prejudices which are in fact coherent, though he does not see that they are; he needs a practical philosophy. He lives in a changing society, and he is socially mobile in that society; he is not exposed to change which is so slow that he cannot perceive it. He lives in a society where men strive deliberately to change their institutions. If he is not to feel lost in society, he needs to be able to take his bearings in it; which involves more than understanding what society is like and how it is changing. It also involves having a coherent set of values and knowing how to use them to estimate what is happening; it involves having a practical philosophy, which cannot, in the modern world, be adequate unless it is also a social and political philosophy.

In the past practical philosophy was rooted in religion and metaphysics; men derived, or purported to derive, their beliefs about how they should behave and how government should be organized from God's intentions for man or from the nature of the world or from man's being a rational creature. But many of the teachings of religion and metaphysics have been undermined by science or by logic; they have been shown to be incompatible with the facts or to rest on confusions of thought and bad argument. Not all religious and metaphysical doctrines have been directly controverted; for many have referred to an order of realities supposed to be beyond the realm of ordinary experience, with which alone science is concerned. They are beyond the reach of science, and logic cannot touch them if they are self-consistent. Yet the spread of science disposes many people to reject even these doctrines. They reject not only what science can show to be false, they also reject what science does not show to be true. Though there is, perhaps, nothing irrational about having both unverifiable and verifiable beliefs about the world, provided the first beliefs do not conflict with the second, many people find it difficult to do this, and feel the need to reject all beliefs for which there is no evidence. They may, of course, reject them consciously, and yet also behave as if they believed them; which is irrational. But that possibility does not concern us.

With the decay of religion and metaphysics there has gone a depreciation of the practical philosophies so long connected with them. There has even been a change of attitude to the moral principles contained in these philosophies. Let me give an example to illustrate my meaning. 'All men are equal in the sight of God' is a statement about God's feelings and intentions for man; it purports to be a statement of fact. It is not, on the face of it, a value-judgement; it is descriptive and not prescriptive, and yet it is unverifiable. Connected with this statement are beliefs about how men should behave. These beliefs do not follow logically from the bare statement about God's feelings and intentions; they follow only if it is assumed (as of course it always is) that men ought to behave in ways that further God's intentions for them. Though, when a man ceases to believe in God, he is not committed to rejecting these beliefs, since they do not follow logically from the statement that God has certain intentions, he is inclined to feel less strongly about them. It is only when these beliefs are put before him in some other connexion, as parts of some other intellectual structure, that he is again disposed to accept them as fervently as he did before.

The attempt to derive moral principles from theology or metaphysics is a time-honoured way of putting them forward as principles which all men everywhere o or ought to accept. Therefore, when this manoeuvre is rejected, so too is the idea that there are universal principles. It is admitted that there always are moral principles and that there always will be, it is admitted that the study of what they are and how they arise is valuable. But the task of elaborating a systematic practical philosophy is depreciated, it is what the theologians and metaphysicians used to do. It is what they still do, though with less conviction now than when their labours were not greeted with scepticism. The task made sense to them; but how can it make sense to men thoroughly imbued with the scientific spirit?

Now, this attitude to practical philosophy is quite irrational. The need for it is there, whether or not it is possible to derive universal principles from beliefs about God or the world or man; it is there, whether or not it can be shown that there are principles which men do or ought to accept everywhere. Man today, much more than in the past, must get his own bearings in the world; he must *make* himself at home in the world, for he can no longer be at home in it merely by conforming to the conventions and acquiring the prejudices of his station in society. Indeed, he no longer has a station, as his ancestors did; he is much more socially mobile in a much more quickly changing society.

Self-conscious, sophisticated man's conception of himself does not consist only of what he knows about himself or thinks he knows; it consists also of what he aspires to be. Admittedly, he is not what he aspires to be; he is what he is. But the kind of image he has of himself depends largely on what he aspires to be. He does not get his aspirations from the sciences, not even the social sciences; he gets them, directly or indirectly, from practical philosophy, whether or not that philosophy is tied to religion or to metaphysics. He cannot live from hand to mouth, following custom and accepting all current prejudices as they come. He lives in a kind of society which makes him critical and self-critical. To be happy, he must have aspirations, and must also feel that he can live up to them; he must be true to some image of himself. If he wants what he cannot get, or wants incompatible things, or has ambitions that bring him into conflict with other men, he cannot be happy.

Not everyone is capable of acquiring for himself a coherent practical philosophy. Not everyone feels the need for it. There are doubtless some people—and who knows how many they are?—who are quite content to drift through life. There are others who need guidance but are incapable of philosophy. They seek guidance from churches, from political parties, and from other organizations, and also from friends. There are still others who make for themselves a practical philosophy without engaging in controversy or adding anything to the stock of ideas and arguments. But some there must be who do the systematic thinking which goes to the making of practical philosophies. They are not scientists; their business is not to explain what happens in the world. And they are not philosophers in the rather narrow contemporary sense; their business is not to explain how we use language or how we get knowledge or what exactly it is that we are doing when we pass moral or aesthetic judgements or when we make decisions. They are philosophers in a quite different sense: they try to produce a coherent system of principles and to establish what needs to be done to enable men to live in conformity with them. They do not merely examine and compare the principles, showing where they are incompatible and explaining their consequences; they do not, like honest shopkeepers, display a large variety of goods, describing them all accurately and leaving it to the customer to choose what pleases him best. They produce a hierarchy of principles, and try to explain how men should use them to make their choices. This is how they help to provide them with a practical philosophy.

If the producers of these theories were like honest shopkeepers, if they were mere purveyors of ideas, they could not meet the need which it is their function to meet. If their business were merely to explain what this or that principle amounts to, how it fits in with other principles, and what is likely to happen when it is acted upon; if their business were to offer a large variety of principles, or even philosophies, for consideration, inviting every man to make his own choice among them, they would only bewilder and annoy. But they are not mere purveyors of ideas; they are preachers and propagandists. They are people who have, or who believe they have, discovered how men should live; and they will not be listened to unless they speak with conviction. They need not all speak with one voice, but each of them must take his stand. This is a condition of their effectiveness. If every missionary were to explain several different religions to his listeners, leaving it to them to make a choice, religion would take no hold. A man must already be committed before he can do much to help other people to commit themselves. As it is with missionaries, so it is with philosophers of this kind. Their business is to help people commit themselves. Freedom of thought is preserved, not because each thinker offers several theories for inspection and choice, but because different thinkers offer different theories with equal conviction. It is not the variety of strongly held convictions among the intellectual *élite* which is bewildering and depressing; it is the lack of conviction among them. Strong convictions attract and repel; they do not leave people indifferent. They encourage those who have the ability to do so to make up their own minds, to know where they stand. They do what science and linguistic analysis cannot do.

It is not enough that practical philosophies should be strongly held; they should also be well thought out and realistic. They should aim at self-consistency and at taking account of the facts.[1] The more thoughtful they are, the more they encourage thought in the persons who take stock of them. It does not matter that very few people should swallow them whole. Whoever considers them seriously will usually want to do more than establish their merits and defects, he will also want to construct a practical philosophy for himself, and the more they challenge thought in him, the more thoughtful that philosophy will be.

The more men live in societies which change quickly, the more mobile they are in those societies, and the more accustomed to the idea that they can, by taking thought, change their social environment to come closer to their ideals, the greater the part of social and political thought in practical philosophy. Its business is to relate a coherent body of principles to government; its business is to tell us what government should do to realize those principles and how it should be organized to do it. Political theory, as distinct from political science, is not fantasy or the parading of prejudices; nor is it an intellectual game. Still less is it linguistic analysis. It is an elaborate, rigorous, difficult, and useful undertaking. It is as much needed as any of the sciences. Its purpose is not to tell us how things happen in the world, inside our minds or outside them; its purpose is to help us decide what to do and how to go about doing it. To achieve that purpose, it must be systematic, self-consistent, and realistic. We learn to cope with the world, not by collecting principles at random, but by acquiring a coherent practical philosophy, which we acquire largely in the process of considering other philosophies of the same kind.

[1] Practical philosophy is deeply affected by psychology and the social sciences. Though we do not logically derive our values from what we know (or think we know) about ourselves and our social environment, we do change them as we change our minds about the facts. No one has done more than Freud to change our standards of sexual morality. Though these changed standards do not follow logically from his psychological theories, people who accept the theories are more disposed than they would otherwise be to accept the standards. But this detracts nothing from the importance or the distinctive character of practical philosophy. Art, too, is deeply affected by science and by practical philosophy, and yet it is an activity of a quite different kind which seems unimportant only to people who do not understand what it is. The more our standards are liable to change, the greater our need for practical philosophy. The greater our need, not just to understand how they have changed, but to introduce order among them. The need for practical philosophy is part of man's need to be his own master, to make up his own mind how he shall live and what he shall be.

No doubt only a small minority acquire, or are capable of acquiring, a coherent practical philosophy. But then only a small minority are capable of becoming scientists. We do not show that an activity is unnecessary or useless by showing that only a few persons engage in it.

IV

It may well be that no practical philosophy, and therefore no political theory, is universally acceptable. There may be no set of principles of which we can say: if men understood these principles, and also understood what human nature is and might be, they would accept them. I suspect that Marx and Engels believed the contrary. They denied that a practical philosophy can be derived logically from theology or from the nature of man, but they believed, none the less, that the fundamental rules and values of the classless society are universally acceptable, in the sense that men who understand what man and society are and might become do accept them. They expected the morality of classless societies to be everywhere the same and unchanging.

To defend my thesis I need not go as far as Marx and Engels went. I say only that the need for practical philosophy exists in all sophisticated societies. Just as sophisticated man is a scientist and an artist and an analytical philosopher, so too is he a practical philosopher and a political theorist. Most men, of course, are not so, but some are. Modern society creates a need for what they do which can neither be destroyed nor met by science and analytical philosophy.

There is nothing illiberal about practical philosophy and political theory, thus conceived. Admittedly, they are indoctrination; they are not the mere sorting out of ideas and their implications. But there need be no monopoly of indoctrination. In a liberal society there are some principles common to all or most of the political theories current in it. There is both community and variety of beliefs. But the beliefs held in common are as much open to question as the others. For society to remain liberal, it is not necessary that these beliefs should not be questioned; all that is needed is that they should be widely accepted. The more men differ, and the longer they have been accustomed to differing, the more likely they are to accept principles which make it possible for those who differ to live peacefully together. The principles commonly accepted are not more strongly held than the others; they are merely held along with the others. The Catholic or the Protestant who believes in toleration is not a liberal first and a Catholic or a

Protestant afterwards, nor is he a less fervent believer than he would be if he were intolerant. So it is also with political creeds; they are not the less strongly held merely because those who hold them are tolerant.

II

POLITICS, PHILOSOPHY, IDEOLOGY[1]

P. H. PARTRIDGE

MY object is to comment upon what seem to me to be some typical
trends in current English and American political theory, having in
mind the view that has recently been constantly asserted, that political
theory has been in decline or may even have expired during the last
few decades.[2] I will argue that the report of death, even of decline,
is grossly exaggerated, that in fact the present period is unusually
fertile in thinking about politics that is not only original and
important, but is also, at any rate in many significant respects, entirely
in the traditions of 'classical' political theory. That is one half of
my thesis; the other half is that during the past few years some very
important shifts in interest, approach, and emphasis have certainly
occurred; and I shall make some suggestions about the character of
these shifts, and the reasons for them.

Unfortunately, those who have been announcing the decay or death
of classical political theory have as a rule taken less trouble to
establish the fact of death or decay than to assert its causes. I do not
know what kind or amount of evidence is necessary to prove that
political theory has declined in volume or quality, but the assertion
does not seem to be very plausible on its face. For one thing, changes
of this somewhat radical kind do not occur quite so dramatically as

From *Political Studies*, Vol. 9 (Clarendon Press, 1961), pp. 217–35. Reprinted by
permission of the author and the Clarendon Press.

[1] The writer is very deeply indebted to Professor Wilfrid Harrison for many suggestions for the improvement of the form of this article.

[1] This is a selection from some of the more recent books and articles which have
discussed the present condition of political theory: A. Cobban. 'The Decline of
Political Theory' (*Pol. Sci. Q.*, vol. lxviii, no. 3, 1953); J. C. Rees, 'The Limitations of
Political Theory' (*Pol. Studies*, vol. ii, no. 3, 1954); P. Laslett (ed.), *Philosophy, Politics and
Society* (1956); G. C. Field, 'What is Political Theory?' (*Proc. Arist. Society*, vol. liv);
G. E. G. Catlin, 'Political Theory: What is It?' (*Pol. Sc. Q.*, vol lxxi, no. 1. 1957):
D. Braybrooke, 'The Expanding Universe of Political Philosophy' (*Review of Metaphysics*,
vol. xi, no. 4, 1958); J. P. Plamenatz, 'The Use of Political Theory' (*Pol. Studies*, vol.
vii, no. 1, 1960); H. R. Greaves, 'Political Theory Today' (*Pol. Sc. Quarterly*, vol.
lxxv, no. 1, 1960); A. Brecht, *Political Theory* (1959); H. V. Jaffa, 'The Case Against
Political Theory' (*Journal of Politics*, vol. 22. no. 2. 1960); L. Strauss, *What is Political
Philosophy, and Other Studies* (1959).

this one is sometimes supposed to have occurred. Or, again, if we call to mind the very large number of books that have dealt quite recently with such central problems as the nature and conditions of democracy, the group theory of political action and structure, and the theory of bureaucracy, one might have thought that there has never been a time when so much theoretical speculation about politics has been going on. Clearly, when writers nevertheless maintain that political theory is in decline, they must have something else in mind. Hence, we should perhaps begin by considering briefly what are some of the different things that political theory has meant, what different sorts of thinking about politics the name has been applied to. Some kinds may have become unfashionable, while others have continued to flourish.

I

Classical political theory has usually been a mixture of different kinds of inquiry or speculation. One could distinguish three different impulses—philosophical, sociological, ideological. This paper will be mainly about the third, but I want to say something first about all three. The political speculation of Plato, Hobbes, Locke, or Hegel is philosophical chiefly because each of these writers has tried to connect his conclusions about political organization, or about the 'ends' of political life, with a wider philosophical system. He has tried to derive political and social conclusions from more general beliefs about the nature of reality, to show that every sphere of reality, including the political, possesses certain common features or 'categories', that all these spheres can be spoken about in the same logical language, that, in short, political conclusions follow from or are supported by more general logical and metaphysical principles. And one obvious reason for the current impression that classical political theory is in decay is that there is not so much of this sort of argument now: many philosophers now insist that one cannot deduce the 'rightness' or 'rationality' of a form of political organization, or of a political policy, from more ultimate principles. For example, that section of Weldon's *Vocabulary of Politics* which deals with what he calls 'foundations' has this main philosophical purpose.

As I have said, one special form of the traditional connexion between philosophy and politics starts from the conception that it is the task of philosophy to exhibit what is common between the social and other 'spheres' of reality. Historically, of course, this has been a most important link between philosophy and politics; for instance, philosophical atomism has lent support to social individualism, the dialectic and the concrete universal are as important in Hegel's social theory as in the more philosophical parts of his work; and more recently some of the earlier political pluralists gained some support from the criticisms of philosophical monism developed by William James and others.

But clearly, a great deal of political theory has not been philosophical in this sense. Although de Tocqueville or Graham Wallas discussed some of the problems that political philosophers also discussed, their political views were not systematically connected with a philosophical position. A lot of de Tocqueville's writing we should now describe as sociological; he asserts generalizations, including causal generalizations, about the behaviour of social phenomena. Naturally, this is not only true of the de Tocquevilles, Bagehots or Maines; even in the writings of the political philosophers in the more technical sense, there is much sociological generalization—Hobbes is a notable example. Political philosophy was, of course, one of the parents of contemporary sociology. And no one doubts that the development of sociology as a specialized, altogether more rigorous, subject has also affected general political and social speculation.

By the ideological impulse I mean merely the form of political thinking in which the *emphasis* falls neither on philosophical analysis and deduction, nor on sociological generalization, but on moral reflection—on elaborating and advocating conceptions of the good life, and of describing the forms of social action and organization necessary for their achievement. Of course one cannot draw a sharp line between ideological and philosophical political writing: almost all political philosophy has been 'practical philosophy' in that it has had the practical object of persuading readers of the 'rationality' or moral superiority of some specific form of social organization. Even the *Leviathan* has such a practical aim, although Hobbes's practical conclusions are grounded upon philosophical and other argument which has usually been taken to be of greater interest than the practical purpose. But Rousseau, unlike Hobbes and Hegel, was not primarily a philosopher. The *Social Contract* introduces some general distinctions and conceptions of a philosophical kind, the significance and limitations of which were more developed by later writers, including Green and Bosanquet. But one would not expect much to be said about Rousseau in a history of philosophy—not, at least, in one written by an Englishman. In his case it would be very easy to detach and stress the ideological element. In fact, this is what seems to have happened: the image or model of democratic society drawn from the *Social Contract* has been very much more influential historically than any philosophical conceptualization or argument that the book contains.

But no matter how we choose to classify any theorist, I think it will be agreed that we can distinguish these three different impulses and interests, and these three 'orders' of political thinking. Nor will anyone dispute that one very powerful interest throughout the course of European social thinking has been the 'ideological'—moral argument about ends and ways of life, and about the institutional conditions of the good life.

II

Possibly each one of these impulses has grown weaker in recent years. Undoubtedly the progress of detailed empirical political and social inquiry has shaken the habit of speculative sociological generalization of the 'philosophical' kind, the concoction of what Dahl has called 'macrotheory' in politics.[1] Part of what is to be found in classical political philosophy has now been absorbed into political science and sociology. Again, many philosophers now reject the conception of philosophy, and of the resulting connexion between philosophy and politics, on which most of classical political philosophy (in the strict sense) rests. I cannot here discuss the technical reasons for the rejection: I shall make just one remark—addressed to many political writers who have been lamenting the decay of traditional political philosophy: this lament is idle if you have no answer to the technical philosophical arguments which can be deployed against the practice of supporting conclusions about the 'functions' of the State or about the rational ordering of social life by resting upon 'higher' or 'more ultimate' logical and philosophical principles.

But does it follow that these philosophical arguments have produced a decay of philosophical political theorizing? I should argue that there has not been such a decay. While philosophers have been disclaiming competence in political discussion, political scientists have been delighted to accept their disclaimer; and it can be argued that what is now happening is only an example of the familiar separation of a distinct subject from the parent philosophical stem.

[1] See his review article on de Jouvenel's *Sovereignty*—'Political Theory: Truth and Consequences' (*World Politics*, vol xi, no 1, 1958).

Political science, like economics, and other sciences, has reached the point where the specialists must themselves deal with the very general matters, including conceptual analysis, popularly or traditionally called 'philosophical'; and they do so at a level of sophistication and complexity which the philosopher *qua* philosopher could hardly approach. The boundaries between philosophy and politics are being redrawn. A number of twentieth-century philosophers have drawn a very sharp line indeed between 'philosophical' questions (or conceptual analysis) and 'empirical' questions; between 'second order' and 'first order' statements about politics. By and large, the political scientists have been sensible enough to see that the drawing of this sharp boundary is hopelessly disabling for the study of social theory, and have ignored it. On the other hand, the philosophers who have imposed it have been left in occupation of only a wafer-thin slice of the territory of politics—as *The Vocabulary of Politics* clearly demonstrates.

The philosophical impulse, in fact, is not the most important part of our inquiry; technical philosophy, after all, has only a limited influence; many of the most important political theorists of the last three centuries were not much influenced, or not influenced at all, by the technical philosophy of their own time. The philosophical impulse or influence is only one of those which have sustained political speculation; others have been equally or even more important. This brings me, then, to the 'ideological impulse' with which, in one way or another, the rest of this essay will be concerned.

III

The writers who have drawn attention to what they interpret as a languishing of philosophical thinking about politics have mainly in mind the political philosophy which has been an extension of moral theory—which inquires into the ends of the State and its morally right organization (What is the State that I should obey it?)—into the morally necessary or morally justifiable ordering of political society. The 'decline of political theory' is taken to be the decline of the moral interest in politics. 'On the one hand, there is a great deal of eagerness to deal with politics in moral terms; on the other, the insights of psychology, anthropology and of political observation have silenced the urge.'[1] It is this fact—if it is a fact—that is most in need of explanation.

[1] Judith Shklar, *Beyond Utopia* (Princeton, 1957), p. 272. J. P. Plamenatz's article 'The Use of Political Theory' (*Pol. Studies*, vol. viii, no. 1, 1960) and H. R. Greaves,

Is it a fact that there has been a 'slackening' of the 'moral urge'? Once again it is not hard to construct a case against. There is, after all, a very large amount of contemporary discussion of the moral foundations and dimensions of politics; for instance, the many fashionable criticisms of secular or positivistic liberalism such as are examined by Frankel in his *Case for Modern Man*. Nor should we overlook the moral discussion to be found in the pages of sociologists who are interested in the *non*-political areas of social life. One striking (and perhaps strange) feature of recent American sociology has been the popularization of the notion of 'alienation'. This, together with the closely connected themes of anomie, depersonalization, the atomization allegedly inherent in large-scale industrial society, the supposed dissolution of 'community' and aggrandizement of the State and other depersonalized, bureaucratized forms of organization, is surely one of the most widely-followed fashions of social thought at present. Perhaps there is a good reason for this; perhaps the social conditions and changes which appear to be morally most significant are not changes, or possible changes, in *political* arrangements or institutions, but those at other levels of society. The kind of lives people live in modern cities, the demands that industrial and other great organizations make upon them, the effects of commercialism, industrialization, and 'mass media' on popular culture—one could argue that it is in such contexts that the more important occasions for moral disquiet and reflection are to be found. In other words, if the moral interest in politics *has* declined, one reason could be that questions of political organization, of allocation of political rights and powers, &c., are not at present generally felt to be morally critical.[1]

IV

I want to develop this. There now prevails in England and the United States and in several other Western-type democracies a quite unusual degree of political relaxation and consensus. I shall not try to state carefully what this consensus embraces; but it obviously embraces the fundamental constitution of the liberal-democratic order. There is no significant social or intellectual movement which calls into question the broad structure of rights and powers under-

'Political Theory Today' (*Pol. Sc. Quarterly*, vol. lxxv, no. 1, 1960) are examples of this line of argument.

[1] I am speaking of course of the Western democracies; the reader will immediately protest against this remark if it is applied to contemporary Africa.

stood to constitute or define a democratic polity. There are no new classes struggling to win a share in political power, none struggling for an enlargement of power in ways that would entail substantial modification of political foundations. In Western Europe since, let us say, the beginning of the seventeenth century, it is not often that this could have been said. One could point, of course, to important contemporary controversies about rights or liberties (e.g. controversies about limitations upon the freedom of action of trade unions), but such controversies tend less and less to raise issues of great generality, and generality has normally been taken to be the work of *philosophical* issue in politics.

Now, if this is roughly true, it is plausible to suppose that this consensus (and not technical changes in philosophy or the growth of empirical social science, or other developments of extremely circumscribed influence) is the main factor affecting the character of contemporary political theory. If classical political theory *has* died, perhaps it has been killed by the triumph of democracy. At any rate, this seems to me to be a very relevant consideration which has not been sufficiently noticed by those who have written about the decay of political theory.[1]

In fact, the consensus appears to include more than the general system of powers and rights and the legally established institutions which give effect to them. It seems to embrace also objectives and justifications of policy. Is there not an all but universal acceptance

[1]May we not suspect the influence of ideological consensus even in some of the arguments employed by recent English philosophers? The late Miss Margaret Macdonald, for example, in her well-known essay, *The Language of Political Theory*, argues that the orthodox question Why should I obey the State, or Why should I obey the law? is in principle unanswerable. I can give reasons why I should obey (or disobey) this particular law; but there is no answer to the general question Why should I obey the law (or the State)? Now, apart from the question whether this argument does justice to what such a philosopher as T. H. Green was really saying, we may ask whether the argument would in fact always hold. If we give the State a content (let us take it to be, for example, a secular political authority claiming ultimate or sovereign political power over all other institutions), have there not been theocrats and anarchists to whom it was by no means obvious that the State, as distinct from other institutions, was entitled to claim final obedience? If there is, then, a real *general* issue, is it pointless to try to make a case in *general* terms for the supremacy of the State and its law, though we may admit that it is a general case only, and that there may quite well be conditions—as Green, along with other political philosophers admitted—under which the case for the State's final authority does not hold? May not Miss Macdonald's argument derive some plausibility from the fact that the State and its legal supremacy are now so firmly established as a matter of historical fact that to ask *in general*, Why should I obey the State? seems as sensible as to ask why I should obey the laws of gravity?

of the belief that continuous technological and economic innovation, uninterrupted expansion of economic resources, a continuously rising standard of 'material welfare', are the main purposes of social life and political action, and also the main criteria for judging the success and validity of a social order? No doubt, there is in any of the societies I have referred to some public questioning and criticism of these objectives and criteria; nevertheless, these are the objectives and criteria which define the course of contemporary democratic politics. They are the 'built-in' criteria which render irrelevant and impotent any alternative social philosophy.[1]

To speak of unusual ideological consensus when it is popularly supposed that the world is divided by warring ideologies may seem paradoxical; but the career of communism in England, the U.S.A., and some other democracies reinforces the argument. Communism has had no important effect in these countries as an alternative political philosophy; in England, as Miss Iris Murdoch has put it, communism has been left to the communists: one of the chief forces in creating and consolidating democratic consensus has been the repudiation of the consequences of communist revolutions. And one might document the growth of consensus in England by examining the history of socialist thought over the past three or four decades. There are now few socialist writers who advocate any systematic alternative to the basic *political* assumptions and arrangements of a liberal-democratic system. Most of the specifically socialist notions of extended democratic rights and institutions which had some currency earlier in the century—industrial democracy, workers' participation in management, guild socialism, and so on—are not much heard of now in serious politics. One of the most interesting points about such recent English works as Crosland's *The Future of Socialism* and Strachey's *Contemporary Capitalism* is that they disclose very plainly indeed how the standard institutions and procedures of liberal parliamentary democracy are now accepted as common ground.

[1] It is possible, of course, that the political and moral consensus may be more superficial than appears; and that there may be conflicts or frustrations growing in the deeper social soils that most of us are not sensitive enough to perceive. If the sociologists to whom I earlier referred are right in much of what they say about the psychological dissatisfactions and social dislocations of industrial society, then this may be so. At any rate, they have not yet become significant in practical politics, and, except for a few writers of the 'new Left' in England and America, they have not provided material for new political formulations. In his *Beyond the Welfare State*, Myrdal tries to describe in more detail the consensus that exists in the stable democracies; he seems to have no doubt about the stability of the prevailing agreement upon the arrangements and objectives of the Welfare State.

V

But, further, there is the even more interesting and important fact that some of the most influential political theorists of the day have become consciously *anti*-ideological. A closer look at some of the arguments which have been brought to bear against ideological politics will help us to see more clearly what is happening in contemporary English and American political theory.

By and large, the ruling trend of contemporary theory has been reacting against the more optimistic philosophies or ideologies of the past two centuries; consciously or implicitly, it has set about deflating the larger ideas of human possibilities that recommended themselves to many thinkers in the past, and has engaged in the job of cutting down our notions of man's nature to size.

The argument against 'ideological politics' has taken a number of different lines. It may simply assert that ideological ways of formulating political attitudes and objectives have declined in the course of this century as a matter of fact. But most writers who have touched on this theme have intended to do more; they have produced an account of what they believe to be *rational* political action. One argument is that ideologically-dominated thinking has no relevance to the controlling facts of contemporary social structure and change. 'Grand alternatives' like capitalism and socialism are irrelevant, because our choice is not between all-inclusive and mutually exclusive alternatives; in any society, there may be an indefinite number of ways in which different institutions and social mechanisms may be arranged and administered. Sometimes, this point is connected with a wider point—that ideological thinking has usually been totalistic; that is, that it has assumed that every important characteristic of a society is connected with a single governing mechanism, and that the whole of human life can be transformed from a central point. Thus, it is suggested, ideological thinking tends to adopt global views of social structure and political action.[1]

Again, it has been argued that this totalistic illusion has been responsible, in those countries which have suffered ideologically-inspired revolution, for much of the barbarism of the twentieth-century upheavals. The attempt to transform society globally can never be successful, and demands the employment of force on a monstrous scale and in a never-ending process. The logic of the idea

[1] This is suggested by the way in which some followers of Marx have talked about 'the' revolution; as if there were one revolution that would transform society, and the eradication of all social evils waited upon 'the' revolution.

of total transformation leads to perpetual force, apart from the fact that ideological conviction is often associated with moral and political fanaticism.

Finally, I must mention the criticism of ideological politics that Edward Shils has developed because it is theoretically the most penetrating and interesting. Shils's criticism connects with his theory of social groups and kinds of social cohesion. His argument is meant to suggest, I think, that those who have defined political action (or the change to be accomplished by political action) ideologically have erred by imposing upon civil society a character repugnant to it, one which rather characterizes other types of social grouping and adhesion. Civil society, according to Shils, is characterized by a plurality of groups, interests, and values, and the attachment of the members of civil society to the common set of values is normally moderate, luke-warm, sporadic, and intermittent. Thus, those who envisage a civil society as embodying a shared and intensely experienced set of common values are really imputing to civil society the emotional, psychological, or moral qualities that are characteristic of quite different types of social group, for instance, the sect or the community bound by 'primordial' ties of blood or propinquity. The attempt to create a civil society possessing a heightened emotionalism, and a more intense, inclusive, and continuous integration around a common 'centre', is thus bound to be destructive of liberty and other political values of civil society.[1]

For such reasons, much recent British and American political theory has been concerned with the devaluation of ideology and ideologies, with showing the importance of 'technique' as opposed to ideology, or with showing that 'incrementalism' (Dahl and Lindblom), or 'piecemeal engineering' (Popper), are the most rational methods of political change. Now, this quite considerable body of recent writing obviously raises some very important questions (the question of the nature and function of ideologies in politics has certainly not been exhausted); and it seems odd, therefore, that there should be so much talk about the decline or decay of political

[1]The reference is primarily to the article, 'Primordial, Personal, Sacred and Civil Ties', in *British Journal of Sociology*, vol. 8, no. 2. Some of the bearings of this view upon questions of political philosophy are suggested in *The Torment of Secrecy*. Many other lines of contemporary political thinking are allied to those I have summarized. For example, Talmon's studies of the history of political ideas, *Totalitarian Democracy* and *Political Messianism*, have a similar tendency; as have the various articles that have recently appeared discussing the positive functions of political apathy in democracies, for example, W. H. Morris Jones, 'In Defence of Apathy' (*Pol. Studies*, vol. iv, no. 6, 1954).

theory. Nor does this particular line of thought justify the suggestion that political theory has been entirely supplanted by factual or purely descriptive and explanatory political 'science'; for these writers are concerned with the justification of forms of political action and organization, just as political philosophers have always been. The method of justification is no doubt different; writers like Shils ground their conclusions on sociological premises rather than on more general philosophical ones. But this is but another illustration of the point already made that in twentieth-century political theory the discussion of the general issues is being detached from 'philosophy' and more and more closely linked with empirical social inquiry.

It could be argued, I think, that the thorough-going pluralism of present-day Anglo-American political theory has tended strongly to inhibit the formulation of general principles, values, or objectives of political life. It is the pervasive belief of current English and American political science that the 'essence' of democratic politics is a process of bargaining and of finding adjustments between competing demands, interests, values, ways of life-adjustments that will be more or less temporary and shifting as conditions change within and without society. In the more stable and affluent democracies this is the character that present political life has assumed. And this, surely, is enough to account for the relaxed atmosphere of modern democratic politics, the absence of political ideas of general range and importance, and of comprehensive political doctrine. In general, the politics of adjustment is one that directs itself to separate and limited issues, most of which affect only limited sections of a community, and any one of which engages rarely, and usually only marginally and casually, the interests or passions of a large span of the public, and which are unlikely, therefore, to generate political movements or coherent bodies of theory which aim to articulate a whole cluster of issues. It is evident that this corresponds very closely to Shils's account of the nature of 'civil society'.[1]

---

[1] It is not only in political thinking that particularism or piecemealism is the prevailing habit of thought. Wright Mill's recent book, *The Sociological Imagination*, may be read as a protest against this habit of thought in a wider context. If I follow him correctly, when he advocates the 'sociological imagination', he is protesting against the practice of many sociologists—the 'abstracted empiricists'—of concentrating upon the separate and circumscribed social phenomenon or problem. He still believes that one can explore the structure of society as a whole; that there are controlling areas (or at least especially strategic areas) through which a wide range of social life can be affected; and that contemporary social theorists fail to attend to those strategic areas within the social system which have the widest influence on freedom and other values of democratic society.

It would take me too far afield to try to examine in detail the now standard arguments against 'ideological politics'; I shall make only one or two observations. One might argue, to begin with, that the writers to whom I am referring are incautious in their acclaim of the passing of ideologies; that they are generalizing too boldly from the special conditions that now happen to obtain in a few societies. Again, it may even be misleading to say that in these societies the function of ideology has vanished. It can be argued that the politics of 'incrementalism', of bargaining and adjustment, of the pursuit of limited objectives, can itself operate as it does only because of the strong and wide ideological consensus that happens to rule in these societies. In his *Preface to Democratic Theory*, Dahl makes the point that the processes of bargaining and adjustment of claims involve agreed values and principles which keep political conflicts within bounds, limit the demands which minorities will seek to have granted, define the range within which acceptable solutions are known to lie, and so on. But this is a point of general importance. Recent political theorists have been apt to under-emphasize the extent to which all the elements which enter into the consensus operate as a necessary condition of effective political bargaining and compromise. Ideology may be no less an important element in a political and social system because it lies below the level of general political controversy.

Again, just because of the special circumstances of our time, we may be too ready to conclude that ideology is a false, irrational, and even disastrous guide to political *action*. We look back over recent history, and we see that the aspirations and expectations of ideological and utopian thinkers or agitators differ ludicrously from the states of affairs that actually came to be: such highly-charged ideas as equality, fraternity, 'positive' freedom in the sense of general participation in the control of social affairs, and notions about a classless society, common ownership and the like, seem to have come to very little. And these large moral intimations have apparently not only been held to be irrelevant to the actual course of events: it is often argued that they have been pernicious in their effects: they have encouraged colossal blundering, they have blinded men to the understanding of their own limitations, to the reality of original sin (Reinhold Niebuhr's account of the human situation accords with many of the other fashionable currents of present-day social thought); they have provided facile justifications for ruthlessness and terror.

Michael Polanyi has somewhere argued that the revolutionary excesses of this century have resulted partly from 'the excess of theoretical aspiration over practical wisdom'. Consequently, it is not hard to find grounds for arguing, as Popper does in effect in *The Open Society and its Enemies*, that gradual, piecemeal, 'experimental' attack on limited and particular problems, the pragmatic alleviation of particular evils, is the only rational method of political change.

In a sense, this sort of argument is incontrovertible. Political ideology has often been mainly faith, myth, superstition, political and moral dogmatism and fanaticism; when at full flood it has sometimes produced the most appalling destruction of existing institutions, traditions, and values. It would indeed be difficult to hold that there was anything rational about such ideology-impregnated social upheavals: to say that they are a 'rational' way of bringing about desired social change would be as strange as to say that an earthquake is a good way of producing a lake.

Yet it seems to me that none of these arguments suffices to dismiss 'ideological politics' as an obsolete and irrational method of social change. They cannot be 'justified'; but they may be inevitable in some circumstances; and we may also be able to argue—with the wisdom of hindsight and from the point of view of historical determinism—that they were the necessary condition for the production of certain social changes now accepted as desirable. 'Justification' and 'rationality' are categories applicable only within spheres of social action and change where calculated choice can be made; they apply only within the means-end model of social change and explanation. But could we not argue that there are certain types of social change which are (or were) desirable changes, but which could not have come about as a result of rational calculation and piecemeal adjustment, but only as the short- or long-term consequences of widespread ideological and even utopian upsurge and agitation?

I am aware that in these very swift remarks I have run together with nothing like sufficiently careful definition and discrimination some exceedingly hard questions of political analysis and theory. And I confess that I do not know how to prove that phases or periods of intense ideological activity (such as the activity of the Levellers and the Diggers in the English civil war, or the ideological ferment that preceded and accompanied the French Revolution, or the swell of socialist myth-making, moralizing, and social criticism that grew throughout the nineteenth century) are a necessary lever of political change, even though they never succeed in bringing about the results that ideologists believe they are bringing about. But one can argue negatively. One can argue that the 'unideological' politics of adjustment and piecemeal change must necessarily accept limited goals and types of social change, or again, that the many built-in pressures that support order and stability, the natural need and desire to go on living the daily life, operate to sift and narrow the objectives that are likely to be put on the agenda of responsible politics. (This, in fact, was one of the stock Marxist arguments against the politics of gradualism and reform—that the policy of incrementalism or rational calculation will involve us in accepting as constants certain structural features of the existing system, and certain moral or ideological elements that are embedded in that structure.)

To put this in another way—in any given state of society there will be well-established institutions and habits of moral thinking, which are central in the sense that they protect important elements, and which operate to limit the objectives, methods and types of change which are accepted as matters for political policy and governmental action, so that at any given time that part of the social structure that is at all generally *recognized* as subject to political action and change is always comparatively small. But it is in relation to what must be called the institutional and ideological *infrastructure* that ideological ferment and ideological politics have a very important function. They have their important effects below the level of 'rational' or programmatic political action, in eroding or loosening established moral and ideological habits and certainties, in producing the climate of opinion in which it is ultimately possible for new sorts of political or social objectives, new forms of social control and organization, new techniques of social action, to be accepted as parts of the ordinary programmes of political parties.[1]

However, it is not my intention in this article to embark upon a thorough examination of this question. My comments are simply meant to illustrate two main points: (*a*) That recent political scientists

[1] The only support that one could give to this assertion would be in the form of extended historical analysis. One would have to show how prolonged periods of ideological ferment, no matter how 'utopian' the ideologies might have been, ultimately produced important political results in the form of quite common-place programmes and policies. Examples are the revolutionary current in France from the late eighteenth century to the end of the nineteenth, or the nineteenth-century British movement of utopian socialism. A more extreme, and large-scale, example would be the rise, spread and ultimate political effects of the great world religions. There are some interesting remarks about some of the topics I have touched on in the last few paragraphs in Howard Horsburgh's article, 'The Relevance of the Utopian' (*Ethics*, vol. lxvii, no. 2).

have in fact been raising interesting and important problems of political theory and their discussion is a continuation of discussions that have been going on in Western political theory for centuries. (It is evident that some of the issues raised are very close to those raised by Burke about the French Revolution or by Marxists in their controversies with 'gradualists' and reformers.) (*b*) Yet, at the same time, this example does illustrate an important shift of interest in recent political speculation. In the democratic countries practical politics are mainly concerned for the time being with limited object-ives and adjustments: many political scientists have come to accept this style of politics as the rational norm for all political activity: the discounting of ideology has been accompanied by a scepticism concerning general speculation about the moral issues of politics, a disposition to assume that thinking about 'techniques' alone qualifies as really rational or practical political thinking.

VI

Let me take two other examples. The anti-ideological trend of so much recent political theory ('anti-ideological' both in the sense of discounting the importance of ideologies in politics, and in the sense of attacking and debunking political ideologies that have been very influential) is very plain in much of what is now being said about the nature of democracy and about the working of democratic institutions, especially political parties.

I will start with Schumpeter's brilliant discussion in *Capitalism, Socialism and Democracy* which expresses a line of thought and an emphasis which reappears substantially in later books.[1] Schumpeter begins, it will be remembered, by rejecting 'The Classical Theory of Democracy' which he formulates in this way: 'The democratic method is that institutional arrangement for arriving at political decisions which realizes the common good by making the people itself decide issues through the election of individuals who are to assemble in order to carry out its will.' He rejects this view because it involves assumptions and concepts about non-existents—a common good, a popular will, &c. He goes on to expound and defend 'Another Theory of Democracy' of which the formula is: 'The democratic method is that institutional way for arriving at political decisions in which individuals acquire the power to decide by means of a competitive struggle for the people's vote.'

[1] For example, Dahl's *Preface to Democratic Theory* and Down's *An Economic Theory of Government Decision-Making in a Democracy*.

Obviously, this involves a very different notion of the functions of the 'elements' in a democratic system and the relations between them. The leaders of the political parties decide, not 'the people'. It is the more or less organized groups of men competing for power who have the initiative and supply the political drive: 'so far as there are genuine group-wise volitions at all . . . [they] do not assert themselves directly . . . [but] remain latent, often for decades, until they are called to life by some political leader who turns them into political factors' (p. 270, 2nd edition). Policies and programmes are to be viewed as weapons employed in the competition for office, taken up or discarded according as they help or prejudice the party's competitive position; some question will become an 'issue' in politics when a leader or party judges it to be 'a good horse to back'. And a political party 'is a group whose members propose to act in concert in the competitive struggle for political power' (p. 283).[1]

A model like Schumpeter's is not to be criticized for being unrealistic. Any model involves selection and simplification: it is to be judged by its capacity to explain (and perhaps predict) the facts it is intended to explain. No doubt we could explain within the limits of Schumpeter's assumptions a great many of the political events of a democratic state. Nevertheless, I want to comment on a couple of the interesting features of his simplification.

In the first place, his model places heavy emphasis on manipulation and leadership—on the making and propagating of policy—and its tendency is to draw attention away from the 'infrastructure'. I do not intend to imply that he would deny the importance of the infrastructure; nevertheless, it is important to be quite explicit that this special emphasis is there.

Now, if we like, we may apply the word 'politics' to one level of activity only—to the level where policy operates, where individuals and groups more or less explicitly and deliberately seek adjustments and arrangements of their particular interests and activities. But, if we define the political in this way, it is very important to remember that the range of the political is always oscillating, and may at times oscillate somewhat violently.[2] And for Schumpeter to say that 'so far

---

[1] So also Downs, on *Economic Theory and Democracy*, p. 28: 'parties formulate policies in order to win elections, rather than win elections in order to formulate policies'. This is described as 'the fundamental hypothesis of our model'.

[2] It seems to me that recent political science has suffered from concentrating so heavily on the study of short-term political events (e.g. the study of the single election), on the act of 'decision-making', on 'bargaining models' and so on. This may have had advantages from the point of view of concreteness, empirical exactness and rigour.

as there are genuine group-wise volitions at all . . . they do not assert themselves directly . . . but remain latent often for decades until they are called to life by some political leader who turns them into political factors' is to be guilty of a very considerable over-simplification. It is true, of course, that this is how things often happen; political leaders formulate policies which are not formulated by other social groups; they crystallize or focus attitudes or demands that would otherwise remain uncrystallized; they may propose solutions that no one else has proposed. But to leave the matter there would be to postulate a gap between the politician (and the political party) and other social organizations which may be wider in some societies than in others, but which is not an invariable feature of all democracies. The party politician who appears in the political theory of Schumpeter and many other present-day political theorists is an abstraction. In 'real life' not all politicians are members only of a political party, or committed only to the success of a party (as 'success' is defined in the sort of model I am discussing). They are often also members of other social organizations; and very often they may be said to belong to a *movement*—and a movement is a social as well as a political phenomenon, and something it would be difficult to define except (at least partly) by reference to doctrine.

Now it is a matter of common observation that politicians are very often in the grip of a conflict between the beliefs or interest of their organizations or movements and of their party. And how they act in the end will not always be explicable solely by reference to the conditions of party success in the competition for power. Moreover, democratic societies differ from one another as regards the latitude for manoeuvre that parties enjoy. Within the one society there is an oscillation over time: the relations between parties and 'society' change, and there are occasions when the impact of demands, or of more general social and political ideas generated within social movements or organizations, upon the life and actions of parties is much greater than at others.[1] This being so, the model of democratic

But it has brought about a very drastic abstraction from a great deal of political reality. Rostow, it will be remembered, in his *British Economy in the Nineteenth Century* suggests an outline of the relations between economic change and political action. His schema involves two inter-related tripartite divisions: one between long term, trend or medium term, and short-term economic processes, the other a division between economy, society and politics; his suggestions concerning the different ways in which the three types of economic change operate at the political level could be profitably explored further by political theorists.

[1] And sometimes a difference as regards the current 'issues' of politics: as regards some issues, a party may have no alternative but to obey pressure 'from below';

politics which Schumpeter proposes will be helpful for explanation only in certan cases. And, even with this limitation, it is more likely to be helpful in the understanding of *short-term* runs of political decisions than in the understanding of a long-term direction of political change.

This, then, is the kind of emphasis and selection which the now fashionable Schumpeterian model of democracy contains. It is relatively uninterested in the important Marxian notion of 'shifts in the foundation' or infrastructure and their long-run political effects; or, if we may use a different image, it largely ignores the series of concentric circles within which, in some societies and at some times, the generation of social attitudes, ideas, and ideologies takes place. Perhaps the most important point I want to make is that these circles oscillate as conditions change: they grow wider or narrower, as regards both the range of social institutions or conditions which become subjects of social questioning and idea-making, and the numbers of those who are to some degree caught up in social criticism.[1]

One thing that may be said about Schumpeter's account is that it tends to stress the specialized and professional character of political activity; that its intention and effect is one of ideological deflation. And this brings me to the other comment I wish to make about his theory. Most of the so-called theories of democracy in the history of political thought have been primarily normative or prescriptive.

as regards others, it may be able to play the electoral market in the manner Schumpeter describes.

[1] In his review of de Jouvenel's *Sovereignty* in *World Politics* to which I have already referred, Dahl employs this concept of oscillation in speculating about the nature of democratic 'consensus'. His point, of course, is very closely related to mine. It would be a legitimate comment that Schumpeter does not pretend to be providing a model of *any* political system but only of democratic systems. And he might argue—indeed, there are plain indications that he would argue—that a democratic system will operate successfully (in the sense of maintaining over a long period its character or structure) only if conditions are as I have described them, in particular, only if the range of matters that come up for political decision and action remains narrow. This is now, of course, a widely-held view; one aspect of the reaction against socialist ideologies, or against notions of 'holistic' planning, is the argument that democracy is a method and system of government which requires as a condition that 'the effective range of political decision should not be extended too far' (Schumpeter). It is dubious whether this particular hypothesis can be given any hard meaning: what I have already said about the way in which consensus oscillates suggests that how much a government can do and get away with—or a party propose and get away with—will be affected by many different conditions which are far from being stable. However, it will be clear that this particular theory about democracy is closely allied with Shils's account of the nature of 'civil society' to which I referred earlier.

One important strain of democratic thought has connected democracy with the enlargement and greater equalization of opportunities for participating in the control or management of common affairs for sharing effective social responsibility. On this view, part of the task of a theory of democracy would be to investigate the means by which self-government or participation in the direction of affairs could be more widely extended. Mill puts very succinctly what has been a pretty constant problem and theme in the growth of democratic theory: 'A democratic constitution not supported by democratic institutions in detail, but confined to the central government, not only is not political freedom, but often creates a spirit precisely the reverse, carrying down to the lowest grade in society the desire and ambition of political domination.' This is not only succinct, but also perceptive—as the post-Millian growth of party discipline and party machines, of political bosses, and of publicity agents and carefully managed publicity campaigns remind us.

Perhaps there is no logical incompatibility between this and the Schumpeterian model; one might, for instance, say that Schumpeter is specifying the minimum conditions of democracy at the level of central government, and that his specification is not affected by how much or how little decentralization and diversification of control there might be down below. But I doubt it. I suspect that the more the two positions were developed, the more theoretical conflict would become apparent. On Schumpeter's view, it is *the* function of political parties to compete for votes by raising issues and proposing policies; it is *the* function of the public to express a preference between competing leaders and would-be governments. He appears to be saying that so far as democracy is concerned, this is not merely how democratic systems happen to work now, but that it is *the most that can be expected*. In effect, his model has a normative or prescriptive ring about it; and this is the more so when it is examined in the context in which he places it, viz. the rejection of the 'classical theory of democracy' with its very different conception of the meaning of self-government and of individual political participation and responsability.

My second example is Dahl's model in *Preface to Democratic Theory*. This differs a little from Schumpeter's in that Dahl assigns a less prominent place to parties and the electoral competition and a more prominent place to organized minorities and pressure groups. He warns us against attributing too rich a function to elections; in his view, the main function of elections in the democratic system is that they extend the range of the minorities which exert an influence on governmental decisions. According to Dahl, democracy is neither rule by the majority nor rule by a minority, but rule by *minorities*. 'Thus the making of governmental decisions is not a majestic march of great majorities united on certain matters of basic policy. It is the steady appeasement of relatively small groups' (p. 146). (Dahl at least has it in common with Schumpeter that he rejects the majority and anything that smacks of the notion of the general will.)

One might say that Dahl's assertion is just not true as a universal proposition; that there are not a few occasions and issues on which a majority does form and exert its influence. Recent political theory has no doubt gained in getting rid of loose and muddled concepts like 'the general will' and the 'common good', and uncriticized, question-begging ones like 'the majority'; but it is another matter whether it is fortunate in what it has substituted. In Dahl (and in the whole tribe of 'pressure group' analysts) the emphasis falls heavily on the notion of the determinate, relatively 'given', or impermeable, minority or group, possessing its own clear and determinate interests which have to be attended to by parties and governments. This, no one will want to deny, is *one sub-system* within the very complex system of democratic politics; but it exists in interplay with other sub-systems, including the interaction of interests, institutions, movements, ways of life within a process of general influence, and 'discussion' (if I may fall back on one of the governing conceptions of older theorists of democracy), and the resulting slow spread of general attitudes or bodies of belief which certainly affect the course of politics in the long run. In rejecting the categories and assumptions of the older philosophical idealists and monists, some of the more recent school of pluralists have tended to play down the social processes by means of which some sort of common denominator of sentiment and idea is created within a society, processes which are undoubtedly important for politics, and which their idealist predecessors rightly took to be pretty central for political theory, even if they misrepresented or unduly magnified them.

In an earlier section I illustrated the general reaction against ideology which has marked recent political and sociological thought. Correspondingly, then, in some recent democratic theory there has been an undermining of versions of *democratic* ideology which have been very prominent until quite recently.

VII

I have already explained that it is not my object to examine the theoretical strength of the views I have been considering. My main object has been to draw attention to some very common characteristics of recent political thought with a view to explaining the widely shared impression that political theory or political philosophy has lost its inspiration. If we take the work of such writers as Schumpeter and Dahl, it is absurd to say that the energy or the rigour of political theorizing have declined; on the contrary, it has acquired an analytical thoroughness and sharpness, a closeness in argument, that is pretty new. But what this more recent work *does* show is a narrowing of moral interests and expectations, a dismissal of wider notions of equality, freedom, participation, &c.,[1] and, accompanying this, the tendency to be most interested in the existing machinery of democratic systems. This is not simply a matter of science replacing the more philosophical interest in principles, values, or objectives. The ambition to lay the foundations of an empirical science of politics is no doubt a very important intellectual influence; but the present trend is also critical: it expresses an ideological or philosophical standpoint of its own, an inclination to accept as inevitable, or at least as more rational than any alternative, the broad types of organization, the distribution of rights and roles, the methods of adjusting existing interests, which have by now come to *define* democracy in the Anglo-Saxon democracies. In short, as I have said before, the current feeling that there is no very persuasive alternative to the prevailing methods and orthodoxies of Anglo-American democracy is at least one of the reasons for the shortcomings (if shortcomings they are) of contemporary political theory.

[1] Instead of illustrating my general thesis by dealing with recent theories of democracy, I might have taken recent writing about liberty, one striking feature of which has been an emphasis on the value or importance of 'negative freedom' and the distrust of notions of 'positive freedom'. Berlin's *Two Concepts of Liberty* is quite typical in this respect. Berlin's way of reviewing somewhat indiscriminately many different concepts of 'positive freedom', ranging from the special views of Hegel to much more prosaic attempts to connect liberty with the exercise of political initiative, is surprising and questionable; all the same, in his sensitiveness to the possibly illusory and dangerous character of ideas of 'positive freedom', he is very much in tune with his time. On a different point: the trend of thought I describe in the text is not of course entirely novel, as readers of Michels's *Political Parties* will be well aware; the argument between the supporters of a radical democratic ideology and those who insist upon the hard logic of social organization has been going on for some time. What is perhaps characteristic of more recent years is the unusual weakness of the strain of moral criticism and speculation.

III

ARE THERE ANY NATURAL RIGHTS?[1]

H. L. A. HART

I SHALL advance the thesis that if there are any moral rights at all, it follows that there is at least one natural right, the equal right of all men to be free. By saying that there is this right, I mean that in the absence of certain special conditions which are consistent with the right being an equal right, any adult human being capable of choice (1) has the right to forbearance on the part of all others from the use of coercion or restraint against him save to hinder coercion or restraint and (2) is at liberty to do (i.e., is under no obligation to abstain from) any action which is not one coercing or restraining or designed to injure other persons.[2]

I have two reasons for describing the equal right of all men to be free as a *natural* right; both of them were always emphasized by the classical theorists of natural rights. (1) This right is one which all men have if they are capable of choice: they have it *qua* men and not only if they are members of some society or stand in some special relation to each other. (2) This right is not created or conferred by

From *Philosophical Review*, Vol. 64 (1955), pp. 175–91. Reprinted by permission of the author and the *Philosophical Review*.

[1] I was first stimulated to think along these lines by Mr. Stuart Hampshire, and I have reached by different routes a conclusion similar to his.

[2] Further explanation of the perplexing terminology of freedom is, I fear, necessary. *Coercion* includes, besides preventing a person from doing what he chooses, making his choice less eligible by threats; *restraint* includes any action designed to make the exercise of choice impossible and so includes killing or enslaving a person. But neither coercion nor restraint includes *competition*. In terms of the distinction between 'having a right to' and 'being at liberty to', used above and further discussed in Section I, B, all men may have, consistently with the obligation to forbear from coercion, the *liberty* to satisfy if they can such at least of their desires as are not designed to coerce or injure others, even though in fact, owing to scarcity, one man's satisfaction causes another's frustration. In conditions of extreme scarcity this distinction between competition and coercion will not be worth drawing; natural rights are only of importance 'where peace is possible' (Locke). Further, freedom (the absence of coercion) can be *valueless* to those victims of unrestricted competition too poor to make use of it; so it will be pedantic to point out to them that though starving they are free. This is the truth exaggerated by the Marxists whose *identification* of poverty with lack of freedom confuses two different evils.

men's voluntary action; other moral rights are.[1] Of course, it is quite
obvious that my thesis is not as ambitious as the traditional theories
of natural rights; for although on my view all men are *equally* entitled to be free in the sense explained, no man has an absolute or
unconditional right to do or not to do any particular thing or to be
treated in any particular way; coercion or restraint of any action may
be justified in special conditions consistently with the general principle. So my argument will not show that men have any right (save the
equal right of all to be free) which is 'absolute', 'indefeasible', or
'imprescriptible'. This may for many reduce the importance of my
contention, but I think that the principle that all men have an equal
right to be free, meagre as it may seem, is probably all that the political philosophers of the liberal tradition need have claimed to
support any programme of action even if they have claimed more. But
my contention that there is this one natural right may appear unsatis-
fying in another respect; it is only the conditional assertion that *if* there
are any moral rights then there must be this one natural right. Perhaps
few would now deny, as some have, that there are moral rights; for the
point of that denial was usually to object to some philosophical claim
as to the 'ontological status' of rights, and this objection is now
expressed not as a denial that there are any moral rights but as a
denial of some assumed logical similarity between sentences used to
assert the existence of rights and other kinds of sentences. But it is
still important to remember that there may be codes of conduct quite
properly termed moral codes (though we can of course say they are
'imperfect') which do not employ the notion of *a* right, and there is
nothing contradictory or otherwise absurd in a code or morality con-
sisting wholly of prescriptions or in a code which prescribed only what
should be done for the realization of happiness or some ideal of personal perfection.[2] Human actions in such systems would be evaluated
or criticized as compliances with prescriptions or as *good* or *bad*,
right or *wrong*, *wise* or *foolish*, *fitting* or *unfitting*, but no one in such a
system would have, exercise, or claim rights, or violate or infringe
them. So those who lived by such systems could not of course be

[1] Save those general rights (cf. Section II, B) which are particular exempli-
fications of the right of all men to be free.

[2] Is the notion of *a* right found in either Plato or Aristotle? There seems to be
no Greek word for it as distinct from 'right' or 'just' (δικαίον), thought expressions
like τὰ ἐμὰ δικαία are I believe fourth-century legal idioms. The natural expressions in Plato are τὸ ἑαὑτὸν (ἔχειν) or τὰ τινὶ ὀφειλόμενα, but these seem
confined to property or debts. There is no place for a moral right unless the moral
value of individual freedom is recognized.

committed to the recognition of the equal right of all to be free; nor, I think (and this is one respect in which the notion of a right differs from other moral notions), could any parallel argument be constructed to show that, from the bare fact that actions were recognized as ones which ought or ought not to be done, as right, wrong, good or bad, it followed that some specific kind of conduct fell under these categories.

I

(A) Lawyers have for their own purposes carried the dissection of the notion of a legal right some distance, and some of their results[1] are of value in the elucidation of statements of the form 'X has a right to . . .' outside legal contexts. There is of course no simple identification to be made between moral and legal rights, but there is an intimate connexion between the two, and this itself is one feature which distinguishes a moral right from other fundamental moral concepts. It is not merely that as a matter of fact men speak of their moral rights mainly when advocating their incorporation in a legal system, but that the concept of a right belongs to that branch of morality which is specifically concerned to determine when one person's freedom may be limited by another's[2] and so to determine what actions may appropriately be made the subject of coercive legal rules. The words '*droit*', '*diritto*', and '*Recht*', used by continental jurists, have no simple English translation and seem to English jurists to hover uncertainly between law and morals, but they do in fact mark off an area of morality (the morality of law) which has special characteristics. It is occupied by the concepts of justice, fairness, rights, and obligation (if this last is not used as it is by many moral philosophers as an obscuring general label to cover every action that morally we ought to do or forbear from doing). The most important common characteristic of this group of moral concepts is that there is no incongruity, but a special congruity in the use of

---

[1] As W. D. Lamont has seen: cf. his *Principles of Moral Judgement* (Oxford, 1946); for the jurists, cf. Hohfeld's *Fundamental Legal Conceptions* (New Haven, 1923).

[2] Here and subsequently I use 'interfere with another's freedom', 'limit another's freedom', 'determine how another shall act', to mean either the use of coercion or demanding that a person shall do or not do some action. The connexion between these two types of 'interference' is too complex for discussion here; I think it is enough for present purposes to point out that having a justification for demanding that a person shall or shall not do some action is a necessary though not a sufficient condition for justifying coercion.

force or the threat of force to secure that what is just or fair or some-one's right to have done shall in fact be done; for it is in just these circumstances that coercion of another human being is legitimate. Kant, in the *Rechtslehre*, discusses the obligations which arise in this branch of morality under the title of *officia juris*, 'which do not require that respect for duty shall be of itself the determining principle of the will', and contrasts them with *officia virtutis*, which have no moral worth unless done for the sake of the moral principle. His point is, I think, that we must distinguish from the rest of morality those principles regulating the proper distribution of human freedom which alone make it morally legitimate for one human being to determine by his choice how another should act; and a certain specific moral value is secured (to be distinguished from moral virtue in which the good will is manifested) if human relationships are conducted in accordance with these principles even though coercion has to be used to secure this, for only if these principles are regarded will free-dom be distributed among human beings as it should be. And it is I think a very important feature of a moral right that the possessor of it is conceived as having a moral justification for limiting the freedom of another and that he has this justification not because the action he is entitled to require of another has some moral quality but simply because in the circumstances a certain distribution of human freedom will be maintained if he by his choice is allowed to determine how that other shall act.

(B) I can best exhibit this feature of a moral right by reconsidering the question whether moral rights and 'duties'[1] are correlative. The contention that they are means, presumably, that every statement of the form 'X has a right to . . .' entails and is entailed by 'Y has a duty (not) to . . .', and at this stage we must not assume that the values of the name-variables 'X' and 'Y' must be different persons. Now there is certainly one sense of 'a right' (which I have already mentioned) such that it does not follow from X's having a right that X or someone else has any duty. Jurists have isolated rights in this sense and have re-

[1] I write 'duties' here because one factor obscuring the nature of a right is the philosophical use of 'duty' and 'obligation' for all cases where there are moral reasons for saying an action ought to be done or not done. In fact 'duty', 'obligation', 'right', and 'good' come from different segments of morality, concern different types of conduct, and make different types of moral criticism or evaluation. Most important are the points (1) that obligations may be voluntarily incurred or created, (2) that they are *owed* to special persons (who have rights), (3) that they do not arise out of the character of the actions which are obligatory but out of the relationship of the parties. Language roughly though not consistently confines the use of 'having an obligation' to such cases.

ferred to them as 'liberties' just to distinguish them from rights in the centrally important sense of 'right' which has 'duty' as a correlative. The former sense of 'right' is needed to describe those areas of social life where competition is at least morally unobjectionable. Two people walking along both see a ten-dollar bill in the road twenty yards away, and there is no clue as to the owner. Neither of the two are under a 'duty' to allow the other to pick it up; each has in this sense a right to pick it up. Of course there may be many things which each has a 'duty' not to do in the course of the race to the spot— neither may kill or wound the other—and corresponding to these 'duties' there are rights to forbearances. The moral propriety of all economic competition implies this minimum sense of 'a right' in which to say that 'X has a right to' means merely that X is under no 'duty' not to. Hobbes saw that the expression 'a right' could have this sense but he was wrong if he thought that there is no sense in which it does follow from X's having a right that Y has a duty or at any rate an obligation.

(C) More important for our purpose is the question whether for all moral 'duties' there are correlative moral rights, because those who have given an affirmative answer to this question have usually assumed without adequate scrutiny that to have a right is simply to be capable of benefiting by the performance of a 'duty'; whereas in fact this is not a sufficient condition (and probably not a necessary condition) of having a right. Thus animals and babies who stand to benefit by our performance of our 'duty' not to ill-treat them are said *therefore* to have rights to proper treatment. The full consequence of this reasoning is not usually followed out; most have shrunk from saying that we have rights against ourselves because we stand to bene-fit from our performance of our 'duty' to keep ourselves alive or develop our talents. But the moral situation which arises from a promise (where the legal-sounding terminology of rights and obli-gations is most appropriate) illustrates most clearly that the notion of having a right and that of benefiting by the performance of a 'duty' are not identical. X promises Y in return for some favour that he will look after Y's aged mother in his absence. Rights arise out of this transaction, but it is surely Y to whom the promise has been made and not his mother who *has* or *possesses* these rights. Certainly Y's mother is a person concerning whom X has an obligation and a person who will benefit by its performance, but the person *to whom* he has an obli-gation to look after her is Y. This is something *due to* or *owed to* Y, so it is Y, not his mother, whose right X will disregard and to whom

X will have done *wrong* if he fails to keep his promise, though the mother may be physically injured. And it is Y who has a moral *claim* upon X, is *entitled* to have his mother looked after, and who can *waive* the claim and *release* Y from the obligation. Y is, in other words, morally in a position to determine by his choice how X shall act and in this way to limit X's freedom of choice; and it is this fact, not the fact that he stands to benefit, that makes it appropriate to say that he has *a right*. Of course often the person to whom a promise has been made will be the only person who stands to benefit by its performance, but this does not justify the identification of 'having a right' with 'benefiting by the performance of a duty'. It is important for the whole logic of rights that, while the person who stands to benefit by the performance of a duty is discovered by considering what will happen if the duty is not performed, the person who has a right (to whom performance is *owed* or *due*) is discovered by examining the transaction or antecedent situation or relations of the parties out of which the 'duty' arises. These considerations should incline us not to extend to animals and babies whom it is wrong to ill-treat the notion of a right to proper treatment, for the moral situation can be simply and adequately described here by saying that it is wrong or that we ought not to ill-treat them or, in the philosopher's generalized sense of 'duty', that we have a duty not to ill-treat them.[1] If common usage sanctions talk of the rights of animals or babies it makes an idle use of the expression 'a right', which will confuse the situation with other different moral situations where the expression 'a right' has a specific force and cannot be replaced by the other moral expressions which I have mentioned. Perhaps some clarity on this matter is to be gained by considering the force of the preposition 'to' in the expression 'having a duty to Y' or 'being under an obligation to Y' (where 'Y' is the name of a person); for it is significantly different from the meaning of 'to' in 'doing something to Y' or 'doing harm to Y', where it indicates the person affected by some action. In the first pair of expressions, 'to' obviously does not have this force, but indicates the person to whom the person morally bound is bound. This is an intelligible development of the figure of a bond (*vinculum juris: obligare*); the precise figure is not that of two persons bound by a chain, but of *one* person bound, the other end of the chain lying in the hands of another to use if he chooses.[2] So it appears

---

[1] The use here of the generalized 'duty' is apt to prejudice the question whether animals and babies have rights.

[2] Cf. A. H. Campbell, *The Structure of Stair's Institutes* (Glasgow, 1954), p. 31.

absurd to speak of having duties or owing obligations to ourselves—of course we may have 'duties' not to do harm to ourselves, but what could be meant (once the distinction between these different meanings of 'to' has been grasped) by insisting that we have duties or obligations *to* ourselves not to do harm to ourselves?

(D) The essential connexion between the notion of a right and the justified limitation of one person's freedom by another may be thrown into relief if we consider codes of behaviour which do not purport to confer rights but only to prescribe what shall be done. Most natural law thinkers down to Hooker conceived of natural law in this way: there were natural duties compliance with which would certainly benefit man—things to be done to achieve man's natural end—but not natural rights. And there are of course many types of codes of behaviour which only prescribe what is to be done, e.g., those regulating certain ceremonies. It would be absurd to regard these codes as conferring rights, but illuminating to contrast them with rules of games, which often create rights, though not, of course, moral rights. But even a code which is plainly a moral code need not establish rights; the Decalogue is perhaps the most important example. Of course, quite apart from heavenly rewards human beings stand to benefit by general obedience to the Ten Commandments: disobedience is wrong and will certainly harm individuals. But it would be a surprising interpretation of them that treated them as conferring rights. In such an interpretation obedience to the Ten Commandments would have to be conceived as due to or owed to individuals, not merely to God, and disobedience not merely as wrong but as *a wrong to* (as well as harm to) individuals. The Commandments would cease to read like penal statutes designed only to rule out certain types of behaviour and would have to be thought of as rules placed at the disposal of individuals and regulating the extent to which *they* may demand certain behaviour from others. Rights are typically conceived of as *possessed* or *owned by* or *belonging to* individuals, and these expressions reflect the conception of moral rules as not only prescribing conduct but as forming a kind of moral property of individuals to which they are as individuals entitled; only when rules are conceived in this way can we speak of *rights* and *wrongs* as well as right and wrong actions.[1]

---

[1] Continental jurists distinguish between '*subjektives*' and '*objektives Recht*', which corresponds very well to the distinction between *a* right, which an individual has, and what it is right to do.

II

So far I have sought to establish that to have a right entails having a moral justification for limiting the freedom of another person and for determining how he should act; it is now important to see that the moral justification must be of a special kind if it is to constitute a right, and this will emerge most clearly from an examination of the circumstances in which rights are asserted with the typical expression 'I have a right to . . . '. It is I think the case that this form of words is used in two main types of situations: (A) when the claimant has some special justification for interference with another's freedom which other persons do not have ('*I* have a right to be paid what you promised for my services'); (B) when the claimant is concerned to resist or object to some interference by another person as having no justification ('*I* have a right to say what I think').

(A) *Special rights*. When rights arise out of special transactions between individuals or out of some special relationship in which they stand to each other, both the persons who have the right and those who have the corresponding obligation are limited to the parties to the special transaction or relationship. I call such rights special rights to distinguish them from those moral rights which are thought of as rights against (i.e., as imposing obligations upon)[1] everyone, such as those that are asserted when some unjustified interference is made or threatened as in (B) above.

(i) The most obvious cases of special rights are those that arise from promises. By promising to do or not to do something, we voluntarily incur obligations and create or confer rights on those to whom we promise; we alter the existing moral independence of the parties' freedom of choice in relation to some action and create a new moral relationship between them, so that it becomes morally legitimate for the person to whom the promise is given to determine how the promisor shall act. The promisee has a temporary authority or sovereignty in relation to some specific matter over the other's will which we express by saying that the promisor is under an obligation *to* the promisee to do what he has promised. To some philosophers the notion that moral phenomena—rights and duties or obligations—can be brought into existence by the voluntary action of individuals has appeared utterly mysterious; but this I think has been so because they have not clearly seen how special the moral notions of a right and an obligation are, nor how peculiarly they are

[1] Cf. Section (B) below.

connected with the distribution of freedom of choice; it would indeed be mysterious if we could make actions morally good or bad by voluntary choice. The simplest case of promising illustrates two points characteristic of all special rights: (1) the right and obligation arise not because the promised action has itself any particular moral quality, but just because of the voluntary trans-action between the parties; (2) the identity of the parties concerned is vital—only *this* person (the promisee) has the moral justification for determining how the promisor shall act. It is *his* right; only in relation to him is the promisor's freedom of choice diminished, so that if he chooses to release the promisor no one else can complain.

(ii) But a promise is not the only kind of transaction whereby rights are conferred. They may be *accorded* by a person consenting or authorizing another to interfere in matters which but for this consent or authorization he would be free to determine for himself. If I consent to your taking precautions for my health or happiness or authorize you to look after my interests, then you have a right which others have not, and I cannot complain of your interference if it is within the sphere of your authority. This is what is meant by a person surrendering his rights to another; and again the typical characteristics of a right are present in this situation: the person authorized has the right to interfere not because of its intrinsic character but because *these* persons have stood in *this* relationship. No one else (not similarly authorized) has any *right*[1] to interfere in theory even if the person authorized does not exercise his right.

(iii) Special rights are not only those created by the deliberate choice of the party on whom the obligation falls, as they are when they are accorded or spring from promises, and not all obligations to other persons are deliberately incurred, though I think it is true of all special rights that they arise from previous voluntary actions. A third very important source of special rights and obligations which we recognize in many spheres of life is what may be termed mutuality of restrictions, and I think political obligation is intelligible only if we see what precisely this is and how it differs from the other right-creating transactions (consent, promising) to which philosophers have assimilated it. In its bare schematic outline ·it is this: when a number of persons conduct any joint enterprise according to rules and thus restrict their liberty, those who have submitted to these restrictions when required have a right to a similar submission from those who have benefited by their submission. The rules may provide

[1] Though it may be *better* (the lesser of two evils) that he should: cf. p. 62 below.

that officials should have authority to enforce obedience and make further rules, and this will create a structure of legal rights and duties, but the moral obligation to obey the rules in such circumstances is *due to* the co-operating members of the society, and they have the correlative moral right to obedience. In social situations of this sort (of which political society is the most complex example) the obligation to obey the rules is something distinct from whatever other moral reasons there may be for obedience in terms of good consequences (e.g., the prevention of suffering); the obligation is due to the co-operating members of the society as such and not because they are human beings on whom it would be wrong to inflict suffering. The utilitarian explanation of political obligation fails to take account of this feature of the situation both in its simple version that the obligation exists because and only if the direct consequences of a particular act of disobedience are worse than obedience, and also in its more sophisticated version that the obligation exists even when this is not so, if disobedience increases the probability that the law in question or other laws will be disobeyed on other occasions when the direct consequences of obedience are better than those of disobedience.

Of course to say that there is such a moral obligation upon those who have benefited by the submission of other members of society to restrictive rules to obey these rules in their turn does not entail either that this is the only kind of moral reason for obedience or that there can be no cases where disobedience will be morally justified. There is no contradiction or other impropriety in saying 'I have an obligation to do X, someone has a right to ask me to, but I now see I ought not to do it'. It will in painful situations sometimes be the lesser of two moral evils to disregard what really are people's rights and not perform our obligations to them. This seems to me particularly obvious from the case of promises: I may promise to do something and thereby incur an obligation just because that is one way in which obligations (to be distinguished from other forms of moral reasons for acting) are created; reflection may show that it would in the circumstances be wrong to keep this promise because of the suffering it might cause, and we can express this by saying '*I ought not* to do it though *I have an obligation to him* to do it' just because the italicized expressions are not synonyms but come from different dimensions of morality. The attempt to explain this situation by saying that our real obligation here is to avoid the suffering and that there is only a prima facie obligation to keep the promise seems to me to confuse two quite different kinds of moral reason, and in practice such a terminology obscures the precise character of what is at stake when 'for some greater good' we infringe people's rights or do not perform our obligations to them.

The social-contract theorists rightly fastened on the fact that the obligation to obey the law is not merely a special case of benevolence (direct or indirect), but something which arises between members of a particular political society out of their mutual relationship. Their mistake was to identify *this* right-creating situation of mutual restrictions with the paradigm case of promising; there are of course important similarities, and these are just the points which all special rights have in common, viz., that they arise out of special relationships between human beings and not out of the character of the action to be done or its effects.

(iv) There remains a type of situation which may be thought of as creating rights and obligations: where the parties have a special natural relationship, as in the case of parent and child. The parent's moral right to obedience from his child would I suppose now be thought to terminate when the child reaches the age 'of discretion', but the case is worth mentioning because some political philosophies have had recourse to analogies with this case as an explanation of political obligation, and also because even this case has some of the features we have distinguished in special rights, viz., the right arises out of the special relationship of the parties (though it is in this case a natural relationship) and not out of the character of the actions to the performance of which there is a right.

(v) To be distinguished from special rights, of course, are special liberties, where, exceptionally, one person is *exempted* from obligations to which most are subject but does not thereby acquire a *right* to which there is a correlative obligation. If you catch me reading your brother's diary, you say, 'You have no right to read it'. I say, 'I have a right to read it—your brother said I might unless he told me not to, and he has not told me not to'. Here I have been specially *licensed* by your brother who had a right to require me not to read his diary, so I am exempted from the moral obligation not to read it, but your brother is under no obligation to let me go on reading it. Cases where *rights*, not liberties, are accorded to manage or interfere with another person's affairs are those where the licence is not revocable at will by the person according the right.

(B) *General rights*. In contrast with special rights, which constitute a justification peculiar to the holder of the right for interfering

with another's freedom, are general rights, which are asserted defen-
sively, when some unjustified interference is anticipated or threatened,
in order to point out that the interference is unjustified. 'I have the
right to say what I think'.[1] 'I have the right to worship as I please'.
Such rights share two important characteristics with special rights.
(1) To have them is to have a moral justification for determining how
another shall act, viz., that he shall not interfere.[2] (2) The moral
justification does not arise from the character of the particular action
to the performance of which the claimant has a right; what justifies
the claim is simply—there being no special relation between him and
those who are threatening to interfere to justify that interference—
that this is a particular exemplification of the equal right to be free.
But there are of course striking differences between such defensive
general rights and special rights. (1) General rights do not arise out
of any special relationship or transaction between men. (2) They are
not rights which are peculiar to those who have them but are rights
which all men capable of choice have in the absence of those special
conditions which give rise to special rights. (3) General rights have
as correlatives obligations not to interfere to which everyone else is
subject and not merely the parties to some special relationship or
transaction, though of course they will often be asserted when some
particular persons threaten to interfere as a moral objection to that
interference. To assert a general right is to claim in relation to some
particular action the equal right of all men to be free in the absence
of any of those special conditions which constitute a special right
to limit another's freedom; to assert a special right is to assert in
relation to some particular action a right constituted by such special
conditions to limit another's freedom. The assertion of general rights
directly invokes the principle that all men equally have the right to
be free; the assertion of a special right (as I attempt to show in
Section III) invokes it indirectly.

[1] In speech the difference between general and special rights if often marked
by stressing the pronoun where a special right is claimed or where the special right
is denied. 'You have no right to stop him reading that book' refers to the reader's
general right. '*You* have no right to stop him reading that book' denies that the
person addressed has a special right to interfere though others may have.

[2] Strictly, in the assertion of a general right both the *right* to forbearance from
coercion and the *liberty* to do the specified action are asserted, the first in the face
of actual or threatened coercion, the second as an objection to an actual or anticipated demand that the action should not be done. The first has as its correlative
an obligation upon everyone to forbear from coercion; the second the absence in any
one of a justification for such a demand. Here, in Hohfeld's words, the correlative
is not an obligation but a 'no-right'.

III

It is, I hope, clear that unless it is recognized that interference with another's freedom requires a moral justification the notion of a right could have no place in morals; for to assert a right is to assert that there is such a justification. The characteristic function in moral discourse of those sentences in which the meaning of the expression 'a right' is to be found—'I have a right to . . .', 'You have no right to . . .', 'What right have you to . . .?'—is to bring to bear on interferences with another's freedom, or on claims to interfere, a type of moral evaluation or criticism specially appropriate to interference with freedom and characteristically different from the moral criticism of actions made with the use of expressions like 'right', 'wrong', 'good', and 'bad'. And this is only one of many different types of moral ground for saying 'You ought . . .' or 'You ought not . . .'. The use of the expression 'What right have you to . . .?' shows this more clearly, perhaps, than the others; for we use it, just at the point where interference is actual or threatened, to call for the moral *title* of the person addressed to interfere; and we do this often without any suggestion at all that what he proposes to do is otherwise wrong and sometimes with the implication that the same interference on the part of another person would be unobjectionable.

But though our use in moral discourse of 'a right' does pre-suppose the recognition that interference with another's freedom requires a moral justification, this would not itself suffice to establish, except in a sense easily trivialized, that in the recognition of moral rights there is implied the recognition that all men have a right to equal freedom; for unless there is some restriction inherent in the meaning of 'a right' on the type of moral justification for interference which can constitute a right, the principle could be made wholly vacuous. It would, for example, be possible to adopt the principle and then assert that some characteristic or behaviour of some human beings (that they are improvident, or atheists, or Jews, or Negroes) constitutes a moral justification for interfering with their freedom; *any* differences between men could, so far as my argument has yet gone, be treated as a moral justification for interference and so constitute a right, so that the equal right of all men to be free would be compatible with gross inequality. It may well be that the expression 'moral' itself imports some restriction on what can constitute a moral justification for interference which would avoid this consequence, but I cannot myself yet show that this is so. It is, on the other hand, clear to me that the moral justification for interference which is to constitute a *right* to interfere (as distinct from merely making it morally good or desirable to interfere) is restricted to certain special conditions and that this is inherent in the meaning of 'a right' (unless this is used so loosely that it could be replaced by the other moral expressions mentioned). Claims to interfere with another's freedom based on the general character of the activities interfered with (e.g., the folly or cruelty of 'native' practices) or the general character of the parties ('We are Germans; they are Jews') even when well founded are not matters of moral right or obligation. Submission in such cases even where proper is not *due to* or *owed to* the individuals who interfere; it would be equally proper whoever of the same class of persons interfered. Hence other elements in our moral vocabulary suffice to describe this case, and it is confusing here to talk of rights. We saw in Section II that the types of justification for interference involved in special rights was independent of the character of the action to the performance of which there was a right but depended upon certain previous transactions and relations between individuals (such as promises, consent, authorization, submission to mutual restrictions). Two questions here suggest themselves: (1) On what intelligible principle could these bare forms of promising, consenting, submission to mutual restrictions, be either necessary or sufficient, irrespective of their content, to justify interference with another's freedom? (2) What characteristics have these types of transaction or relationship in common? The answer to both these questions is I think this: If we justify interference on such grounds as we give when we claim a moral right, we are in fact indirectly invoking as our justification the principle that all men have an equal right to be free. For we are in fact saying in the case of promises and consents or authorizations that this claim to interfere with another's freedom is justified because he has, in exercise of his equal right to be free, freely chosen to create this claim; and in the case of mutual restrictions we are in fact saying that this claim to interfere with another's freedom is justified because it is fair; and it is fair because only so will there be an equal distribution of restrictions and so of freedom among this group of men. So in the case of special rights as well as of general rights recognition of them implies the recognition of the equal right of all men to be free.

IV

THE USES OF 'SOVEREIGNTY'

STANLEY I. BENN

I

JEAN BODIN defined 'sovereignty' as 'supreme power over citizens and subjects, unrestrained by law'. Since then criticisms of theories in which the term has been employed have led to repeated attempts to redefine it and to distinguish different kinds of 'supreme power' and examine the relations between them. For Austin the sovereign is 'a *determinate* human superior, *not* in a habit of obedience to a like superior, (receiving) *habitual* obedience from the *bulk* of a given society'.[1] Applying this notion to the British Constitution Dicey finds it necessary to distinguish 'legal sovereignty' and 'political sovereignty'.[2] Lord Bryce employs a different distinction. 'Legal sovereignty', he says, is primarily the concern of the lawyer: 'The sovereign authority is to him the person (or body) to whose directions the law attributes legal force.'[3] This kind of sovereignty, Bryce says, 'is created by and concerned with law, and law only'.[4] But it is also possible to detect a 'practical sovereign': 'The person (or body of persons) who can make his (or their) will prevail whether with the law or against the law. He (or they) is the *de facto* ruler.'[5] More recently Mr. W. J. Rees has attempted an exhaustive analysis of the ways in which 'sovereignty' has been used and has tried to establish three possible senses.[6] He begins with 'power': 'To exercise power . . . is to determine the actions of persons in certain intended ways. There are, however, different species of power, and these may be distinguished according to the means used to determine persons' actions.'[7] He

From *Political Studies*, Vol. 3 (Clarendon Press, 1955), pp. 109–22. Reprinted by permission of the author and the Clarendon Press.

[1] J. Austin, *Lectures on Jurisprudence* (5th ed.), p. 221.

[2] A. V. Dicey, *Law of the Constitution* (9th ed.), p. 72.

[3] Lord Bryce, *Studies in History and Jurisprudence*, vol. ii (1901), p. 51.

[4] Ibid., p. 56.

[5] Ibid., p. 59–60.

[6] W. J. Rees, 'The Theory of Sovereignty Restated', in *Mind*, vol. lix (1950).

[7] Ibid., p. 511.

distinguishes three such species to each of which corresponds a species of supreme power, or sovereignty.

'*Legal sovereignty*' is a capacity 'to determine the actions of persons in certain intended ways by means of a law . . . where the actions of those who exercise the authority, in those respects in which they do exercise it, are not subject to any exercise by other persons of the kind of authority which they are exercising.[1] 'A person or a body of persons may be said to exercise *coercive sovereignty*, or supreme coercive power, if it determines the actions of persons in certain intended ways by means of force or the threat of force, and if the actions of the persons who exercise the power, in those respects in which they do exercise it, are not themselves capable of being similarly determined.'[2] 'To exercise *political influence* . . . is to determine in certain intended ways the actions, jointly or severally, of the legal and coercive sovereigns, provided always that their actions are determined by some means other than a rule of law or a threat of force. . . . To exercise *sovereignty* in this sense is to exercise political influence, as now defined, to a greater degree than anyone else . . . .'[3]

'Legal sovereignty', it seems, might be attributed to Parliaments or amending organs or constitutions;[4] 'coercive sovereignty' to armies or similar organized forces or a socially coercive power such as existed under the frank-pledge system;[5] 'influential sovereignty' to a ruling class, the majority of the electorate, a priesthood, or some other such group.[6]

I propose in this paper to isolate and examine these and other usages, to try to discover in what kinds of study, if any, each is likely to be useful; and to determine whether they possess any common element that would justify the use of the one word 'sovereignty' to cover them all.

II. *Legal Sovereignty*

It has often been said that a 'legal sovereign' is necessary in every

---

[1] W. J. Rees, 'The Theory of Sovereignty Restated', in *Mind*, vol. lix (1950), p. 508. (My italics S.I.B.)

[2] Ibid., p. 511. (My italics S.I.B.)

[3] Ibid., p. 514. (My italics S.I.B.)

[4] Ibid., pp. 516–17. It is not clear from this passage that Mr. Rees would ascribe legal sovereignty to a constitution. Such an ascription has been made by other writers, however (e.g. by Sir Ernest Barker in *Principles of Social and Political Theory*, p. 61, and Lord Lindsay in *The Modern Democratic State*, pp. 222–9), and I propose to examine the implications of this usage.

[5] W. J. Rees, op. cit., p. 509.

[6] Ibid., p. 513.

state if legal issues are to be settled with certainty and finality.[1] From one point of view, this necessity derives from the nature of a judicial decision understood as one determining a dispute within the framework of established rules (as distinct from one made according to subjective criteria). The judge called upon to settle a dispute sees law as a system of rules to guide his decision; and such a system needs criteria of validity determining which rules belong to it; it needs a supreme norm, providing directly or indirectly the criteria of validity of all other norms, and not itself open to challenge.[2]

Where a written constitution exists, it is approximately true to say that the constitution itself provides such a supreme norm; and in this sense one may speak of the 'legal sovereignty of the constitution'. An amendable written constitution will provide criteria for

[1] E.g. Sir Ernest Barker, op. cit., p. 59: 'There *must* exist in the State, as a legal association, a power of final legal adjustment of all legal issues which arise in its ambit.' W. J. Rees, op. cit., p. 501: 'Laws can only be effectively administered if there exists some final legal authority beyond which there is no further legal appeal. In the absence of such a final legal authority no legal issue could ever be certainly decided, and government would become impossible.' J. W. Salmond: *Jurisprudence* (10th ed. by Glanville Williams), App. I, p. 490: 'It seems clear that every political society involves the presence of supreme power . . . . For otherwise all power would be subordinate, and this supposition involves the absurdity of a series of superiors and inferiors *ad infinitum*.' But contrast John Chipman Gray, *The Nature and Sources of the Law*, p. 79 (quoted by W. Friedmann, *Legal Theory*, 2nd ed., p. 147): 'The real rulers of a political society are undiscoverable. They are the persons who dominate over the wills of their fellows. In every political society we find the machinery of government . . . . We have to postulate one ideal entity to which to attach this machinery, but why insist on interposing another entity, that of a sovereign? Nothing seems gained by it, and to introduce it is to place at the threshold of Jurisprudence a very difficult, a purely academic, and an irrelevant question.' Gray seems to argue (*a*) that the influential sovereign is undiscoverable; (*b*) that the jurist is needlessly multiplying the entities by postulating a legal sovereign. But (*b*) is not a necessary inference from (*a*).

[2] Cf. H. Kelsen, *General Theory of Law and State* (1945), p. 124: 'The legal order . . . is therefore not a system of norms coördinated to each other, standing, so to speak, side by side on the same level, but a hierarchy of different levels of norms. The unity of these norms is constituted by the fact that the creation of one norm—the lower one— is determined by another—the higher—the creation of which is determined by a still higher norm, and that this *regressus* is terminated by a highest, the basic norm which, being the supreme reason of validity of the whole legal order, constitutes its unity.' And Salmond, op. cit., sec. 50: 'It is requisite that the law should postulate one or more first causes whose operation is ultimate, and whose authority is underived. In other words, there must be found in every legal system certain ultimate principles from which all others are derived, but which are themselves self-existent. . . . Whence comes the rule that Acts of Parliament have the force of law? This is legally ultimate; its source is historical only, not legal. . . . No Statute lays it down. It is certainly recognized by many precedents, but no precedent can confer authority upon precedent. It must first possess authority before it can confer it. If we enquire as to the number of these ultimate principles, the answer is that a legal system is free to recognize any number of them, but it is not bound to recognize more than one.'

identifying valid amendment. But even so the constitution may not be altogether identified with the supreme norm; for there may be rules for its interpretation which judges accept as binding but which are not prescribed in the constitution. Effectively, therefore, it is the traditional judicial interpretation of the constitution that is the supreme norm.

The absence of a written document does not vastly alter the situation. The supreme norm in English law is provided in part by the maxim 'Parliament is sovereign'. But this leaves open the question 'What is an Act of Parliament?' A judge must be able to refer to a criterion superior in status to an Act, which will establish which rules are Acts. (In a recent article[1] Mr. Geoffrey Marshall has drawn attention to the way in which the interpretation of Parliamentary sovereignty is changing. The critical question, in his view, is: 'What is Parliament?' This seems to me to put the problem the wrong way. A judge requires not a definition of the organ Parliament, but a criterion by which to recognize a norm of the type 'Act of Parliament'. For judicial decisions are reached in the light of norms, not of organs. Mr. Marshall seems to argue that there is a difference in principle between the view typified by Lord Campbell's dictum that the Parliament roll provides conclusive evidence of a statute's validity[2] and the rule in *Harris* v. *Dönges* which implies that a rule issuing from Parliament by a procedure other than that legally prescribed is not an Act.[3] But the difference is not that Parliament is held, in the one view, to be above the law, and, in the other, to be subject to law; it lies in the stringency of the criteria which, in the view of the court, a rule must satisfy in order to be deemed an Act of Parliament.)

An Act of Parliament, therefore, is subordinate to the supreme constitutional norm. It is, however, a rule of a special type in that its binding force cannot be challenged on the grounds that it is in *substantial* conflict with any superior norm. (In this respect it differs from an Act of Congress or a statutory instrument.) In view of this

---

[1] G. Marshall, 'What is Parliament? The Changing Concept of Parliamentary Sovereignty', in *Political Studies*, vol. ii, no. 3 (1954), pp. 193–209.

[2] In *Edinburgh and Dalkeith Rly. Co.* v. *Wauchope* (1842): 'All that a Court of Justice can do is to look to the Parliamentary roll: if from that it should appear that a bill has passed both Houses and received the Royal assent, no Court of Justice can inquire into the mode in which it was introduced into Parliament, nor into what was done previous to its introduction, of what passed in Parliament during its progress in its various stages through both Houses.'

[3] See G. Marshall, op. cit., for a full discussion of this and other relevant cases.

peculiarity, it might be useful to ascribe to Acts of Parliament *immediate* supremacy as decisive rules in questions of substance, while the norm from which their validity derives might be termed *ultimately* supreme. This is a reinterpretation of a distinction made by Sir Ernest Barker, who ascribes ultimate sovereignty to the constitution and immediate sovereignty to a supreme legislative organ; but it avoids the awkward asymmetry of his ascription:[1] the word 'sovereignty' can scarcely be precisely and unambiguously defined and yet fit with equal comfort both an organ and a norm.[2]

The interpretation of 'legal sovereignty' I have offered has, I believe, the advantage that while meeting the judicial need for an ultimate point of reference, it avoids the criticisms directed against the command theory with which the notion of sovereignty has traditionally been associated. Whether law is command is irrelevant. For the judge is interested in the 'source' of a law only if by 'source' is meant the higher norm from which its validity derives; its legislative origin is a fact to be assessed according to established legal criteria. Further, 'legal sovereignty', as I conceive it, need not imply that law is 'effective', i.e. generally observed in an actual community. A student might apply ancient legal principles to hypothetical cases; in so doing he would be acting in a way closely parallel to a judge on an English bench, and would find the same necessity for a supreme norm. The same would apply to the student of Utopian or Erewhonian law. Again, 'sanction' is non-essential to 'sovereignty' in this sense, and the difficulties which arise in applying some legal theories of sovereignty to constitutional and administrative law thus do not arise here.[3]

This notion of the 'supreme norm' is essential to any study of the rules governing decisions within a normative order. It is of primary importance for the practising lawyer, and for the jurist. It is also

---

[1] Sir Ernest Barker, op. cit., bk. ii, sec. 5. Sir Ernest recognizes the asymmetry, but considers it 'inherent in the nature of the case' (p. 63).

[2] Ibid., loc. cit.; and W. J. Rees, op. cit., pp. 516–17.

[3] Cf. L. Duguit, *Law and the Modern State*, p. 31: 'In those great state services which increase every day . . . the state . . . intervenes in a manner that has to be regulated and ordered by a system of public law. But this system can no longer be based on the theory of sovereignty. It is applied to acts where no trace of power to command is to be found. Of necessity a new system is being built, attached indeed by close bonds to the old, but founded on an entirely new theory. Modern institutions . . . take their origin not from the theory of sovereignty, but from the notion of public service.' (Quoted in H. E. Cohen, *Recent Theories of Sovereignty*, p. 40.) This notion is in no way incompatible with the view of sovereignty I am suggesting.

of significance to the administrator, and to the student of administration interested in the legal sources and limitations of administrative discretion rather than in the motives which determine the
exercise of discretion.

In historical or sociological studies and those concerned with
moral questions the notion of a supreme norm is at most only
indirectly relevant. If we ask such questions as 'How do laws
develop?', 'What governs the content of law in this (or any) community?', 'What is the role of law in this (or any) society?',[1] we shall
need a way of distinguishing law from other modes of social control,
but the judicial criterion of validity will not necessarily be an element
in such a principle of differentiation. Of course, any description of
the life of a community must, to be complete, include an account of
its judicial system, and so of the assumptions made by the men whose
business it is to reach decisions within this normative order; but the
supreme norm will figure in a sociologist's account as a feature of the
conceptual apparatus employed by lawyers, not as part of his own.

Similarly, in asking the moral question 'What ought laws to be like?'
we need to distinguish laws from, say, conventional moral rules. But
the principle of differentiation must now be related to those aspects
of law which constitute it a distinct problem (e.g. the coercive
sanction, or the presumption that most people will obey it), and the
judicial criterion of validity will not necessarily figure as part of it.

The questions of political science are both normative and descriptive. If the political scientist is concerned with the state as a
normative order, the idea of the supreme norm will have the same
relevance for him as it has for the lawyer; but if his questions concern
men's actual political behaviour, his view of law will be much more
that of the sociologist.

III. *Legislative Sovereignty*

The approach to 'legal sovereignty' that I have suggested derives
from reflection upon the activities of a judge, for whom the law
appears, at any particular moment, as a body of given rules to guide
his judgement. For the political scientist, however, law appears in the
process of creation; he is concerned with law-making and law-

---

[1] Cf. R. Wollheim's distinction between questions about law which are in Jurisprudence, and those which are not, in 'The Nature of Law', in *Political Studies*, vol. ii
(1954), pp. 139–40.

makers;[1] he is interested in 'legislative organs', and not merely in 'legal norms'. I propose accordingly to inquire now whether there is a place in the political scientist's vocabulary for 'supreme legislative organ', and what it might mean to attribute 'supremacy' in this way. To distinguish the supremacy of a norm from that of a legislative organ, I propose to use 'legal sovereignty' for the former and 'legislative sovereignty' for the latter.

A political scientist might significantly classify legislative organs in a legal order into superior and inferior (or subordinate), and he might arrange them hierarchically as a sort of reflection of the judge's hierarchy of norms. The judge will deem an Act of Parliament superior in status to a statutory instrument; the political scientist will deem Parliament superior in competence to a minister acting as legislator. But does it follow that the necessity which leads the judge to postulate a supreme norm is paralleled by a similar necessity leading the political scientist to postulate a supreme legislative organ? Such an organ would be omnicompetent, that is, competent to legislate on all matters without the possibility that any of its rules might be invalidated by reason of conflict with some other rule not of its own making.[2] It might reasonably, therefore, be called 'legislative sovereign'. But such a sovereign is not logically necessary to a legal order. A constitution might allocate fields of legislative competence between co-ordinate organs, or place certain matters beyond the competence of any organ (e.g. by a Bill of Rights); and in respect of such limitations the constitution might be unamendable. (This qualification is important, since the competence to amend the constitution in these respects would be, on an ultimate analysis, omnicompetence.) In such a case, there would be no omnicompetent organ. On the other hand, one might speak of one organ with supreme competence *in a particular field* or of several such organs; and that would mean that though the rules of such an organ might be invalidated by reason of conflict with the constitution they could not be invalidated through conflict with the rules of any other *organ*. But one cannot say a priori that every legal order *must* possess one or more 'supreme legislative organs' even

---

[1] Cf. Kelsen, op. cit., p. 39: 'If we adopt a static point of view, that is, if we consider the legal order only in its completed form or in a state of rest, then we notice only the norms by which the legal acts are determined. If, on the other hand, we adopt a dynamic outlook, if we consider the process through which the legal order is created and executed, then we see only the law-creating and law-executing acts.'

[2] Except for a rule of another organ to which this one had expressly delegated a limited competence to make rules, in a given field, of equal status to its own (e.g. by a 'Henry VIII' clause).

in this sense. A constitution that is unamendable (at least in respect of its allocation of fields of competence) might constitute two (or more) organs co-ordinate in the same field, so that a rule enacted by either might set aside a rule of the other. A judge operating such an order would require only some general prescription to show which of conflicting rules enacted by different organs he should deem binding; and this could be met by the principle that in case of conflict a later rule should repeal an earlier. This might be highly inconvenient if the co-ordinate organs were operated by men of different opinions, and competition developed for the latest place. But this could be avoided without making one organ supreme in each field, if, for example, co-ordinate organs were operated by members of one highly disciplined political party, or by men who reached decisions by mutual agreement before legislating. The judge need not then be faced with conflicts any oftener than he is in England.

There is thus neither logical nor practical necessity for a legislative sovereign in every state, though there may be states in which such organs are discoverable. But it should be stressed that to ascribe 'sovereignty' to a legislative organ in either of the senses just considered is to attribute to it not 'power', in the sense of ability 'to determine the actions of persons in certain intended ways',[1] but legal capacity or 'competence'; it is to say no more than that a judge will set an organ's rules in a particular kind of relation to the rules of other organs. It is, indeed, a statement about the formal structure of a legal order. It does not presuppose any actual ability possessed by the men acting through an organ to determine the actions of other persons in intended ways. It does not even require that the action of the judge himself should be so determined; for the person occupying judicial office may disregard the law. Law is normative: it prescribes how a person must act to function as a judge within the legal order; it does not predict that he *will* so act.

Yet it is true that law-making is one way of 'determining the actions of persons in certain intended ways'. A sociologist seeking to explain behaviour in a community would need to take its statutes

---

[1] 'Power' suffers from a systematic ambiguity. When we refer to 'the powers of Local Authorities', 'Parliament's power to legislate on any subject whatsoever', or 'legislative powers of Ministers', we mean 'competence' or 'entitlement'—i.e. that they are 'empowered' to act in this or that way. This is a quite different sense from that implied by Mr. Rees's definition: 'to determine the actions of persons in certain intended ways'. The 'power' possessed by a Local Authority to orginize concerts is clearly not power in this second sense. Neither is it a species of a 'power' genus. Mr. Rees's argument suffers from his failure to make this distinction. *Vide* op. cit., p. 511.

into account, since the knowledge that a particular rule is a statute may condition the behaviour of those subject to it. Consequently, legislators can often be regarded as determining the actions of persons in intended ways. But there is no warrant for automatically transferring 'supremacy' as applied to competence to any power deriving from such competence. It is not, for instance, necessarily true that the men who operate the organ termed 'supreme' receive more obedience than those operating a 'subordinate' organ. The amending organ of the U.S.A.—Congress together with three-fourths of the States—is omnicompetent (or very nearly so), yet the Eighteenth Amendment was much less effective than most Acts of Congress.[1] 'Supremacy', then, is relevant, when applied to legislative organs, only when a legislative act is considered as a directive to a judge: in all other contexts it is out of place.

IV. *The Sovereignty of the State in its international aspect*

There remains to be considered, before leaving the juristic field, the sense of 'sovereignty' as applied in international relations.

It has often been argued that state 'sovereignty' is incompatible with international law. The term implies that the state is a self-sufficient legal order; and this must mean that a judge operating that order need seek no further than its own supreme norm. The traditional problem then arising is put by Kelsen in the following terms:

'That the State is sovereign means that the national legal order is an order above which there is no higher order. The only order that could be assumed to be superior to that of the national legal order is the international legal order. The question whether the State is sovereign or not thus coincides with the question whether or not international law is an order superior to national law.'[2]

---

[1] This is not to suggest that 'supreme legislative power' is necessarily meaningless. It could conceivably be used in historical and sociological studies. To attribute it to A might mean (1) that all the laws he made were invariably effective and could not be overturned (which would be the 'power' equivalent to 'supreme competence'); (2) that they were more generally effective than anyone else's (though the use of 'superior' rather than 'supreme' might accord better with common usage); or (3) that his laws were usually effective, and his conduct was not determined by laws made by others. Examples of (1) probably cannot be found; (2) would be useful only if the effectiveness of laws depended on their sources, which seems improbable; (3) might be true of a few autocrats, but must be unusual. A fourth apparent possibility, viz. that in consequence of A's possessing supreme legislative competence his laws are more likely to be effective, *ceteris paribus*, than rules liable to invalidation, is really only another way of saying that the legal order is effective. None of these senses seems important and I shall not consider them further.

[2] Kelsen, op. cit., p. 384.

A pluralistic position, he argues, is inadmissible: two legal orders with conflicting norms cannot be simultaneously valid for the same territory.[1] The choice lies, therefore, between the primacy of international law, with non-'sovereign' national legal orders deriving validity from it, and the primacy of national law endowing international law with validity to the extent that it recognizes it. But the consequence of the second view is 'state solipsism',[2] for now only one State can be held to be sovereign; other legal orders exist for it only as derivatives of itself, either directly or indirectly through its recognition of international law. Kelsen adds:

'It is, however, logically possible that different theorists interpret the world of law by proceeding from the sovereignty of different States. Each theorist may presuppose the sovereignty of his own State, that is to say, he may accept the hypothesis of the primacy of his own national legal order. Then he has to consider the international law which establishes the relations to the legal orders of the other States and these national legal orders as parts of the legal order of his own State, conceived of as a universal legal order. This means that the picture of the world of law would vary according to what State is made the basis of the interpretation. Within each of these systems, erected on the hypothesis of the primacy of national law, one State only is sovereign, but in no two of them would this be the same State.'[3]

Kelsen appears to regard this solution as irrefutable but unsatisfactory. I believe, however, that otherwise stated it can throw light on the place of 'sovereignty' in international law, and of international law within the structure of 'sovereign' national orders.

Within the English legal framework an English judge will take cognizance of international law as a part of English law to the extent that its rules do not conflict with other rules of English law; the national laws of other states will equally be subject to the criteria of validity of the English legal order, and in so far as they are recognized by a judge will become parts of that order. In this sense, then, it is true that for the English judge, the only sovereign order is his own. But *mutatis mutandis* the same is true of a French or any other national judge. Each can operate only within his own order, and for him it is self-sufficient. This is again true of the international lawyer. His order is a self-sufficient order embracing national orders as subordinate parts. A given rule may well be valid in one of these orders

[1] Ibid., p. 363.
[2] Ibid., p. 387.
[3] Ibid., p. 386.

(national or international) and invalid in another. But there is not here, as Kelsen supposes, any contradiction, and if it involves 'State solipsism', this need cause no embarrassment. Kelsen's argument, that 'two norms which by their significance contradict and hence logically exclude one another, cannot be simultaneously valid', misses the point. He requires that there shall be only one *objectively valid* legal order. But to ascribe 'self-sufficiency' to an order rules out the ascription to it of 'validity', which for Kelsen is meaningful only *within* an order. Accordingly, many such systems can logically exist, side by side, and none can claim greater legal validity than another.

It follows, as a corollary to this analysis, that if the international lawyer refers to 'sovereign orders', or the national lawyer to '*other* sovereign states', then the sense of the word 'sovereign' as here used must be different from that in which either applies the term to his own order, as self-sufficient. He is now using it of a particular type of partial order, analogous to other partial orders, like 'corporations', recognized by various legal orders. The precise definition of 'a sovereign state' in any given legal order is a question of particular not of general jurisprudence and cannot be settled by reflection upon the nature of legal systems in general.

V. *Sovereignty as 'supreme coercive power'*

'Sovereignty' as 'supreme coercive power' is not, I believe, relevant to or meaningful in a normative study of political institutions.

If we begin by defining the state as a coercive order, that is, as an order maintained by the exercise or threat of physical force, then coercive power is, by definition, necessary to it. If we define it in some other way, then, in Mr. Rees's phrase, coercive power is 'causally necessary' to it, if it is to be capable of surviving violent opposition. In either case, the coercive power attributed is a mode of operation, or an institutional framework, within which action is undertaken by whatever men happen to occupy the appropriate offices or to fit the constitutional categories which the order provides.

For instance, to say that in a particular state the coercive power is exercised by the Army is to say that this mode of state action is the proper function of any group which satisfies a set of legal or conventional conditions constituting it the coercive organ of the state, and which acts according to the procedures proper to such an organ (e.g. under orders from the Minister for War or the Commander-in-Chief). In this context only one coercive power is possible in a state:

for the term must refer either to a mode of action within the single normative order, or to the organs whose mode of action it is. If several organs employ this mode, they all operate within the same order, and so jointly constitute its coercive power. The state's coercive power may therefore in a sense be divided, but so long as we think of the state as an order there is no point in saying of one or other organ, or of a group of organs, that it is supreme. For 'supremacy' implies the possibility of conflict, and a conflict of coercive organs is incompatible with the conception of the state as an order. Thus if conflict does arise between groups qualified to act as coercive organs, then at least one group must be acting otherwise than as a state organ. For example, an army in rebellion against the established Government is not acting as a state organ. (Of course, in any territory at any moment there may well be more than one actual coercive organization: in 1932, besides the coercive forces of the German Republic there existed the Brown Shirts. But the Brown Shirts were not part of the state order.)

One further point—the distinction drawn by Mr. Rees between political orders in which coercive sovereignty is exercised by an institutionally coercive power and those in which it is exercised by a socially coercive power[1] is misleading in two ways. To reserve the term 'institutional' for coercive power exercised by professional armies, &c., obscures the fact that where all, or nearly all, the members of a community collectively constitute the coercive organ, their function *is* 'institutional'. Secondly, inasmuch as Mr. Rees has in mind the classification of political orders, the attribution of 'supremacy' to coercive organs is redundant, and nothing is lost by abandoning the term.

In historical and sociological studies, 'supreme coercive power' may well be meaningfully used. A statement like: 'By 1649, the New Model Army had emerged as the supreme coercive power in England' is not concerned with institutional relations in the English constitutional order, but with power relations between groups of men in a particular territory. In such studies we may well compare the coercive power of one group with that of another. For the historian, Brown Shirts and Communists are as much factors of the 1932 German situation as were the armed forces of the Republic, and he might declare one of them 'supreme', in the sense that, had armed conflict developed, it could have defeated its rivals. It is doubtful, however, whether the term is helpful in describing any but the simplest situa-

[1] W. J. Rees, op, cit., pp. 509–10, and Section I above.

tions. In peaceful conditions we could say that coercive sovereignty
is exercised by the coercive organs of the state; and after a civil war
we could attribute it to a victorious army that remained united. But
it would rather mislead to try to apply it, for example, to Sicily in
the days of the Mafia or France in the days of the Maquis.[1] In any
case, even if the seat of coercive sovereignty can be located, the
possibilities of inquiry opened up are limited. It will give us no way
of understanding the importance in the determination of policy of
those controlling the coercive organs of the state. Taken collectively,
the Germany army, navy, air force, Gestapo, and S.S. may have constituted the coercive sovereign in Hitler's Germany; but to understand
the part played by those controlling these organs in shaping political
events we have to consider them separately, not collectively, and
to examine their mutual relations and rivalries and the power each
exercised at any given moment. To lump in problems of this sort is
to obscure rather than to illumine.

VI. Sovereignty as 'the strongest political influence'

The first question here concerns the type of discussion to which
'influence' may be relevant. I drew a distinction earlier[2] between words
of two logical types—'competence' and 'power' (as ability to determine the actions of persons in intended ways). 'Influence' is a word
of the same type as 'power'. To establish A's *competence* we examine
his status in a normative order; to establish his *influence* we must
observe how men behave in relation to him, whether for instance
they act on his suggestions or consult his wishes. 'Influence', and
consequently 'the strongest political influence', have thus no place
in a normative study. It is only in historical or sociological studies
that they can be meaningfully employed. It is of course true that a
man's status in a normative order may be a source of influence; but
the extent of that influence, and, indeed, its very existence, cannot
be established by normative study.

Is the search for 'an influential sovereign' likely to be fruitful in
historical and sociological studies? We must distinguish, first, two
senses of 'influence': as in (1) 'Climate influences vegetation' and (2)
'Rasputin's influence over Nicholas II'. In (1) no more than 'effect'
is implied: there is no suggestion of intention; in (2) the effect produced
is one intended. When we speak of 'the strongest political influence'

[1] Cf. Lord Bryce, op. cit., p. 63.

[2] Section III above.

we are presumably thinking of some group which can shape governmental policy to its own purposes. We are using 'influence' therefore
in sense (2).

Now we should not say that a group was the 'influential sovereign'
merely because it had occasionally shaped government policy as it
intended. That would multiply sovereigns endlessly and deprive the
term of all point. As Mr. Rees has pointed out, 'sovereignty' resembles
dispositional words in that it implies recurrent capacity to determine
policy in intended ways under understood conditions.[1] In seeking an
influential sovereign, therefore, we should be seeking a stable dominant influence over a fairly wide range of political issues.

In states of one type a single group (e.g. a ruling class), able
decisively to influence policy whenever it operated, could be regarded
as such an influence. The value of this approach, however, would
depend on the range of common interests from which the group's
identity derived and which therefore constituted its field of operation.
In states of another type Governments are sensitive to pressures
from diverse interests, and political decisions are thus the outcome of
an interplay of influences rather than expressions of a single dominant
influence. If we seek an influential sovereign here, then, we are likely
to be seriously misled; terms like 'lobby' and 'pressure group' will
be much more appropriate analytical concepts.

Sometimes influence is attributed to 'the electorate' or 'the
majority' as one might attribute it to 'the bankers' or a 'ruling class'.
This is a mistake. Groups such as 'the bankers' or 'the ruling class'
derive identity from common interest and homogeneity of intention;
'the electorate' denotes a state organ. All that electors have in common
is the right to vote. Severally, or in groups, they may exercise influence
deriving from electoral competence; but there is not therefore one
super-influence of the electorate as such. An election is a procedure
in which influences are pitted against one other; what emerges is a
result, or an 'effect', not a new influence. We cannot say of the electorate that it influences policy as it intends; it has no single intention,
only a multitude of intentions given different weights by the electoral
process. It is no more accurate to assign influential sovereignty to
'the majority' (as Mr. Rees seems to do).[2] In any election a certain
aggregate of interests is more numerous than another, and this
arithmetical relation, corresponding to a recognized legal procedure,
is a source of influence for the groups concerned. But the aggregates

[1] W. J. Rees, op. cit., pp. 514–15.

[2] Ibid., pp. 512–13.

at the next election will be differently constituted; in five elections there will be five majorities; and we should not treat them as though they were one group, *the* majority, exercising a stable dominant influence. Consequently, the inference to be drawn from 'The majority (or the electorate) is sovereign' is not that Government is sensitive to a specified influence but that it is sensitive to *all* influences.

Finally, 'influential sovereignty' might be applied to an organization, like a Church or a Communist party, which has a policy on all, or most, matters, and is able to make it effective. But here again the policy is not the intention of a group identifiable by common interest, but the result of an interplay of influences within the organization. The internal politics of influential organizations need to be interpreted in terms of pressure groups just as much as do the politics of states. To attribute sovereignty to the Communist party is not to provide an explanation of the changes in Soviet policy since 1917: it is the struggle for power within the party that is the point of interest for the student of Soviet history.

The concept 'influential sovereignty' has the disadvantage, then, that it may direct attention to the wrong questions, or conceal the need for inquiry beyond the point where the influential sovereign has been identified.

VII

In this paper I have identified six senses in which 'sovereignty' might be meaningfully employed:

(*a*) to express the supremacy of a norm in a legal hierarchy, as viewed by a lawyer, or by a student concerned with the legal limits of discretion;

(*b*) in a study of constitutions as normative orders, to refer either to the omnicompetence, or to the supreme competence within its field, of a legislative organ;

(*c*) to express the self-sufficency of a legal order from the point of view of a lawyer operating within it;

(*d*) to refer to a particular kind of partial order, the definition of which may vary from one legal order to another (its utility in this sense being limited to particular jurisprudence);

(*e*) to express the ability of bodies such as armed forces to defeat all probable rivals;

(*f*) to express the ability of a sectional interest decisively to influence policy.

The first four senses are relevant to normative studies and cannot be directly utilized in historical or sociological studies without confusion. Each of them is a useful concept in its own field, but they seem to have little in common. The first two share the idea of 'supremacy' but in slightly different senses of that word; the third is an expression of totality, rather than supremacy; the fourth implies neither notion. The fifth and sixth senses, unlike the first four, do imply ability to determine other people's conduct; and it is in these senses alone that sovereignty implies supreme power. These two senses may be relevant to historical or sociological studies, and are not relevant to normative studies; their usefulness where they are relevant is limited, for they can be seriously misleading.

In the light of this analysis it would appear to be a mistake to treat 'sovereignty' as denoting a genus of which the species can be distinguished by suitable adjectives, and there would seem to be a strong case for giving up so Protean a word.

V

AUTHORITY

(1) R. S. PETERS

1. *Authority and Artifice.*

THERE are good reasons as well as personal excuses for ushering in Hobbes at the outset of a discussion on 'authority'; for Hobbes himself introduced the concept to deal with difficult problems connected with the analysis of human institutions. And there is little point in making a list of the different ways in which the term 'authority' can be used unless the distinctions are made with an eye on the problem or cluster of problems that can be clarified by means of them.

Hobbes was impressed by the fact that a civil society is not a natural whole like a rook or a beehive; yet it is not a mere multitude of men. A multitude of men becomes an artificial person when each man *authorizes* the actions of a representative. 'Of persons artificial, some have their words and actions owned by those whom they represent. And then the person is the *actor*; and he that owneth his words and actions is the AUTHOR: in which case the actor acteth by authority . . . and as the right of possession, is called dominion; so the right of doing any action, is called AUTHORITY. So that by authority, is always understood a right of doing any act; and *done by authority*, done by commission, or licence, from him whose right it is.' (*Leviathan*, Ed. Oakeshott pp. 105–6.) De Jouvenel, also, uses the concept of 'authority' in the context of the same type of problem. Having rejected the view that civil societies come into being through voluntary association or through domination from without, he claims that authority is 'the efficient cause of voluntary associations' . . . 'Everywhere and at all levels social life offers us the daily spectacle of authority fulfilling its primary function—of man leading man on, of the ascendancy of a settled will which summons and orients uncertain wills . . . Society in fact exists only because

Symposium by R. S. Peters and Peter Winch. From *Proceedings of the Aristotelian Society*, Supp. Vol. 32 (1958), pp. 207–40. Reprinted by courtesy of the authors and the Editor of the Aristotelian Society, with a postscript to his paper by Peter Winch.

man is capable of proposing and affecting by his proposals another's dispositions; it is by the acceptance of proposals that
contracts are clinched, disputes settled and alliances formed
between individuals ... What I mean by "authority" is the
ability of a man to get his proposals accepted'. (*Sovereignty* pp.
29–31.)

2. *The* de jure *and* de facto *senses of 'authority'.*

I have chosen to start off with these quotations from Hobbes and
de Jouvenel partly because they both introduce the concept of 'authority' in the context of the attempt to elucidate what is meant by a
society as distinct from a multitude of men, and partly because the
two quotations illustrate an important difference in the ways in which
the term 'authority' is used in the context of the same sort of problem.
For Hobbes 'authority' is what might be called a *de jure* concept; for
de Jouvenel it seems to be a *de facto* one. In other words, for Hobbes
the term indicates or proclaims that someone has a *right* to do something. 'Done by authority' means 'done by commission or licence from
him whose right it is'. Now I am not concerned to defend Hobbes'
odd conception of the handing over of rights or his account of
'authorization'. But, whatever the correct analysis of the connexion
between 'authority' and 'right', it is quite clear that there is a very
important use of the term 'authority', which is favoured by Hobbes,
which connects the two concepts. A man who is 'in authority' for
instance, clearly has a right to do certain sorts of things. This use of
'authority' is to be contrasted with the *de facto* use favoured by de
Jouvenel. For he says 'What I mean by "authority" is the *ability* of
a man to get his proposals accepted'. The Oxford English Dictionary
seems to permit both usages; for it gives 'power or right to enforce
obedience'. It also speaks of 'power to influence the conduct and
actions of others; ... personal or practical influence; power over the
opinion of others; intellectual influence'; as well as 'moral or legal
supremacy; the right to command or give an ultimate decision ...
title to be believed'. And in ordinary conversation the two senses
can be used without danger of misunderstanding in one sentence when
we say things like 'The headmaster and others in authority had,
unfortunately, no authority with the boys'. The question quite naturally arises how these two senses of 'authority' are related and whether
both senses are important, as Hobbes and de Jouvenel maintain, for
saying certain sorts of things about specifically human relationships
and organizations.

3. *Hobbes' rendering of the* de jure *sense.*

The *de jure* concept of authority presupposes a system of rules which determine who may legitimately take certain types of decision, make certain sorts of pronouncements, issue commands of a certain sort, and perform certain types of symbolic acts. Hobbes brings this out by saying that the actions of a representative are authorized. He relies on the sense of 'authorize' which assimilates it to commissioning or giving a warrant to a man to do certain types of things. The subjects are conceived of as having words and actions which they own, of which they are the 'authors', and to which they have a right. They then appoint a representative to whom they transfer their right. He is now commissioned or 'authorized' to act on their behalf. 'So that by authority is always understood a right of doing any act; and done by authority, done by commission or licence from him whose right it is.' Now Hobbes, as is well known, and as Mr. Warrender has recently shown in such stimulating detail, had a very strange view of natural rights which permeates this picture of authority. He was led by it to conceive of authority *in general* in terms of the particular case where a man is the author of a word or act, to which he also has a right, and where he commissions someone else to act in this matter on his behalf. This is indeed a case of an authorized act; but there is a more general meaning of 'authorize' which is to set up or acknowledge as authoritative; to give legal force or formal approval to. Similarly 'authorized' in its most general meaning is equivalent to 'possessed of authority'. 'Authorization' is better understood in terms of the general concept of 'authority' rather than vice-versa. Hobbes pictured 'authority' in terms of 'authorization' which is one of its derivatives. But he did bring out the obvious connexion between 'authority' and the existence of an 'author' in the realm of acts and words, which is the key to seeing how the concept works.

4. *'Auctoritas' as the key to 'authority'.*

The concept of 'authority' is obviously derived from the old concepts of 'auctor' and 'auctoritas'. An 'auctor' was, to quote Lewis and Short, 'he that brings about the existence of any object, or promotes the increase or prosperity of it, whether he first originates it, or by his efforts gives greater permanence or continuance to it'. 'Auctoritas' which is a producing, invention, or cause, can be exercised in the spheres of opinion, counsel or command. The point of this little excursion into philology is to stress not only the sphere of opinion, command and so on, in which 'auctoritas' is regarded as

being exercised, but also the connexion of the concept with 'producing', 'originating', 'inventing'—in short, with there being an author.

Now in some spheres of social life it is imperative to have such
'auctores' who are producers or originators of orders, pronouncements, decisions and so on. It is also the case that in social life,
whether we like it or not, there are such 'auctores' to whom commands,
decisions and pronouncements are to be traced back in any factual
survey of how social regulation is brought about. This is the sense of
'authority' stressed by de Jouvenel. The notion of 'authority' involves
therefore either a set of rules which determine who shall be the *auctor*
and about what, or, in its *de facto* sense, a reference to a man whose
word in fact goes in these spheres. The *de jure* sense of 'authority'
proclaims that a man has a right to be an 'auctor'; the *de facto* sense
states that he is a matter of fact one. Hobbes' account of 'authorization' relates to the particular case where a man has a right to be an
'auctor', as laid down by a set of rules, and where he commissions
someone else to do what he himself has a right to do. Indeed, often, as
in a bureaucratic system, there are subordinate sets of rules which lay
down procedures for the granting of such warrants and commissions.
But all authority cannot adequately be conceived in this fashion.

5. *Weber's legal-rational and traditional rules for determining who is IN authority.*

Indeed, one of the great services done by the sociologist, Max
Weber, has been to stress the *different* types of normative systems
which are connected with different types of authority. For legitimacy
may be bestowed in different ways on the commands or decisions or
pronouncements issuing from an 'auctor'. In what he calls a legal-
rational system the claim to legitimacy rests on 'a belief in the
"legality" of patterns of normative rules and the right of those
elevated to authority under such rules to issue commands'. (*Theory of
Economic and Social Organization*, Ed. Talcot Parsons, pp. 300/1.) There
is also, however, traditional authority 'resting on an established
belief in the sanctity of immemorial traditions and the legitimacy of
the status of those exercising authority under them'.

There are most important and interesting differences between these
types of authority but this is not the place to investigate the difference
between traditional and legal rules, or to comment on the adequacy
of Weber's analysis—but in both cases to speak of 'the authorities' or
'those in authority' or those who 'hold authority' is to proclaim that
on certain matters certain people are entitled, licensed, commissioned

or have a right to be *auctores*. And the right is bestowed by a set pattern of rules.

6. *Weber's charismatic authority*.

This type of authority is to be distinguished clearly from other types of authority where the right derives from personal history, personal credentials, and personal achievements, which, as will be argued later, are intimately bound up with the exercise of authority in its *de facto* sense. There is a gradation from the pure *de jure* sense of 'authority' as when we say that 'Wittgenstein held a position of authority in Cambridge', through the notion of '*an* authority' as when we say 'Wittgenstein was an authority on William James' to the *de facto* sense as when we say 'Wittgenstein exerted considerable authority over the Moral Science Club'. Both the last two senses of 'authority', unlike the first, imply something about the attributes or qualifications of the individual in question. But the details of this transition are very difficult to make explicit.

Weber, as a matter of fact, made much of authority deriving from personal characteristics when he spoke of 'charismatic authority'— 'resting on devotion to the specific and exceptional sanctity, heroism or exemplary character of an individual person, and of the normative patterns or order revealed or ordained by him' (op. cit. p. 301). He was thinking primarily of the outstanding religious and military leaders like Jesus and Napoleon. He therefore pitched his account rather high and personal 'authority' is decked with the trappings of vocation, miracles and revelation. Nevertheless, there is something distinctive about the charismatic leader which he shares in an exaggerated form with other 'natural' leaders who exercise authority in virtue of personal claims and personal characteristics. For he is unlike the moral reformer who gives reasons of a general kind for his innovations, reasons which he expects everyone to appreciate. He appeals to revelation or claims that he has a call. These are not really justifications of his innovations; they are ways of stressing that he need give no justification because he is *a special sort of man*.

7. *Gradations in the concept of 'AN authority'*.

This notion of presenting credentials of a *personal* sort is an intermediary between the purely *de jure* and the *de facto* senses of 'authority'. For the reference to personal characteristics is a way of establishing that a man has a right to make pronouncements and issue commands because he is a special sort of person. And, although in some societies a man who sees visions and goes into trance states is in danger of electric shock treatment, in other societies pointing to such peculiarities of personal biography are ways of establishing a man as *an* authority in certain spheres. In societies where the claim to vocation or revelation is acceptable there are also, usually, collateral tests for eliminating charlatans and the mentally deranged. But his claims rest, as it were, on some kind of personal initiation into mysteries that are a closed book to most men. In a similar way years of study of inaccessible manuscripts would establish a man as 'an authority' on a special period of history, or years spent in Peru might establish a man as 'an authority' on the Incas. Collateral tests would, of course, be necessary to vouch for his trustworthiness. But in many fields people become 'authorities' by some process of personal absorption in matters that are generally held to be either inaccessible or inscrutable. Dodds suggested that the Forms were objects of this sort for Plato—objects which the initiated had to scrutinize by a kind of bi-location of personality as practised by shamans. And the scrutiny of such objects gave the philosopher kings a right to make decisions and issue commands—in short, made them authorities. (*The Greeks and the Irrational*, pp. 210/11.)

Weber stresses the importance of success as a necessary condition for the maintenance of charismatic authority. If success deserts the leader he tends to think of his god as having deserted him or his exceptional powers as failing him. And his authority will be correspondingly reduced. The disciples, it is said, were in despair when Jesus had been crucified. It was only when he accomplished the supreme feat of rising from the dead that they recovered their faith in him and in his claims. To a certain extent the charismatic leader is in the position of a man who keeps spotting Derby winners without a system. His authority depends on always being right by virtue of a 'flair' or a 'hunch'—words which point to his inability to give grounds for his pronouncements. It is because his authority derives from such *personal* pecularities that failure tends to be fatal. This is a very important empirical generalization about a necessary condition for the exercise of authority which applies at much more mundane levels.[1]

The point, however, is that in the case of these extreme types of charismatic authority revelation and success are not simply necessary conditions for the exercise of authority *de facto*. They are also *grounds*

---

[1] Ernest Gellner has pointed out to me that in many societies there are institutional devices for covering up failure so that the authority *can't* be wrong.

for establishing the right to be an *auctor*. This can be shown, too, in more mundane spheres where we speak of a person being *an* authority. He has not been put *in* authority; he does not hold authority according to any system of rules. But because of his training, competence and past success in this sphere he comes to be regarded as *an* authority. He has a right to speak. It may be the case that people do not exercise authority in various spheres unless they are competent and successful *as a matter of fact*; but it is also the case that they come to be regarded as authorities because these necessary conditions come to be regarded as grounds for a right. The notion of *an* authority, therefore, implies, as it were, a self-generating system of entitlement which is confined to specific spheres of pronouncement and decision. We speak of an authority on art, music or nuclear physics. The grounds which entitle a man are directly connected with his *personal* history and achievements in a specific sphere. These grounds vary from the extremes of revelation, initiation and vocation, through less esoteric grounds like study of inaccessible material in history, to the more public and accessible training of a scientist. But in all these spheres success seems to be a usual ground of entitlement.

8. De facto *authority: its necessary conditions and meaning.*

It was suggested by reference to the Wittgenstein example, that there was a gradation from the purely *de jure* sense of 'authority', through the concept of 'an authority' to the *de facto* sense of 'authority'. The analysis of *de facto* authority must now be tackled and the question faced whether the term 'authority' can ever be used properly if there is no suggestion of a *right* to make decisions and issue commands or pronouncements. Does the exercise of authority *de facto* presuppose that the person who exercises it must be in authority or an authority? In the Admirable Crichton situation the butler, in fact, exercised authority, though the lord was in authority. Are we to assume that, in some sense the butler had a right to make decisions? Or does saying that the butler had authority over the lord mean simply that the lord accepted the butler's decisions just because they issued from a particular man in whose presence his 'genius was rebuked'?

Of course most people who exert authority *de facto* do so because of the deference paid to their office or status rather than because of any outstanding personal characteristics. But there is often a mixture of both as in the case of Julius Caesar or Queen Elizabeth the First. Indeed there is subtle interweaving of these institutional and personal conditions for the exercise of authority *de facto*. For, as we say, the office makes the man; and often the man gives dignity to the office. The same tendency is to be observed in cases where it is more appropriate to speak of there being *an* authority. The entitlement accorded has a snowball effect. Often the outcome is disastrous—portentous pronouncements which are unquestionably accepted but which turn out to be erroneous. The generalization to other spheres is also a well-known phenomenon—one which Socrates spent so much time attacking.

There is, therefore, a widespread connexion between being in authority or an authority and the *de facto* exercise of authority. But this is a contingent connexion, not a necessary one. And as Admirable Crichton situations are not unusual, it looks as if being in authority or an authority are only frequently conditions for exercising authority; it does not look as if they are even necessary conditions.

What then of the cases where a man exercises authority *de facto* purely because of certain personal characteristics—when either there is no deference paid to his office if he is an official, or when he is not in a position of authority at all? There are two questions here which need to be distinguished. The first is about the conditions other than being in authority or an authority which are necessary to the exercise of authority *de facto*. The second is the logical question of what it *means* to exercise authority *de facto* in this tenuous sense. Is it the case that always the exercise of authority implies that in *some* sense, a man must be regarded as entitled to command, make decisions and so on? Are there necessary conditions which, as in the case of 'an authority' come to be regarded as grounds for a right? To answer this it will be as well to deal briefly with the sorts of things which might be suggested as necessary conditions.

A variety of generalizations can be made about necessary conditions for bringing about unquestioning conformity—for instance, that a man's decisions tend to be accepted in proportion to the extent to which he has been proved right before. Success, too, strengthens another necessary condition for the exercise of authority—the expectation of being believed, followed or obeyed. People will tend to accept decisions and obey orders in proportion as the man who makes them or gives them expects that they will. The more successful he is, the less questioning there will be and the greater will be the confidence with which he utters them. We have phrases like 'an air of authority', 'an authoritative voice', and Jesus, it is said, produced consternation because as a boy he spoke 'with authority' in the temple. Such descriptions draw attention to the outward signs of the inner certitude which is usually necessary for the exercise of authority. For it is not sufficient for a man to be in fact wise or shrewd or a felicitous prophet, if he is to exercise authority. He must also be known to be so. It is said that Attlee's authority in the country suffered in his early days as Prime Minister because he did not have a good public relations officer. A man cannot exercise authority if he hides his light under a bushel.

Such empirical generalizations are the province of the social psychologist. The question of philosophical interest is whether any such empirical conditions must come to be regarded as *grounds* for a right if a man is to be said properly to exercise authority without being in authority or an authority. A concrete case will help here. Suppose there is an explosion in a street or a fire in a cinema. Someone comes forward who is not a policeman or a fireman or manager of the cinema and who is quite unknown to all present—i.e. he is not regarded as 'an authority' in virtue of his personal history or known competence in an emergency. Suppose he starts issuing orders and making announcements. And suppose that he is unquestioningly obeyed and believed. Would we say that such a man exerted authority in a crisis? I think we would only say so if we thought that his orders were obeyed *simply because they were his*. There would have to be something about him in virtue of which his orders or pronouncements were regarded as being in some way legitimately issued. Maybe it would be his features; maybe it would be the tone of his voice.[1] Maybe he would have a habit of command. But those who heard him would have to think in an embryonic way that he was the sort of man who could be trusted. It would put the matter altogether too strongly to say that they thought he had a right to take control. For obviously, in any useful sense of 'right', he has not got a right. He has not been appointed; he is not a status-holder; he possesses no credentials of a more personal sort. All that can be said is that there is something about him which people recognize in virtue of which they do what he says simply because he says it. Perhaps the word 'faith' is required here; for, as Hobbes put it, the word 'faith' is required when our reasons for assent derive 'not from the proposition itself but from the person propounding'.

It may be, however, that the search for some vague ground for the acceptance of orders in this unquestioning way is to approach the

---

[1] Cf. *King Lear*, Act. 1 Sc. IV. *Lear:* Who wouldst thou serve? *Kent:* You. *Lear:* Dost thou know me fellow? *Kent:* No sir: but you have that in your countenance which I would fain call master. *Lear:* What's that? *Kent:* Authority.

analysis of 'authority' in its *de facto* sense in too positive a manner. Perhaps the use of the term 'authority' is to *deny* certain characteristic suggestions rather than to assert a positive ground for unquestioning obedience. People often do what they are told because they are threatened or bribed or physically forced. After all, obedience in a crisis can be produced by a fire-hose or machine gun, irrespective of who is manning it. Maybe the term 'authority' is necessary for describing those situations where conformity is brought about *without* recourse to force, bribes, incentives or propaganda and *without* a lot of argument and discussion, as in moral situations. We describe such situations by saying that an order is obeyed or a decision is accepted *simply because* X gave it or made it. This is a way of excluding *both* that action was taken on moral grounds *and* that the person acted under constraint or pressure or influence. The use of authority, in other words, is a manner of regulating human behaviour which is an intermediary between moral argument and the use of force, incentives and propaganda.

9. *Common features of all uses of 'authority'*.

There are, therefore, features which all uses of the term 'authority' have in common. In so far as the *de facto* sense implies that, in an indeterminate and embryonic sense, the person who exercises authority is regarded as 'having a right' to be obeyed, and so on, the *de facto* sense is parasitic on the *de jure* sense. But the common features of both senses are, perhaps, best brought out by summarizing and making explicit the peculiar nature and rôle of authority in the regulation of human behaviour—the point at which I embarked on this analysis in the company of Hobbes and de Jouvenel.

(a) *In contrast to 'power'*. The first feature to stress is the connexion between 'authority' and the use of certain types of regulatory utterances, gestures and symbolic acts. A person *in* authority has a right to make decisions, issue pronouncements, give commands and perhaps perform certain sorts of symbolic significant acts. To *have* authority with another man is to get him to do things by giving orders to him, by making pronouncements and decisions.

The main function of the term 'authority' in the analysis of a social situation is to stress these ways of regulating behaviour by certain types of utterance *in contrast* to other ways of regulating behaviour. This is to reject the more usual attempts to analyse 'authority' in terms of 'power' as exemplified by Weldon, for instance, who claims that 'authority' means power exercised with the general approval of those concerned. (*Vocabulary of Politics*, p. 56.) This, of course, is not to deny that it may be important, as Warrender stresses, to distinguish physical power from political power, the latter being confined to cases where an element of 'consent' is involved, as when a man does something because he is threatened, cajoled or duped, in contrast to when he is physically coerced—e.g., bound and put into prison. (See *The Political Philosophy of Hobbes* pp. 312/3.) It might, therefore, be tempting to regard the exercise of authority as a species of the exercise of political power distinguished by approval as opposed to mere acceptance on the part of the victim. But this, surely, is an over-simplification. For often what we want to bring out when we say that men are in authority or exert authority over other men is that they get their way or ought to get their way by means *other than those* of force, threats, incentives and propaganda, which are the usual ways of exercising *power*. It is only when a system of authority breaks down or a given individual loses his authority that there must be recourse to power if conformity is to be ensured. The concept of 'authority' is necessary to bring out the ways in which behaviour is regulated *without* recourse to power—to force, incentives and propaganda. These ways are intimately bound up with issuing pronouncements, making decisions and giving commands. I suppose the concept of 'power' can be extended to cover these ways of influencing people. But my claim is that 'power' usually has meaning by contrast with 'authority' rather than as a generic term of which 'authority' is just one species.

In so far as there is a *positive* connexion between 'power' and 'authority' it is better conceived along other lines. For instance, it might well be true that a common condition for the exercise of authority *de facto* is the ability to dispose of overwhelming power, if necessary. Or, alternatively, power might be regarded as a ground of entitlement. The old saying that there can be no legitimacy without power might be interpreted in this second way—as claiming that one of the grounds which give a man a right to command must always be, directly or indirectly, the ability to dispose of power, if necessary. Or it could be interpreted in the first way as an assertion that the possession of power is a necessary condition for the *de facto* exercise of authority, the legitimacy of which might be established in other ways. And, of course, this necessary condition, like others which I have mentioned before, can come to be regarded as a ground of entitlement. There is, however, no need to explore this positive connexion in detail. For my claim is that these are answers to other questions— questions about the grounds of entitlement or about the necessary conditions for the exercise of authority, not questions about the meaning of 'authority'.

There is little mystery about why authority should be so intimately connected with the problem of the analysis of human institutions. For men, *pace* Aristotle, are rule-following animals; they talk and regulate their own behaviour and that of others by means of speech. Men perform predictably in relation to each other and form what is called a social system to a large extent because they accept systems of rules which are infinitely variable and alterable by human decision. Such systems can only be maintained if there is general acceptance of procedural rules which lay down who is to originate rules, who is to decide about their concrete application to concrete cases, and who is entitled to introduce changes. In other words, if this peculiarly human type of order is to be maintained there are spheres where it is essential that decisions should be accepted simply because *somebody*, specified by rules of procedure, has made them. It is very difficult to play cricket without an umpire, just as it is difficult to conceive of an army working without a hierarchical system of command. The term 'authority' is essential in those contexts where a pronouncement, decision or command must be accepted simply because some person, conforming to specifications laid down by the normative system, has made or given it—where there must be a recognized 'auctor'. More liberal societies, of course, guard against injustice and stupidity by instituting further procedures for appealing against decisions of those in authority. But this is merely a device whereby a higher authority is instituted to correct the mistakes of a lower one. It is still a regulatory device which relies on the institution of authority and in no way abrogates the duty of obedience to the lower authority, provided that the lower authority is acting *intra vires*.

(b) *In contrast to moral and scientific regulation of conduct and opinions.* This analysis of 'authority' accounts also for a long tradition which stresses the incompatibility between authority and certain specific human enterprises like science and morality. For it would be held that in science the importance of the 'auctor' or originator is at a minimum, it never being justifiable in scientific institutions to set up individuals or bodies who will either be the originators of pronouncements or who will decide finally on the truth of pronouncements made. The procedural rules of science lay it down, roughly speaking, that hypotheses must be decided by looking at the evidence, not by appealing to a man. There are also, and can be, no rules to decide who will be the originators of scientific theories. In a similar way, it would be held that a rule cannot be a moral one if it is to be accepted just because someone has laid it down or made a decision between competing alternatives. Reasons must be given for it, not originators or umpires produced. Of course, in both enterprises provisional authorities can be consulted. But there are usually good reasons for their choice and their pronouncements are never to be regarded as final just because they have made them. In science and morality there are no appointed law-givers or judges or policemen. This is one of the ways in which life in the laboratory differs from life in the army and law-courts.

This analysis of 'authority' readily explains, too, the connexions so often made between 'authority' and 'command'. For commands, roughly speaking, are the sorts of regulatory utterances for which no reasons need to be given. A man can only give a command if he is in a position of authority or if he exerts authority in a *de facto* sense. For as an occupant of an office or as a status holder he has a right to make decisions which are binding and to issue orders. Similarly, if the *de facto* sense of authority is being used, to say that a man has authority over other men is to say, amongst other things, that they will do what they are told without questioning the prudence, wisdom and good sense of the decision. They may, of course, question its legality; for questions can be raised about a man's right to issue commands in general or in a particular sphere. These are questions about his right to an office or status, or about the sphere of its competence or his prerogative. But once it is granted that he occupies an office or holds a status legitimately, and once it is made clear that he is not straying from its sphere of competence or exceeding his prerogative, there can be no further question of justifying his commands. For commands just are the type of regulatory utterance where questions of justification are ruled out.

Authority, however, is not exercised *only* in the giving of commands. There are also the spheres of making pronouncements and decisions and the performance of symbolic acts. Behaviour or opinion in these spheres is regulated by the utterance of a man which carries with it the obligation for others to accept, follow or obey. The claim put forward by Hobbes and Austin, that law is command, is right in stressing the connexion between law and authority but wrong in conceiving of commands as the only form of authoritative utterance. Similarly those who speak of 'the authority of the individual conscience' cannot be supposed merely to be saying that in moral matters a man must give himself orders, which sounds, in any case, a little quaint; rather they are saying that in moral matters a man must decide himself between conflicting claims and principles and not accept the pronouncements and decisions of others simply because they issue from determinate sources. In morals a man must be his own 'auctor'.

10. *Conclusion.*

To conclude: my thesis is that the concept of 'authority' can be used in a *de jure* and a *de facto* sense. Amongst the former uses it is very important to distinguish the kind of entitlement implied in being *in* authority from that implied in being *an* authority. Authority in a *de facto* sense is parasitic on the *de jure* sense in that it implies that decisions are in fact accepted or commands obeyed simply because they issue from a certain person whose attributes are in some way regarded as bestowing legitimacy on them. The grounds for this legitimacy are often much more indeterminate than those more impersonal grounds characteristic of *de jure* authority. There are, however, more general negative features which all senses of 'authority' share. The term is always used to speak of ways in which conduct is regulated as distinct from the mere use of power—e.g. the giving of commands, the making of decisions and pronouncements, as distinct from the use of force, incentives and propaganda. Secondly, within the sphere of decisions, pronouncements and other such regulatory utterances, authority is confined to those which are or must be obeyed simply because someone has made them. This second feature of 'authority' brings out the contrast between laws, commands and religious utterances, on the one hand, and those of science and morality on the other. Both these features of 'authority' are rooted in the Latin word 'auctoritas' which implies an originator in the sphere of opinion, counsel and command.

The concept of authority does not merely give rise to isolated philosophical difficulties of its own. It is intimately connected with some of the most central issues in philosophy. Hence Dr. Peters is right to start with Hobbes: for Hobbes' account of authority is closely bound up with his general philosophical account of the nature of human life, thought and society. Indeed, the connexions between the philosophy of society and politics on the one hand and metaphysics and epistemology on the other have probably never been so clearly brought out as they were by Hobbes. (Thus I think it is a great mistake to try, as some have lately tried, to treat Hobbes' account of politics as if it had nothing logically to do with his epistemological presuppositions. It is not merely a mistaken interpretation of Hobbes but is also a symptom of wrong ideas about the relevance of philosophy to politics. Of course, in saying this I should not be taken as endorsing the specific account Hobbes gives of epistemology and of politics.)

But my agreement with Dr. Peters, fortunately for the future of this symposium, ends there. Although I think that he starts off with a genuine philosophical problem, and one which an analysis of the concept of authority should have much to contribute to, I do not accept the analysis which he offers; I should like to suggest, moreover, that the defects in it which I hope to be able to point out arise out of a failure on Peters' part to keep his initial problem clearly in mind and go deeply enough into it. My method, therefore, will be to develop my argument independently from the same starting point as Peters', trying to show *en passant* what seems to me wrong with the account of authority which he offers.

What light then does the notion of authority throw on the nature of the cohesion or unity which is characteristic of societies of human beings as opposed to what Peters calls 'natural wholes'? As Peters notes, Hobbes uses the notion in a legalistic way: for him, the unity of a society is a sort of legal *fiction*, involving the quasi-legal notion of representation, which he regards as closely analogous to authorization and hence as involving the notion of authority.

A multitude of men, are made *one* person, when they are by one man, or one person, represented; so that it be done with the consent of every one of that multitude in particular. For it is the *unity* of the representer, not the *unity* of

the represented, that maketh the person *one*, And it is the representer that beareth the person, and but one person; and *unity*, cannot otherwise be understood in multitude.
(*Leviathan*, Ed. Oakeshott, p. 107.)

What is important here for my purposes is that the real *unit*, in Hobbes' conception, is the individual will. His problem is to say how a large number of wills can be conceived as co-ordinated in the way with which we are familiar in human societies. Now M. de Jouvenel equally, in those passages which Peters cites, seems to take the individual will as his starting point: he thinks of a society in terms of the mutual influence of such wills. Social movements, for him, start as the projects of individual wills; authority is the faculty of interesting the wills of others in one's own projects.

Peters himself does not, I think, explicitly declare himself on this issue. Nevertheless, I think it is fair to ascribe to him too the view that the starting point in the analysis of authority should be the success of the individual in getting his decisions accepted by other individuals. This is implicit, for instance, in his account of the notion of 'natural', '*de facto*' authority, with his stress on the importance of purely *personal* qualities.

My paper starts from a point of view which is opposed to this. Although a man who exercises authority does indeed influence the wills of other men, authority cannot be understood as a peculiar sort of influence of one will upon another. If that sounds paradoxical, let us recall that although a man who has knowledge does indeed believe something, knowledge cannot be understood as a peculiar kind of belief. This analogy points to a parallel, which I think may be quite illuminating, between the problem in political philosophy of giving an account of the distinction between authority and power and the problem in epistemology of giving an account of the distinction between knowledge and belief. The connexions between these questions are brought out in the argument of Plato's *Gorgias*; I shall return to the parallel subsequently.

Authority is not a sort of influence. It is not a kind of *causal* relation between individual wills but an *internal* relation. The very notion of a human will, capable of deliberating and making decisions, presupposes the notion of authority. I shall try to show this by considering the whole question of the nature of the unity of a human society from a different point of view.

I want to say first that the chief way in which this unity differs from that of what Peters calls 'natural' wholes is that it is a unity essentially involving *concepts*. It would obviously be going much too far to say that a human society *is* a conceptual unity in the sense in which one can say this of a system of ideas; but there are analogies. For the interaction of human beings in society, unlike that of animals, involves communication, speech and mutual understanding (or, of course, *mis*understanding). It is a type of interaction which can be accounted for adequately neither in terms of instinct nor of conditioned reflex.[1]

It follows from this that one cannot give a full account of the nature of a human society without giving an account of the way in which concepts enter into the relations which men have to each other in such a society.

Wittgenstein has shown how notions like communication and understanding presuppose the notion of *following a rule*. He has also offered an account of this latter notion which brings out the peculiar kind of social interaction which it involves: what he calls 'agreement to go on in the same way'. Now Peters mentions, in Section 9 of his paper, that activities which are governed by rules can be carried on only if there is agreement that somebody should be in authority to make crucial decisions. But he does not seem to me to see the full bearing of this fact on the analysis of the concept of authority. It is not clear whether he regards the connexion between rule-governed activities and authority as merely contingent (arising out of the tendency of men to come into mutual conflict), or whether he is making a grammatical statement about what is involved in the very notion of a rule. I think it is important to see that the connexion is conceptual rather than contingent.

The acceptance of authority is not just something which, as a matter of fact, you cannot get along without if you want to participate in rule-governed activities; rather, to participate in rule-governed activities *is*, in a certain way, to accept authority. For to participate in such an activity is to accept that there is *a right and a wrong way of doing things*, and the decision as to what is right and wrong in a given case can never depend *completely* on one's own caprice. (Cf. Wittgenstein: *Philosophical Investigations*, I, 258.) For instance, *pace* Humpty Dumpty, I cannot (at least *in general*) make words mean what I want them to mean: I can use them meaningfully only if other people can come to understand how I am using them. Of course, I can decide, in a certain context, to make the sound 'red' mean what is commonly meant by the

---

[1] For reasons of space much must be taken for granted here. I have argued the point at greater length in *The Idea of a Social Science* (Routledge & Kegan Paul, 1958).

sound 'blue'; but I can do this only in so far as I also understand the meanings of a great many words which *I* have not decided upon. In other words, when it comes to following rules I must (as a matter of logic) accept what certain other people say or do as authoritative.

This approach suggests that there is an intimate conceptual connexion between the notion of authority on the one hand and, on the other hand, the notion of there being a right and a wrong way of doing things. That is the position that I propose to maintain and develop in what follows.

It may sound far-fetched to start a discussion of the concept of authority at this point; for the activity of speaking a language is not one in which the exercise of authority is at all obtrusive.[1] When we use words in the right way we do not think of ourselves as bowing to the dictates of an alien will. No; but then I want to say that to submit to authority (as opposed to being subjected to power) is not to be subject to an alien will. What one does is directed rather by the idea of the right way of doing things in connexion with the activity one is performing; and the authoritative character of an individual's will derives from its connexion with that idea of a right way of doing things. (This, I think, is part of the truth beind Collingwood's odd, but in some ways illuminating, definition of authority in *The New Leviathan*, 20. 45: 'Something capable of ruling itself sometimes appears to be (but is not in fact) ruled by something else. I refer to the case in which one thing is said to have *authority* over another.')

The rôle of authority in activities like speaking a language is obscured by the fact that the authority in question is not esoteric. All educated Englishmen are authorities on the correct speaking of English. This makes it particularly easy to, and important not to, overlook the interwovenness of the idea of there being a correct way of speaking, on the one hand, and the established practice of a certain group of people (the 'authorities': in this case a very wide group), on the other.

All characteristically human activities involve a reference to an *established* way of doing things. The idea of such an established way of doing things in its turn presupposes that the practices and pronouncements of a certain group of people shall be authoritative in connexion with the activity in question. Further, we can give no account of the

[1] Though, as Max Weber several times emphasizes, the exercise of authority (in a more obvious sense) is certainly essential to the maintenance of a language. *Cf. Wirtschaft und Gesellschaft*. Kapitel III: 'It is the authority exercised in school which puts the seal on what counts as the orthodox, correct way of writing and speaking' etc.

nature of the wholes which we call human societies, as opposed to that of 'natural' wholes, except by giving an account of what is involved in characteristically human activity. It is in this way, I suggest, that the notion of authority is important to the conception of a human society. It should be noted that I have made no explicit reference here to the idea of one individual human will's influencing another. A relation of authority, as opposed to one of power, is an *indirect* relation between X and Y involving as an intermediary the established way of performing the activity on which X and Y are engaged.

I can now amplify my earlier remark that authority is an internal rather than a causal relation. It is so because of its connexion with the *ideas* embodied in the form of activity within which it is exercised. (I use the notion of a 'form of activity' here in an extended sense to include not merely activities like tree-felling, chess-playing, etc., but also moral and political behaviour, which constitute forms of activity in a somewhat different sense. De Jouvenel's distinction, to which I shall return shortly, between the 'team of action' and the 'milieu of existence', may be helpful in explicating this distinction.) If N is trying to teach me chess and I am trying to learn, N and I are internally related by way of my acceptance of his authority on the right way to play chess. Again, if N is a judge trying a case in which I am litigating, his authority over me is an internal relation which can only be understood in terms of the system of (legal, moral and political) ideas which give such legal processes their sense in our society. In neither of these two examples can the relation of authority between N and me be understood in purely causal (sociological or psychological) terms.

Much of Peters' argument turns on his belief that 'it is very important to distinguish the kind of entitlement implied in being *in* authority from that implied in being *an* authority' (Section 10). His Weberian idea of 'natural' authority, depending on purely personal qualities, commits him to a denial of my assertion that the notion of an 'established' way of doing things is essential to the notion of authority as such. I am saying, in a sense, however, that someone who is *in* authority is always an authority *on* something. I am aware of the difficulties this way of speaking raises, especially in connexion with those situations where Weber speaks of the exercise of 'charismatic' authority; I shall reserve discussion of these until later. I should like first to show that the kind of analysis I propose is capable of easing certain long-standing philosophical difficulties which the notion of authority gives rise to.

Earlier I cited a remark of Collingwood's to the effect that to be subject to authority is not to be in somebody else's power. This brings us face to face with the whole question of how the necessity for authority in human affairs fits in with men's freedom of choice. To be subject to somebody else's will is for one's own freedom of choice to be reduced; but there is a powerful philosophical tradition to the effect that the exercise of legitimate authority is not a curtailment of this freedom. De Jouvenel, for instance, writes: 'Authority is the faculty of inducing assent. To follow an authority is a voluntary act. Authority ends where voluntary assent ends. There is in every state a margin of obedience which is won only by the use of force or the threat of force: it is this margin which breaches liberty and demonstrates the failure of authority.' (*Sovereignty*, p. 33.) This line of thought seems to me one which it is important to emphasize. I shall now try to show that authority, according to the account I have been giving of it, is not by any means a curtailment of liberty but is, on the contrary, a precondition of it.

The liberty in question is the liberty to choose. Now choice, as Hobbes (though in a misleading way) emphasized, goes together with deliberation (*Leviathan*, Ch. 6). To be able to choose is to be able to consider reasons for and against. But to consider reasons is not, as Hobbes supposed, to be subject to the influence of forces. Considering reasons is a function of acting according to rules; reasons are intelligible only in the context of the rules governing the kind of activity in which one is participating. Only human beings are capable of participating in rule-governed activities, hence other animals cannot be said to deliberate and choose, though Hobbes, consistently with his premises, maintained otherwise. Thus it is only in the context of rule-governed activities that it makes sense to speak of freedom of choice; to eschew all rules—supposing for a moment that we understood what that meant—would not be to gain perfect freedom, but to create a situation in which the notion of freedom could no longer find a foothold. But I have already tried to show that the acceptance of authority is conceptually inseparable from participation in rule-governed activities. It follows that this acceptance is a precondition of the possibility of freedom of choice. Somebody who said that he was going to renounce all authority in order to ensure that he had perfect freedom of choice would thus be contradicting himself. (A conceptual version of the man who thought that he could fly more easily if only he could escape the inhibiting pressure of the atmosphere.)

Consider an example. If I am being taught chess, then the pronouncements of my teacher are authoritative for me because of my recognition of the fact that he is telling me the *correct* way to move the pieces. If I make a wrong move and he corrects me, this is not in any intelligible sense an encroachment on my freedom of action. Until I know how to play chess the question of my being free or not to play the sort of game I choose cannot arise. And I can only learn how to play by accepting the pronouncements or example of some mentor or mentors as authoritative.

I realize that this example loads all the dice in my favour, and it is time now to consider some cases which give me more difficulty. In this connexion I must draw attention to two aspects of the chess example. (1) Playing or not playing chess is itself a matter of choice; but it is certainly not true of all cases of authority that it is accepted voluntarily in *this* sense. Very often authority cannot be accepted or rejected at will because it is not a matter of choice for us to participate or not to participate in the form of activity within which it is exercised. Indeed, one of the most telling criticisms frequently made of social contract theories of authority is precisely that they overlook this point. (2) In the chess example the meaning of the expression 'the *right* way to proceed' is clear and unambiguous. People who know how to play chess do not dispute about what moves of the various pieces are legitimate (and this fact belongs to our idea of the game of chess). But this feature is lacking from many of the cases in which authority is exercised, and particularly from those which give the most philosophical trouble. There will, for example, certainly be no general agreement about whether or not a given exercise of political authority was 'right' or not (and this belongs to our idea of politics). Peters is so impressed by this that he is led to think that the concept of authority becomes applicable precisely where the concept of 'the right way to proceed' ceases to apply. That, at any rate, is how I interpret his insistence that an appeal to authority is a way of avoiding having to give reasons for what one does or says. Now I agree that this lack of agreement about what is right creates philosophical difficulties; but I do not think that Peters' way of dealing with them is satisfactory.

I shall now deal with these two objections in turn.

(1) Consider the following two cases in which the authority exercised over a person clearly does not depend on his choice to participate in any particular form of activity: (*a*) the authority of adults over children; (*b*) political authority.

(*a*) The point about children is that they are not yet in a position to exercise freedom of choice in the full sense, because they have not

yet been sufficiently educated in modes of social life to be able to
deliberate. The exercise of authority over them, therefore, cannot be
an encroachment on their freedom: it is *via* the exercise of authority
that they will be inducted into modes of social life and thus be made
capable of deliberating and exercising choice. A child is obviously
not in a position to *choose* to do this or that until he has *learned how*
to do this and that.

(*b*) The difficulty raised by political authority is quite different.
It is not, characteristically, exercised over children (and any attempt to
derive it from the notion of paternal authority is, I think, completely
misconceived). But still, like the liability of children to adult authority,
one's liability to political authority does not depend on a decision to
subject oneself to it; in this way it is unlike the case of someone who
subjects himself to the authority of those who know how to play chess
in deciding to learn chess himself, or the case of someone who
subjects himself to the authority of the priest by deciding to become
a Roman Catholic.

To deal with this I shall use a modified version of de Jouvenel's
distinction, already alluded to, between the 'milieu of existence' and
the 'team of action' (op. cit., Chapter 4). Activities like playing
chess, building bridges, performing religious duties, going to war,
etc., do not take place in isolation. They presuppose an established
social framework. No society can be understood as just one big action
group. But neither can it be properly understood as just the sum of
the various action groups which compose it. For new (political)
problems (that is, problems not specific to any particular action
group) arise out of the fact that action groups influence each other:
either by mutual assistance or by conflict. Moreover, no individual will belong to just one action group, with the result that
(moral) problems of divided loyalty occur within the life of the
individual. Along with those new problems go specific ways of
treating and thinking about them: conventions dealing with right
and wrong ways of settling conflicts, for example. And the carrying
out of those conventions will, in the public sphere, involve the
exercise of authority. This is the sphere of Jouvenel's 'milieu of
existence' and the authority exercised within it is what he calls the
authority of the *rex* as opposed to that of the *dux* who leads the team
of action.

For my purposes it is important to emphasize that our very idea
of the kind of activity carried on by the action group carries with
it the idea of a milieu of existence in which some kind of political

authority is exercised in the settling of conflicts. We do not know what it would be like for such a mode of activity to be carried on in complete isolation: apart, that is, from other modes of activity with which it is in contact, with which it may conflict, and for which conflicts there must be conventions governing their equitable settlement. Although, therefore, one does not choose to accept political authority; although its applicability to one does not depend on any decision one may or may not have made to 'engage in politics'; nevertheless, the fact that one is a human social being, engaged in rule-governed activities and on that account able to deliberate and to choose, is in itself sufficient to commit one to the acceptance of legitimate political authority. For the exercise of such authority is a precondition of rule-governed activities. There would, therefore, be a sort of inconsistency in 'choosing to reject' all such authority. And since the acceptance of such authority is implied in the kind of behaviour to which alone the category of freedom of choice is applicable, it would be absurd to regard it as a derogation from a man's freedom of choice.

(2) I turn now to the other objection: that whereas there is general agreement on what counts as 'right' when we are dealing with the moves of chessmen, this is not true of other situations in which authority is exercised—of politics, for instance. Now I agree that here—and in some other contexts too—general agreement on the right course of action is lacking; I agree, too, that it is precisely here that it is necessary to have someone *in* authority. That is, where we have no agreement about *what* is to be done, we must, unless we are to lapse into chaos, have some agreement about *who is to decide* what is to be done. But I still wish to maintain, in opposition to what I take to be implied by Peters' position, that we have to deal with genuine authority, as opposed to bare power or ability to influence, only where he who decides does so under the idea of what he conceives to be the *right* decision. This fundamental fact is not altered by the controversial character of the distinction between right and wrong here.

Consider for instance the authority of the Pope over Roman Catholics which is, in a sense, absolute in religious matters. All the same, if a Pope were to issue an Encyclical denying the existence of God and advocating the practice of free love, I doubt whether this would be recognized as carrying the papal authority along with it. Papal authority, that is, is not completely beyond the possibility of all criticism;[1] and this, I want to say, is true of all authority, because authority is essentially bound up with systems of ideas, and systems of *ideas* essentially involve the possibility of discussion and criticism.

Again, certainly not everyone would agree that the Labour Government acted rightly in nationalizing the steel industry. Nevertheless part of that act's authoritative character derived from the fact that it was *claimed* to be the *right* thing to do in the circumstances (and some sort of case had to be made out for it). A great deal of authority would have been lost if the action had been generally and seriously regarded as an arbitrary act of dispossession for the sake of personal enrichment or for the sake of a social grudge. An authority can be allowed to make mistakes (up to a certain point) about what is the right course to follow, and still retain its authoritative character; but for it to be thought that it no longer cares about what is right and what is wrong (in the sense appropriate to the context in which it operates) *is* for it to degenerate from authority into force.[2] For reasons connected with this, M. de Jouvenel seems to me to be saying something of considerable philosophical importance, in his book on *Sovereignty*, when he recalls the attention of political philosophers from the problem of *who* is to decide to the problem of *what* is to be decided. This second problem is not merely pragmatically important; it is conceptually interwoven with the first problem *via* the concept of authority.

I shall now consider the implications of what I have been saying for the distinctions which Dr. Peters attempts to draw in his paper. His position appears to be the following. On the one hand we have authority of what Weber called the 'traditional' and 'legal-rational' types. It is characteristic of these that the authority in question attaches to a status or an office defined and held according to some more or less explicit system of rules. On the other hand we have '*de facto* authority' a watered-down version of Weber's 'charismatic' authority, which attaches to a specific person in view of certain personal qualities which he exhibits—as in Peters' quotation from *King Lear*. Intermediately, we have authority which

---

[1] Peters said, in an earlier version of his paper, that a man who supports what he says by claiming to speak with the voice of God (cf. Hobbes, op. cit., p. 243) is trying to rule out the need to produce arguments. Perhaps he is ruling out arguments *of a certain sort*; but what he is producing is itself an argument of a different sort, which a religious man may give (religious) reasons for accepting or rejecting.

[2] *Cf.* G. C. Homans: *The Human Group*, p. 171 for an illuminating illustration of the close connexion between the idea of authority and that of the right way to behave.

is accepted by virtue of what Peters calls 'credentials of a *personal sort*'—a history of outstanding success, for example, in a given field of activity.

Peters has difficulty with the notion of '*de facto* authority'; for while, on the one hand, he is unwilling to say that this may depend on a set of rules of some sort—as this would seem to endanger its distinctness from '*de jure* authority'; yet, on the other hand, in order to distinguish it from mere power, he has somehow to bring in the notion of there being some *right* to exercise it on the part of the person who does so. He concludes: 'All that can be said is that there is something about him (*sc.* the wielder of *de facto* authority) which people recognize in virtue of which they do what he says simply because he says it.' This sounds to me suspiciously evasive. Either people do what he says simply because he says it, or else they do what he says in virtue of something else about him, which they recognize. If the latter, then it will be part of the philosopher's job to say what that 'something else' is. I suggest that the way in which Peters has drawn his distinctions precludes him from doing this.

I can show this better by considering the distinctions of Max Weber's on which Peters leans. According to Weber 'traditional', 'legal-rational', and 'charismatic' authority represent three 'ideal types'. That is, they are conceptually distinct though seldom, if ever, found in their pure forms in actuality. I want to suggest, on the contrary, that these three types are not even conceptually distinct. Both the idea of the 'legal-rational' and that of the 'charismatic' presuppose the idea of a tradition.

I will concentrate here on the notion of charisma. Weber says quite explicitly that charismatic authority is not at all tied to a tradition. (*Cf. Wirtschaft und Gesellschaft*, p. 555.) In the same strain he remarks that the characteristic attitude of the charismatic leader is: 'It is written that.... But I say unto you.... (Ibid., p. 141.) Charismatic authority is conceived as a *revolutionary* force, as one of the main agencies by which *new* ways of living and thinking are introduced into a society.

Granted that this is so, it is still very misleading to *oppose* charisma to tradition. The point about it is not that it stands apart from established ways of doing things but that it stands to them in a very special relation. Apart from the tradition to which it stands in such a relation it is quite unintelligible and inconceivable.

Jesus Christ certainly revolutionized the religion of the Jews. The authority that he exercised was clearly very different from that of an orthodox rabbi. But what Jesus was, what he did and said, and the kind of authority he exercised, are completely unintelligible *apart* from the Jewish religious tradition. He came to *fulfil* the Law. When he opposed what he said to what was written he cannot sensibly be taken to have meant that he was replacing what was written by something *completely* different. Rather, he threw new light on what was written; and what he said could not be understood as it was intended except by someone who had some knowledge of what was written. (This question is discussed with great illumination by Schweitzer in his *The Psychiatric Study of Jesus*.)

Or, to take a very different example, William Webb Ellis when in 1823 he picked up the ball and ran and thereby created the game of Rugby Football, exercised a sort of charismatic authority over his fellow-participants in the game: an authority very different in kind from the legal-rational sort wielded by the duly appointed captain of a football team. But still, Ellis could not have done what he did apart from the rules of the game as they then existed; and we can only understand the nature of the authority which he exercised by considering what he did, and the effects of what he did, in relation to those rules.

Peters says that the charismatic or natural *de facto* leader is unable to give reasons for what he does. Perhaps so. Nevertheless, what he does or proposes has a *sense*; and it derives this sense from the tradition of activity in the context of which it occurs, whether this be a context of religious thought and practice, rules of football, or whatever.

To say that X is exercising *de facto* authority when his decisions are accepted simply because they are his does not go far enough. As Peters implicitly recognizes when he says that his decisions are accepted because people recognize 'something about him', we must look further than the mere *fact* that his decisions are accepted, if we are to account for his authority. We must ask what lies behind that acceptance. And what will be found to lie behind it is the tradition of activity which gives his proposals and decisions, and other people's acceptance of them, their sense. His authority consists in the fact that his followers trust him to show them the *right* course to pursue in the context of that activity. And his exercise of that authority may, in genuinely charismatic cases, result in the giving of a new sense to the notion of 'the right course to pursue'.

Let us consider a little more closely the external marks of natural authority which Peters emphasizes in Section 8 of his paper. Let us ask what makes a certain air, a certain tone of voice, a certain demeanour, a sign of *authority*. Certainly not anything intrinsic to the demeanour itself. In the film about the exploits of H.M.S. *Amethyst*, 'Yangtse Incident', the 'authoritative' demeanour of the rating who dressed up as an officer in order to bluff the Chinese commandant was merely laughed at by his fellow ratings. A given demeanour can only be a sign of authority in a special sort of context.

If we try to explain what (even *de facto*) authority *is* in terms of these external marks—as when Peters wonders 'whether any such empirical conditions must come to be regarded as *grounds* for a right'— we shall get into the same kind of difficulty as Descartes got into in trying to account for knowledge in terms of the clearness and distinctness of ideas. The clearness and distinctness of one's ideas may be a sign that one knows what one is talking about, but will not by itself serve as a *criterion* of the truth of what one is saying. Similarly, the confidence of one's demeanour may be a sign that one knows the right thing to do and that what one proposes may therefore be accepted as authoritative. But even the success of one's confident demeanour in inducing others to do what one proposes is not the ultimate test of one's authority. The test of whether or not other people were right to accept one's authority will be the subsequent assessment of the rectitude of what was done at one's instigation.

The parallels are close between the misguided attempts in political philosophy to account for authority in terms of the properties and relations between individual wills and the equally misguided attempts in epistemology to account for knowledge as a property of the individual mind. Authority is no more a sociological concept than knowledge is a psychological one.

Postscript (1967)

The subject of this symposium was authority *sans phrase*, rather than *political* authority, and I want to emphasize that my paper was concerned with the more general question. This is important for the following reason: what I wrote about specifically political authority is badly mistaken (as I realized as soon as the original paper had gone to the press) and the mistake tends to some extent to give a misleading appearance to my whole argument.

It is a central point of Hobbes's thesis that the answer to the question, 'What constitutes the unity of the *state?*' also provides the answer to the question, 'What are the conditions under which we

are entitled to call a collection of individuals a human *society?*' Now
I believe it is a consequence of my line of argument that Hobbes is
quite mistaken in what he says about this. But this is obscured by the
impression my paper gives that it is concerned with just the same
question as Hobbes was concerned with in the passages quoted by
Peters and myself. The question to which my remarks are relevant is,
'What is it about human life that makes the concept of authority
applicable at all?'; and I tried to show that the answer to *this* question
is also part of the answer to the question 'What is a human society?'
But though these latter questions have to be answered by anyone
who wishes to clarify the peculiar nature of *political* authority,
their answers will not in themselves provide such a clarification,
which requires an analysis not just of the way concepts in general
enter into life in human societies, but of the way a particular
set of political concepts enters into the life of a body politic
and into the binding together of its members under a common
regime.

My failure, in my paper, to make these distinctions clear enough
led me to make the following quite false remark: 'the fact that one is
a human social being, engaged in rule-governed activities and on that
account able to deliberate and to choose, is in itself sufficient to
commit one to the acceptance of legitimate political authority'. This
position is close to Locke's analogy between a political ruler and an
umpire; and there are two considerations which show it to be quite
mistaken. (1) There is, it now seems to me, no good reason to
suppose that social life is impossible in the absence of anything like
the authority of the state. (2) The authority of the state, where it
exists, is *sui generis* and somehow imposed from without on other
social institutions. (This is one of the main points of Hume's criticism
of Locke in his essay 'Of the Original Contract', the argument of which
I think is by and large correct.)

But I still think that Hume's argument needs to be supplemented
by something like the main argument of my paper. Though the state
faces other social institutions as something like an external force
with its own, in a way independent, sources of authority, still this
force and this authority are what they are by virtue of the fact that
there exists a *concept* of the state in the society within which they
are exercised—a concept which enters into what subjects will and will
not submit to from the state and into the activities of the officers of
the state. This concept is not itself *imposed* by the state; it manifests
itself in the spontaneous life of the society, even though its existence

makes possible the imposition of certain things in a way which would not otherwise be possible.

To say this much is to do no more than state a problem: what is the peculiar character of this concept and what difference does its existence make to the life of a society? I do not attempt to answer this question here; the purpose of this postscript is simply to correct the misleading appearance of my original paper to claim to have provided an answer.

VI

THE PUBLIC INTEREST

Brian Barry

I

A TRIBUNAL of·Enquiry claims that the public interest requires journalists to disclose their sources of information; the Restrictive Practices Court invalidates an agreement among certain manufacturers as contrary to the Restrictive Practices Act and therefore contrary to the public interest; the National Incomes Commission says that a proposed rise for the workers in an industry would be against the public interest. These examples could be multiplied endlessly. Each day's newspaper brings fresh ones. In arguments about concrete issues (as opposed to general rhetoric in favour of political parties or entire societies) 'the public interest' is more popular than 'justice', 'fairness', 'equality', or 'freedom'.

Why is this? Roughly, there are two possible answers. One is that 'the public interest' points to a fairly clearly definable range of considerations in support of a policy and if it is a very popular concept at the moment all this shows is that (for better or worse) these considerations are highly valued by many people at the moment. This is my own view. The other answer is that politicians and civil servants find it a handy smoke-screen to cover their decisions, which are actually designed to conciliate the most effectively deployed interest.

These sceptics often buttress their arguments by pointing out that most theoretical writing about 'the public interest' is vague and confused. This theme is copiously illustrated by Frank J. Sorauf in his article 'The Public Interest Reconsidered', *Journal of Politics*, XIX (Nov. 1957) and by Glendon Schubert in his book *The Public Interest: Critique of a Concept*. But it is a familiar idea that people who are perfectly well able to *use* a concept may nevertheless talk rubbish *about* it, so even if many of the writings about the concept are confused it does not follow that the concept itself is. A more cogent line of argument is to construct a definition of 'the public interest' and then

From *Proceedings of the Aristotelian Society*, Supp. Vol. 38 (1964), pp. 1–18. Reprinted by courtesy of the author and the Editor of the Aristotelian Society.

show that, so defined, nothing (or not much) satisfies it. From this, it can be deduced that most uses of the phrase in political discussion must be either fraudulent or vacuous. Like Sorauf and Schubert, the best known expositors of the view are Americans—one may mention A. F. Bentley's *The Process of Government* and D. B. Truman's *The Governmental Process*. But the most succinct and recent treatment is to be found in Chapters Three and Four of *The Nature of Politics* by J. D. B. Miller, and it is to a criticism of these chapters that I now turn.

II

Miller defines 'interest' as follows: 'we can say that an interest exists when we see some body of persons showing a *common concern* about particular matters' (p. 39). On the basis of this he later puts forward two propositions. First, one is not 'justified in going beyond people's own inclinations in order to tell them that their true interest lies somewhere else' (p. 41). It 'seems absurd' to suppose that an interest can exist if those whose interest it is are not aware of it (p. 40). And secondly, a 'common concern . . . must be present if we are to say that a general interest exists'. 'A common concern will sometimes be found in the society at large, and sometimes not. More often it will not be there' (p. 54).

Apart from the last point, which is a statement of fact and one I shall not query here, these propositions follow analytically from the original definition of 'interest', though Miller does not see this clearly. Everything hinges on that slippery word 'concern' which plays such a crucial part in the definition. One can be concerned *at* (a state of affairs) or concerned *about* (an issue) or concerned *with* (an organization or activity) or, finally, concerned *by* (an action, policy, rule, *etc.*). The noun, as in 'so-and-so's concerns' can correspond to any of the first three constructions, and it seems plain enough that in these three kinds of use nobody can be concerned without knowing it. In the fourth use, where 'concerned by' is roughly equivalent to 'affected by', this is not so: someone might well be affected by an economic policy of which he had never heard. But the noun 'concern' does not have a sense corresponding to this, nor does Miller stretch it to cover it. Naturally, if 'interest' is understood in terms of actual striving, no sense can be given to the idea of someone's having an interest but not pursuing it. Similarly, if 'interest' is defined as 'concern' it hardly needs several pages of huffing and puffing against rival conceptions (pp. 52–54) to establish that 'common or general interest' must be equivalent to 'common or general concern'.

Since, then, Miller's conclusions follow analytically from his definition of 'interest', with the addition of a factual premise which I am not here disputing. I must, if I am to reject his conclusions, reject his definition. Miller can, of course, define 'interest' any way he likes; but if he chooses a completely idiosyncratic definition he can hardly claim to have proved much if it turns out that most of the things that people have traditionally said about interests then become false or meaningless. He clearly believes himself to be taking part in a debate with previous writers and it is because of this that he is open to criticism.

Let us start from the other end. Let us begin by considering the things we normally want to say about interests, the distinctions which we normally want to draw by using the concept, and then see whether it is not possible to construct a definition of 'interest' which will make sense of these ordinary speech habits.

The first part of Miller's definition, which makes interests *shared* concerns, conflicts with our normal wish to draw a distinction between someone's private or personal interests on the one hand and the interests which he shares with various groups of people on the other hand. Simply to rule out the former by fiat as Miller does seems to have nothing to recommend it. It might perhaps be argued in defence of the limitation that only interests shared among a number of people are politically important, but it can surely be validly replied that this is neither a necessary nor a sufficient condition.

The second part of the definition equates a man's interests with his concerns. This conflicts with a great many things we ordinarily want to say about interests. We want to say that people can mistake their interests, and that while some conflicts are conflicts of interests, others (e.g., 'conflicts of principle') are not. We distinguish between 'disinterested' concern and 'interested' concern in a particular matter; we find it convenient to distinguish 'interest groups' (e.g., The National Farmers' Union) from 'cause' or 'promotional' groups (e.g., The Abortion Law Reform Association). 'They co-operate because they have a common interest' is ordinarily taken as a genuine explanation, rather than a pseudo-explanation of the '*vis dormitiva*' type, as it would be if co-operation were identified with (or regarded as a direct manifestation of) a common interest. We allow that one can recognize something as being in one's interest without pursuing it. Finally, we do not regard it as a contradiction in terms to say, 'I realize that so-and-so would be in my interests but nevertheless I am against it'. These points are all inconsistent with Miller's definition, and in addition the last of them is inconsistent with any attempt such as that of S. I. Benn to define a man's interests as 'something he thought he could *reasonably* ask for' ('"Interest" in Politics', *Proceedings of the Aristotelian Society*, 1960, p. 127).

Can a definition be found which will make sense of all these uses of 'interest'? I suggest this: a policy, law or institution is in someone's interest if it increases his opportunities to get what he wants—whatever that may be. Notice that this is a definition of '*in* so-and-so's interests'. Other uses of 'interest' all seem to me either irrelevant or reducible to sentences with this construction. Thus, the only unforced sense that one can give to 'What are your interests?', which Benn imagines being put seriously to a farmer, is that it is an enquiry into his favourite intellectual preoccupations or perhaps into his leisure activities—applications of 'interest' whose irrelevance Benn himself affirms. Otherwise, it has no normal application, though a 'plain man' with an analytical turn of mind (such as John Locke) might reply:

'Civil interest I call life, liberty, health and indolency of body; and the possession of outward things, such as money, lands, houses, furniture and the like' (*Letter Concerning Toleration*).

This might be regarded as a specification of the kinds of ways in which a policy, law or institution must impinge on someone before it can be said to be 'in his interests'. Unpacked into more logically transparent (if more long-winded) terms it might read: 'A policy, law or institution may be said to be in someone's interests if it satisfies the following conditions . . . .'

The main point about my proposed definition, however, is that it is always a *policy* that is said to be 'in so-and-so's interest'—not the actual manner in which he is impinged upon. (From now on I shall use 'policy' to cover 'policy, law or institution'.) There are straightforward criteria specifying the way in which someone has to be affected by a policy before that policy can be truly described as being 'in his interests'; but whether or not a given policy will bring about such results may quite often be an open question.

It is this feature of 'interest' which explains how people can 'mistake their interests'—item number one on the list of 'things we want to say about interests'. The stock argument against this possibility is that if you assert it you must commit yourself to the view that 'some people know what's good for other people better than they do themselves'. But this can now be seen to rest on a gross equivocation.

The presumably illiberal, and therefore damaging, view to be saddled with would be the view that policies which impinge on people in ways which they dislike may nevertheless be said to be 'in their interests'. But this is not entailed by the statement that people may 'mistake their interests'. All that one has to believe is that they may think a policy will impinge upon them in a way which will increase their opportunities to get what they want when in fact it will do the opposite. Whether his opportunities are increased or narrowed by being unemployed is something each man may judge for himself; but it is surely only sensible to recognize that most people's opinions about the most effective economic policies for securing given ends are likely to be worthless. In his Fireside Chat on June 28, 1934, President Roosevelt said:

'The simplest way for each of you to judge recovery lies in the plain facts of your own individual situation. Are you better off than you were last year? Are your debts less burdensome? Is your bank account more secure? Are your working conditions better? Is your faith in your own individual future more firmly grounded?'

It is quite consistent to say that people can 'judge recovery for themselves' without respecting their opinions about the efficacy of deficit financing.

The other 'things we normally want to say' also fit the proposed definition. People may want policies other than those calculated to increase their opportunities—hence the possibility of 'disinterested action' and 'promotional groups'. Similarly, a man may definitely not want a policy which will increase his opportunities (perhaps because he thinks that the policy is unfair and that others should get the increase instead). Hence the possibility of someone's not wanting something that he acknowledges would be in his interests. Finally, nothing is more common than for someone to agree that a policy would increase his opportunities if adopted, and to want it to be adopted, but at the same time to say that the addition of his own efforts to the campaign to secure its adoption would have such a small probability of making the decisive difference between success and failure for the campaign that it is simply not worth making the effort; and of course if everyone is in the habit of reasoning like this a policy which is in the interests of a great many people, but not greatly in the interests of any of them, may well fail to receive any organized support at all.

No doubt there is room for amplification of my definition of what it is for a policy to be in someone's interest. In particular the phrase 'opportunities to get what he wants' needs closer analysis, and account should be taken of the expression 'so-and-so's *best* interests' which tends to be used where it is thought that the person in question would make such an unwise use of increased opportunities that he would be better off without them (e.g., a heavy drinker winning a first dividend on the football pools). However, I doubt whether refinements in the definition of 'interest' would alter the correctness or incorrectness of what I have to say about 'the public interest', so I turn now to that expression.

III

If 'interest' is defined in such a way that 'this policy is in A's interest' is equivalent to 'A is trying to get this policy adopted' it is decisive evidence against there being in any but a few cases a 'public interest' that there is conflict over the adoption of nearly all policies in a state. But on the definition of 'interest' I have proposed this would no longer be so. A policy might be truly describable as 'in the public interest' even though some people opposed it. This could come about in a way already mentioned: those who oppose the policy might have 'mistaken their interests'. In other words, they may think the policy in question is not in their interests when it really is. Most opposition in the U.S.A. to unbalanced budgets can be explained in this way, for example. Disagreements about defence and disarmament policy are also largely disagreements about the most effective means to fairly obvious common goals such as national survival and (if possible) independence.

There are two other possibilities. One is that the group opposing the measure is doing so in order to further a different measure which is outside the range of relevant comparisons. The other possibility is that the opposing group have a special interest in the matter which counteracts their interest as members of the public. I do not expect these two descriptions to be clear; I shall devote the remainder of the paper to trying to make them so, taking up the former in this section and IV, and the latter in V.

Comparison enters into any evaluation in terms of interests. To say that a policy would be in someone's interests is implicitly to compare it with some other policy—often simply the continuance of the *status quo*. So if you say that a number of people have a common interest in something you must have in mind some alternative to it which you believe would be worse for all of them. The selection of alternatives for comparison thus assumes a position of crucial importance. Any policy can be made 'preferable' by arbitrarily contrasting it with one sufficiently unpleasant. Unemployment and stagnation look rosy compared with nuclear war; common interests in the most unlikely proposals can be manufactured by putting forward as the alternative a simultaneous attack by our so-called 'independent deterrent' on Russia and the U.S.A. All this need do is remind one that one thing may be 'in somebody's interest' *compared with something else* but still undesirable compared with other possibilities. The problem remains: is there (in most matters) any one course of action which is better for everyone than any other? Fairly obviously, the answer is: No. Any ordinary proposal would be less in my interest than a poll tax of a pound a head, the proceeds to be given to me. And this can be repeated for everybody else, taking each person one at a time. This, however, seems as thin a reason for denying the possibility of common interests as the parallel manoeuvre in reverse was for asserting their ubiquity. In both cases the comparison is really irrelevant. But what are the criteria for relevance? The simplest answer (which will later have to have complications added) is that the only proposals to be taken into account when estimating 'common interests' should be proposals which treat everyone affected in exactly the same way. Take the traditional example of a law prohibiting assault (including murder). If no limitation is imposed upon the range of alternatives it is easy to show that there is no 'common interest' among all the members of a society in having such a law directed equally at everyone. For one could always propose that instead the society should be divided into two classes, the members of the first class being allowed to assault the members of the second class with impunity but not vice versa, as with Spartans and Helots; or each member of the first group might be put in this position only *vis-à-vis* particular members of the second group. (Examples of this can be drawn from slave-holding, patriarchal, or racially discriminatory systems such as the *ante-bellum* South, ancient Rome and Nazi Germany respectively.) It could perhaps be argued that the 'beneficiaries' under such an unequal system become brutalized and are therefore in some sense 'worse off' than they would be under a regime of equality. But the whole point of 'interest'—and its great claim in the eyes of liberals—is that the concept is indifferent to moral character and looks only at opportunities.

Yet even the most sceptical writers often admit that a law prohibiting assault by anyone against anyone is a genuine example of something which is 'in the public interest' or 'in everyone's interest'. This becomes perfectly true when the alternatives are restricted to those which affect all equally, for then the most obvious possibilities are (a) that nobody should assault anybody else and (b) that anybody should be allowed to assault anybody else. And of these two it is hardly necessary to call on the authority of Hobbes to establish that, given the natural equality of strength and vulnerability which prevents anyone from having reasonable hopes of gaining from the latter set-up, the former is 'everyone's interest'.

IV

A convenient way of examining some of the ramifications of this theory is to work over some of the things Rousseau says in the *Social Contract* about the 'General Will'. Judging from critiques in which Rousseau figures as a charlatan whose philosophical emptiness is disguised by his superficial rhetoric, it is hard to see why we should waste time reading him, except perhaps on account of his supposedly malign influence on Robespierre. I doubt the fairness of this estimate, and I am also inclined to deprecate the tendency (often though not always combined with the other) to look on Rousseau through Hegelian spectacles. We need to dismantle the implausible psychological and metaphysical theories (e.g., 'compulsory rational freedom' and 'group mind') which have been foisted on Rousseau by taking certain phrases and sentences (e.g., 'forced to be free' and 'moral person') out of context. As a small contribution to this process of demythologizing Rousseau I want to suggest here that what he says about 'the general will' forms a coherent and ingenious unity if it is understood as a treatment of the theme of common interests.

Rousseau's starting point, which he frequently makes use of, is that any group will have a will that is general in relation to its constituent members, but particular with respect to groups in which it in turn is included. Translating this into talk about interests it means that any policy which is equally favourable to all the members of a given group will be less favourable to member A than the policy most favourable to A, less favourable to member B than the policy most favourable to B, and so on; but it will be more favourable to each of the members of the group than any policy which has to be equally beneficial to an even larger number of people. Suppose, for example, that a fixed sum—say a million pounds—is available for wage increases in a certain industry. If each kind of employee had a separate trade union one might expect as many incompatible claims as there were unions, each seeking to appropriate most of the increase for its own members. If for example there were a hundred unions with a thousand members apiece each employee might have a thousand pounds (a thousandth of the total) claimed on his behalf, and the total claims would add up to a hundred million pounds. At the other extreme if there were only one union, there would be no point in its putting in a claim totalling more than a million pounds (we assume for convenience that the union accepts the unalterability of this amount) and if it made an equal claim on behalf of each of its members this would come to only ten pounds a head. Intermediate numbers of unions would produce intermediate results.

Rousseau's distinction between the 'will of all' and the 'general will' now fits in neatly. The 'will of all' is simply shorthand for 'the policy most in A's interests, taking A in isolation; the policy most in B's interests, taking B in isolation; and so on'. (These will of course normally be different policies for A, B and the rest.) The 'general will' is a *single* policy which is equally in the interests of all the members of the group. It will usually be different from any of the policies mentioned before, and less beneficial to anyone than the policy most beneficial to himself alone.

We can throw light on some of the other things Rousseau says in the one-page chapter II.iii. of the *Social Contract* by returning to the trade union example. Suppose now that the leaders of the hundred trade unions are told that the money will be forthcoming only if a majority of them can reach agreement on a way of dividing it up. A possible method would be for each leader to write down his preferred solution on a slip of paper, and for these to be compared, the process continuing until a requisite number of papers have the same proposal written on them. If each started by writing down his maximum demand there would be as many proposals as leaders—the total result would be the 'will of all'. This is obviously a dead end, and if no discussion is allowed among the leaders, there is a good chance that they would all propose, as a second best, an equal division of the money. (There is some experimental evidence for this, presented in Chapter 3 of Thomas Schelling's *The Strategy of Conflict*.) Such a solution would be in accordance with the 'general will' and represents a sort of highest common factor of agreement. As Rousseau puts it, it arises when the pluses and minuses of the conflicting first choices are cancelled out.

If instead of these arrangements communication is allowed, and even more if the groups are fewer and some leaders control large block votes, it becomes less likely that an equal solution will be everyone's second choice. It will be possible for some leaders to agree together to support a proposal which is less favourable to any of their members than each leader's first choice was to his own members, but still more favourable than any solution equally beneficial to all the participants. Thus, as Rousseau says, a 'less general will' prevails.

In II.iii. Rousseau suggests that this should be prevented by not allowing groups to form or, if they do form, by seeing that they are many and small. In the less optimistic mood of IV.i, when he returns to the question, he places less faith in mechanical methods and more in widespread civic virtue. He now says that the real answer is for everyone to ask himself 'the right question', i.e., 'What measure will benefit me in common with everyone else, rather than me at the expense of everyone else?' (I have never seen attention drawn to the fact that this famous doctrine is something of an afterthought whose first and only occurrence in the *Social Contract* is towards the end.) However, this is a difference only about the most effective means of getting a majority to vote for what is in the common interest of all. The essential point remains the same: that only where all are equally affected by the policy adopted can an equitable solution be expected.

'The undertakings which bind us to the social body are obligatory only because they are mutual; and their nature is such that in fulfilling them we we cannot work for others without working for ourselves . . . . . . What makes the will general is less the number of voters than the common interest uniting them; for, under this system, each necessarily submits to the conditions he imposes on others: and this admirable agreement between interest and justice gives to the common deliberations an equitable character which at once vanishes when any particular question is discussed, in the absence of a common interest to unite and identify the ruling of the judge with that of the party.'

(II.iv. Cole's translation.)

Provided this condition is met, nobody will deliberately vote for a burdensome law because it will be burdensome to him too: this is why no *specific* limitations on 'the general will' are needed. Disagreements can then be due only to conflicts of opinion—not to conflicts of interest. Among the various policies which would affect everyone in the same way, each person has to decide which would benefit himself most—and, since everyone else is similarly circumstanced, he is automatically deciding at the same time which would benefit everyone else most. Thus, to go back to our example of a law prohibiting assault: disagreement will arise, if at all, because some think they (in common with everyone else) would make a net gain of opportunities from the absence of any law against assault, while others think the opposite. This is, in principle, a dispute with a right and a wrong answer; and everyone benefits from the right answer's being reached rather than the wrong one. Rousseau claims that a majority is more likely to be right than any given voter, so that someone in the minority will in fact gain from the majority's decision carrying the day. This has often been regarded as sophistical or paradoxical, but it is quite reasonable once one allows Rousseau his definition of the situation as one in which everyone is co-operating to find a mutually beneficial answer, for so long as everyone is taken as having an equal, better than even chance of giving the right answer, the majority view will (in the long run) be right more often than that of any given voter. (Of course, the same thing applies in reverse: if each one has on average a *less* than even chance of being right, the majority will be *wrong* more often than any given voter.) The formula for this was discovered by Condorcet and has been presented by Duncan Black on page 164 of his *Theory of Committees and Elections*. To illustrate its power, here is an example: if we have a voting body of a thousand, each member of which is right on average fifty-one per cent of the time, what is the probability in any particular instance that a fifty-one per cent majority has the right answer? The answer, rather surprisingly perhaps, is: better than two to one (69%). Moreover, if the required majority is kept at fifty-one per cent and the number of voters raised to ten thousand, or if the number of voters stays at one thousand and the required majority is raised to sixty per cent, the probability that the majority (5,100 to 4,900 in the first case or 600 to 400 in the second) has the right answer rises virtually to unity (99.97%). None of this, of course, shows that 'Rousseau was right' but it does suggest that he was no simpleton.

To sum up, Rousseau calls for the citizen's deliberations to comprise two elements: (a) the decision to forgo (either as unattainable or as immoral) policies which would be in one's own personal interest alone, or in the common interest of a group smaller than the whole, and (b) the attempt to calculate which, of the various lines of policy that would affect oneself equally with all others, is best for him (and, since others are like him, for others). This kind of two-step deliberation is obviously reminiscent of the method recommended in

Mr Hare's *Freedom and Reason*, with the crucial difference that whereas Mr Hare will settle for a willingness to be affected by the policy in certain hypothetical circumstances, Rousseau insists that my being affected by the policy must actually be in prospect. There is no need to construct a special planet to test my good faith—my bluff is called every time. By the same token, the theory I have attributed to Rousseau requires far more stringent conditions to be met before something can be said to be in the common interest of all than the vague requirement of 'equal consideration' put forward by Benn and Peters in their *Social Principles and the Democratic State*.

V

Even if Rousseau can be shown to be consistent it does not follow that the doctrine of the *Social Contract* has wide application. Rousseau himself sets out a number of requirements that have to be met before it applies at all: political virtue (reinforced by a civil religion), smallness of state, and rough economic equality among the citizens. And even then, as he points out plainly, it is only a few questions which allow solutions that touch all in the same way. If only some are affected by a matter the 'general will' cannot operate. It is no longer a case of each man legislating for himself *along with others*, but merely one of some men legislating *for* others. It is fairly obvious that Rousseau's requirements are not met in a great modern nation state—a conclusion that would not have worried him. But since I am trying to show that 'the public interest' is applicable in just such a state it does have to worry me. It is here that I must introduce my remaining explanation of the way in which something can be 'in the public interest' while still arousing opposition from some.

Think again of the examples with which I began this paper. The thing that is claimed to be 'in the public interest' is not *prima facie* in the interests of the journalist whose sources may dry up, the workers whose rise is condemned or the businessmen whose restrictive practices are outlawed. But do first appearances mislead? After all, the journalist along with the rest gains from national security, and workers or industrialists gain along with the rest from lower prices. To avoid a flat contradiction we need more refined tools; and they exist in ordinary speech. Instead of simply saying that some measure is 'in his interests' a man will often specify some rôle or capacity in which it is favourable to him: 'as a parent', 'as a businessman', 'as a house owner' and so on. One of the capacities in which everyone finds himself is that of 'a member of the public'. Some issues allow a policy to be produced which will affect everyone in his capacity as a 'member of the public' and nobody in any other capacity. This is the pure 'Rousseau' situation. Then there are other issues which lack this simplicity but still do not raise any problems because those who are affected in a capacity other than that of 'member of the public' are either affected in that capacity in the same direction as they are in their other capacity of 'member of the public' or at least are not affected so strongly in the contrary direction as to tip the overall balance of their interest (what I shall call their 'net interest') that way. Although this is not quite what I have called the 'Rousseau' situation, the 'Rousseau' formula still works. Indeed, Rousseau sometimes seems explicitly to accept this kind of situation as satisfactory, as when he says (III.xv.) that in a well-ordered state 'the aggregate of the common happiness furnishes a greater proportion of that of each individual'.

Finally, we have the familiar case where for some people a special interest outweighs their share in the public interest. The journalist may think, for example, that compulsory disclosure of sources would indeed be in the public interest but at the same time conclude that his own special interest as a journalist in getting information from people who want to stay anonymous is more important to him than the marginal gain in security that is at stake. In such cases as this Rousseau's formula will not work, for although everyone still has a common interest in the adoption of a certain policy *qua* 'member of the public', some have a net interest in opposing it.

To adopt the policy which is 'in the public interest' in such a case is still different from deliberately passing over an available policy which would treat everyone equally, for in the present case there *is* no such policy available. Even so, it involves favouring some at the expense of others, which makes it reasonable to ask whether it is justifiable to recommend it. Various lines of justification are possible. Bentham seems to have assumed that in most matters there was a public interest on one side (e.g., in cheap and speedy legal procedures) and on the other side the 'sinister' interest of those who stood to gain on balance from abuses (e.g., 'Judge & Co.') and to have believed (what is surely not unreasonable) that a utilitarian calculation would generally give the verdict to the policy favouring 'the public'. On a different tack, it might be argued that it is inequitable for anyone to benefit from 'special privileges' at the expense of the rest of the community. But unfortunately neither of these is as clear as it looks because a hidden process of evaluation has already gone on to decide at what point an interest becomes 'sinister' and how well placed someone must be to be 'privileged'. The cheapest and speediest dispensation of law could be obtained by conscripting the legal profession and making them work twelve hours a day for subsistence rations; but this would no doubt be ruled out by a utilitarian as imposing 'hardship' and by the believer in distributive justice as not giving a 'just reward' for the work done. Thus, by the time one has fixed the level of rewards beyond which one is going to say that 'privilege' and 'sinister interest' lie it is virtually analytic that one has defined a 'good' solution (whether the criteria be utilitarian or those of distributive justice).

It is clearer to say that in these 'non-Rousseauan' situations the public interest has to be balanced against the special interests involved and cannot therefore be followed exclusively. But 'the public interest' remains of prime importance *in politics*, even when it runs against the net interest of some, because interests which are shared by few can be promoted by them whereas interests shared by many have to be furthered by the state if they are to be furthered at all. Only the state has the universality and the coercive power necessary to prevent people from doing what they want to do when it harms the public and to raise money to provide benefits for the public which cannot, or cannot conveniently, be sold on the market: and these are the two main ways in which 'the public interest' is promoted. This line of thought brings us into touch with the long tradition that finds in the advancement of the interests common to all one of the main tasks of the state. The peculiarity of the last two centuries or so has lain in the widespread view that the other traditional candidates—the promotion of True Religion or the enforcement of the Laws of Nature and God—should be eliminated. This naturally increases the relative importance of 'the public interest'.

A contributory factor to this tendency is the still continuing process of social and economic change which one writer has dubbed the 'organizational revolution'. These developments have in many ways made for a more humane society than the smaller-scale, more loosely articulated, nineteenth-century pattern of organization could provide. But they have had the incidental result of making obsolete a good deal of our inherited conceptual equipment. Among the victims of this technological unemployment are 'public opinion' and 'the will of the people'. On most of the bills, statutory instruments and questions of administrative policy which come before Parliament there is little corresponding to the nineteenth-century construct of 'public opinion': the bulk of the electorate holding well-informed, principled, serious views. Even when an issue is sufficiently defined and publicized for there to be a widespread body of 'opinion' about it these opinions are likely to be based on such a small proportion of the relevant data that any government which conceived its job as one of automatically implementing the majority opinion would be inviting disaster.

This does not entail that voting with universal suffrage is not a better way of choosing political leaders than any alternative; but if 'public opinion' is a horse that won't run this means that 'public interest' has to run all the harder to make up, since as we have seen it has the advantage of operating where those affected by the policy in question have not even heard of it and would not understand it if they did. Consider for example the arrangements which enable the staffs of organizations whose members are affected by impending or existing legislation to consult with their opposite numbers in government departments about its drafting and administration. This system of 'functional representation', which now has almost constitutional status, would not get far if each side tried to argue from the *opinions* of its clients (the organization members and 'the public' respectively) on the matter; but their *interests* do provide a basis for discussion, a basis which leaves room for the uncomfortable fact that in a large organization (whether it be a trade union, a limited company or a state) information and expertise are just as likely to be concentrated in a few hands as is the formal power to make decisions.

VI

At the beginning of this paper I suggested that the popularity of 'the public interest' as a political justification could be attributed either to its vacuity or to its being used to adduce in support of policies definite considerations of a kind which are as a matter of fact valued highly by many people. If my analysis of 'the public interest' is correct, it may be expected to flourish in a society where the state is expected to produce affluence and maintain civil liberties but not virtue or religious conformity, a society which has no distinction between different grades of citizen, and a society with large complex organizations exhibiting a high degree of rank and file apathy. I do not think it is necessary to look any further for an explanation of the concept's present popularity.

VII

LIBERTY AND EQUALITY.

E. F. Carritt

In a recently published collection of essays called 'Why am I a Democrat?'[1] Mr. Ronald Cartland says: 'What we must settle at once is whether we rate freedom[2] above equality.' 'Equality involves subjugation and repression.' I select this statement only as a candid and contemporary expression of a doctrine that has always seemed to me both paradoxical and muddled. Left to myself I should have thought that liberty and equality involved one another; indeed I should have found it hard to separate them. Mr. Cartland himself seems not quite free from confusion here for, between the two remarks which I have just quoted, he says: 'Toleration and *equal* justice are possible only in a democracy', where toleration, I suppose, means freedom of speech,—equal freedom,—and democracy means political equality; equal justice, I suppose, is simply justice, for unequal justice would be injustice. So it is implied that freedom should be equal, and that it and justice are only possible with equal political power. What then is the equality with which freedom is supposed to be incompatible? To answer this question I think we must go back to the history of the doctrine. For it is no new one.

Burke paid tribute to liberty, which he thought was conferred and safeguarded by the British Constitution of his day, but to that constitution he thought democracy or political equality was abhorrent. With the enlargement of the franchise during the nineteenth century it began to be assumed, at first by revolutionaries, later by Whigs, young Tories and Tory Democrats, finally by almost all public speakers, not only that we desired liberty but that what conferred and safeguarded it was democracy, that is political equality, which they identified with the British Constitution as revised. Consequently Burke on their view had been wrong. But in the spirit of Burke it was

From *Law Quarterly Review*, Vol. 56 (1940), pp. 61–74. Reprinted by permission of the author's executors and the *Law Quarterly Review*.

[1] Edited by R. Acland (Lawrence and Wishart).

[2] I use the words liberty and freedom in the same sense.

still declared, for instance by both Gladstone and Disraeli,[1] that this freedom was incompatible with some other equality.

These are platform politics, but if we look at the considered statements of political theorists and especially of historians, we find the same thing.

Acton in his *Lectures on Liberty* says that in the course of the French Revolution 'the passion for equality made vain the hope of freedom'. Lecky in *Democracy and Liberty* (I, 212–215) says that 'Democracy (i.e. equality of political power) may often prove the direct opposite of liberty . . . it destroys the balance of classes' (i.e. introduces class equality). Bagehot in *The English Constitution* and Erskine May in *Democracy in Europe* (II, 333) work the same theme, but perhaps the most striking exposition is in Sir James Fitzjames Stephen's *Liberty, Equality and Fraternity* (p. 250):

'I doubt much whether the power of particular persons over their neighbours has ever in any age of the world been so well defined and safely exercised as it is at present. If, in old times, a slave was inattentive, his master might no doubt have him maimed or put to death or flogged; but he had to consider that in doing so he was damaging his own property, that when the slave had been flogged he would continue to be his slave; and that the flogging might make him mischievous or revengeful and so forth. If a modern servant misconducts himself he can be turned out of the house on the spot, and another hired as easily as you would call a cab. To refuse the dismissed person a character may very likely be equivalent to sentencing him to months of suffering and to a permanent fall in the social scale.'

Now what can Sir James have been driving at? I think it is clear that he deplored the power which employers have over their servants, as being so great that the latter have less freedom than slaves. And he seems to attribute this inequality of freedom, which of course is the correlative of an inequality of power, to their equality in some other respect, I suppose to their political equality. He gives no grounds for this attribution, except the suggestion that it is seldom to the interest of a slave-owner or cattle-breeder to injure his chattels. I can hardly think he would have proposed to remedy the insecurity of wage-

---

[1] M. Arnold (*Mixed Essays*, Equality) cites a speech of Lord Beaconsfield to Glasgow students about 1856 and quotes Mr. Gladstone as 'in his copious and eloquent way' saying: 'Call this love of inequality by what name you please,—the complement of the love of freedom, or its negative pole, or the shadow which the love of freedom casts, or the reverberation of its voice in the halls of the constitution,— it is an active, living, and life-giving power.'

earners by substituting an extreme servitude with a legal right in the owner to kill, flog or maim his slaves. Nor does it seem likely that he is consciously arguing for the more obvious remedy, that of increasing freedom by adding economic to political equality. I cannot tell what he wants. All he has shown is, what nobody can have doubted, that majority government does not necessarily and immediately secure the maximum of equal freedom. Nor does any form of government. He might have gone further and said that it is possible for a majority government not only to allow economic inequality and consequent interferences with liberty, but actually itself to be as intolerant as any other government of free speech and action. James Mill (*Government*, Encyclopedia Britannica) is brutally frank: 'Whenever the powers of the Government are placed in any hands other than those of the community, whether those of one man, of a few, or of *several*, those principles of human nature which imply that Government is at all necessary, imply that those persons will make use of them to defeat the very end for which Government exists.' For the word *several* which I have italicized he ought to have substituted *the majority*. But he ought also to have added that those principles of human nature which make stable government at all *possible* may counteract the principles he has described. As Maitland points out (*Liberty*, Collected Papers I) no form of government can *guarantee* liberty, but only 'an opinion of right'. (The phrase is Hume's.) But I know of little reason to think that majority governments are *less* favourable to economic equality and the resulting equal liberty than are plutocracies, aristocracies or despotisms. Even Plato, idealizing aristocracy, thought it must be precluded by communism from the temptation to oppression. And I know of *no* reason to think that democracies are less tolerant of free speech and propaganda than other kinds of government. Such tolerance probably depends upon the amount of security a government feels, which is apt to be in proportion to the equality of political power.

> ἔνεστι γάρ πως τοῦτο τῇ τυραννίδι
> νόσημα, τοῖς φίλοισι μὴ πεποιθέναι
>
> (Aesch. Prom. Desm, 226).

The only way, then, in which I can rationalize the lamentations of Sir James Fitzjames Stephen is to suppose him an unconscious socialist, who so desired equality of liberty to be secured by economic equality that he was willing to sacrifice equality of political power and to institute some class or personal dictatorship.

Perhaps the most influential source for this vague antithesis of freedom to equality is De Tocqueville's *L'Ancien Régime* (1856). He says that countries without an aristocracy are peculiarly liable to despotic or 'absolute' government in its worst forms, and he quotes Mirabeau: 'Cette surface égale facilite l'exercise du pouvoir.' He does not seem to think that an aristocratic government could be despotic. The elements of aristocracy he enumerates are: 'parlement, pays d'état, corps de clergé, privilégiés, noblesse'.

The reason he gives for his view is that 'When men are no longer united by bonds of caste, class, corporation, family, they tend to be wholly preoccupied with their private interests', and in particular with money-making.

The inequality he thinks necessary for freedom is clearly not economic; that existed in the France of his own day, which he considers servile. He must mean political inequality.

He seems to have two points in mind:

(1) A highly centralized government is apt to be oppressive even if unwillingly. But he shows no reason for supposing that democracy (i.e. political equality) is especially favourable to centralization. He emphasizes the high degree of centralization in the *ancien régime*.

(2) A 'privileged nobility' enjoys a good deal of freedom, though the unprivileged masses may have none. This freedom, for instance exemption from taxation, they will certainly try to defend against aggression, and De Tocqueville seems to think that in doing so they may incidentally defend or achieve some freedom for the unprivileged. In England such defence happened to some extent in 1688, and such achievement in 1832. In the 'glorious revolution' a land-owning aristocracy resisted royal encroachment, with some advantage to the liberty of the middle class. In the Reform Bill a new industrial aristocracy by gaining liberty and political equality for itself made them somewhat more accessible to the working classes; but it was opposed by the landed and ecclesiastical aristocracy. Those who had neither political nor economic privileges profited to some extent by the battle between those who had both and those who had one and coveted the other.

What evidence is there that democracy is more susceptible than aristocracy to dictatorship? Napoleon, Hitler, Mussolini perhaps all rose with the aid of something like democracy. Louis XIV, Lenin and Franco did not. England, France, America, the Scandinavian countries, Switzerland, Belgium, Holland are as democratic as any countries, but have as yet no dictators. Whether economic equality favours dictatorship is a question on which there can be little historical evidence, since no near approach to economic equality, unless in the U.S.S.R., as a *result* of 'the dictatorship of the proletariat', has been made. But most countries where the contrasts of wealth are comparatively small, such as the Scandinavian, have remained democratic. Ancient tyrannies generally arose out of economic inequality, to champion those who feared either exploitation or expropriation. Modern dictatorships have found backing both from depressed middle classes and from frightened capitalists. Among a people secure in anything like economic equality such backing would be hard to find. A dictator, thought to have established such equality, as in the U.S.S.R., might indeed be enthusiastically retained, but that would be in the belief, perhaps short-sighted, that he would maintain the liberty he had thereby secured.

How unequal was the liberty which De Tocqueville thought equality endangered can be shown by one or two quotations. In spite of *corvée*, *milice*, arbitrary arrest, aristocratic exemption from taxation, he says: 'Il régnait dans l'ancien régime beaucoup plus de liberté que de nos jours, mais une liberté toujours liée à l'idée d'exception et de privilège, *toujours contractée dans la limite des classes.*' 'France *dans ses classes supérieures* était libre.' 'Les nobles ne se préoccupaient guère de la liberté générale des citoyens.'[1]

De Tocqueville then thinks political equality leads to governmental oppression, and is not afraid of class or personal oppression. Stephen thinks just the opposite; that political equality leads to class or personal oppression. He feared the infraction of one subject's liberty by another more than its restriction by government. But his contemporaries who, like Mr. Cartland to-day, preached the incompatibility of liberty and equality, were mostly in the tradition of *laisser faire*. Like De Tocqueville they were so frightened of any governmental attempt to regulate or reform the economic system of their day that they were careless how much that system itself allowed of personal oppression. Lecky says (op. cit. pp. 212–215): 'Equality is only attained by a stringent repression of natural development.' Nature is a familiar stalking horse for prejudice. It is equally true that peace, order, security of life, limb, property are only attained by a stringent repression of 'natural' development in one sense of nature; and in that sense Hobbes thought the state of nature was one of pretty equal fear and misery. The security of one man's millions or hundreds from crowds of overworked or unemployed is an

[1] My italics.

inequality only maintained by a stringent repression of the 'natural' development called 'helping oneself'.[1] But there is another meaning of the word nature, a meaning which, in the wilderness of the nineteenth century, Matthew Arnold raised his voice to express. In his lecture to the Royal Institution on *Equality* (*Mixed Essays*) he said:

'Property is created and maintained by law. It would disappear in that state of private war and scramble which legal society supersedes. That property should exist and that it should be held with a sense of security[2] and with some power of disposal, may be taken, by us here at any rate, as a settled matter.[3] But that the power of disposal should be practically unlimited, that the inequality should be enormous, or that the degree of inequality admitted at one time should be admitted always—this is by no means so certain. The right of bequest was in early times . . . seldom recognized. In later times it has been limited in many countries . . . . The cause of your being ill at ease is the profound imperfectness of your social civilization . . . . The remedy is social equality. Let me direct your attention to a reform of the law of bequest. On the one side inequality harms by pampering; on the other by vulgarizing and depressing.'

The characteristic Arnoldian refrain of the lecture is 'Choose Equality'. And equality is to be chosen because, far from repressing 'natural' development, it liberates a 'natural and vital instinct' of men, the instinct of 'expansion' or 'humanization'. I think Arnold's diagnosis was right. The equality which his contemporaries thought incompatible with liberty was mainly economic equality. They thought that the promotion of this by law would somehow impair the liberty of more people, or to a greater degree, than does the maintenance of economic inequality (for of course they did not think there should be *no* laws of property). In order to make up our minds how far, if at all, this is so, we must decide as nearly as we can what we mean by liberty. Vaguely of course we all know; that is to say we all agree on extreme cases: that a manacled man is not so free as we are. But there are dubious instances where we might differ from one another, or from ourselves at another time. For example: how far is a man free who cannot throw up an ill-paid job without

[1] Cf. Dickinson, *Justice and Liberty*: 'No regulation is more constant, more crushing, more radical and severe, than that which is involved in property and the police.'

[2] This clause is otiose since Arnold clearly means by 'property' legal security of possession.

[3] Consumption necessitates appropriation.' Locke, *Civ. Govt.* II, 25–51.

losing his house when there is an extreme shortage of housing?[1]

To make discussion profitable we must try to fix precisely the sense in which we are now going to use the word. In this we must be careful to depart as little as possible from normal usage, while avoiding as far as possible its vagueness. Many of the confusions of theorizing on this topic have arisen from arbitrary definitions which went against the very usages where all plain men would agree. But those who adopt such arbitrary definitions seldom succeed in ridding themselves or their readers of the ordinary associations of the word, and so their procedure increases the very ambiguity it was meant to avoid. Hegel, for instance identified freedom with obedience to the laws of my State.[2] But the inescapable associations of the word enabled him to suggest that therefore in obeying my State I am always doing what I really want to do. Hardly less at variance with usage, and consequently hardly less confusing, has been the identification of liberty with the unimpeded power to do what we ought[3] (or perhaps what we think we ought) or to 'contribute to the common good'.[4] But it would go dead against ordinary usage to say that I am quite free if I am forbidden under penalties to smoke or to play tennis on Sunday, though I never thought that either of these were duties or 'contributions to a common good'.

I think our definition of liberty should avoid the use of any moral terms such as 'ought', 'right', 'good'. Only so can we avoid prejudicing the subsequent questions whether liberty is incompatible with equality, and if so, which we *ought* to promote, or which is 'better'.

I offer a preliminary definition of liberty as 'the power of doing what one would choose without interference by other persons' action'.[5]

---

[1] 'We should not be searching for the definition if we already knew precisely the meaning of the term; but the fact that we accept a certain definition as correct shows that we think the definition expresses more clearly the very thing we had in mind when we used the term without knowing its definition. The correctness of a definition is tested by two methods: by asking (i) whether the denotation of the term and that of the proposed definition are the same; (ii) does the definition express explicitly what we had implicitly in mind when we used the term?' Ross, *Foundations of Ethics*, p. 259.

[2] *Phil. d. Rechts.* §§ 15, 140 (e), 206. Cf. Bradley, *Ethical Studies*. My Station and its Duties; and Bosanquet, *Philosophical Theory of the State*, pp. 96, 181, 240, and especially 107, 127. Cf. my *Morals and Politics* under 'Hegel' and 'Bosanquet' and 'Liberty'.

[3] Acton, op, cit. and, inconsistently enough, Hegel and Bosanquet.

[4] Green, *Political Obligation*, §§ 24, 120, etc.

[5] Maitland, Liberty (*Collected Papers*, I) defines it as the absence of 'External restraints on human action which are themselves the results of human action'. This is much the best discussion of Liberty which I know. I assume that by 'restraint'

A maximum interference with liberty would be imprisonment with manacles; a minimum, exclusion from one house or locked safe which I wished to enter. Some of the elements of this definition need justification.

(1) 'Doing'. (a) Our *thinking* cannot be directly constrained (though it can be influenced) by other persons. Thought is always free; (b) Our *feelings* can be very painfully affected by others, for instance if they smack us or whistle out of tune, or (when we love them) by their indifference or neglect. And we do speak of 'freedom from anxiety'; but the qualification is necessary. A lover or anxious parent is not thereby *simpliciter* unfree.

(2) 'What one would choose'. (a) If I am 'prevented'[1] from doing what I should not choose to do, for instance, from cock-fighting or stepping over a cliff in the dark, my freedom is not impaired. A penal law against murder, then, limits the freedom of all who want to murder but not of others. This is acceptable, but less welcome results seem to follow. It might be plausibly argued that many, possibly most people in this country, are so law-abiding that though they would gladly be better fed, and though there is no just reason why they should not be, they would not choose to help themselves, and that therefore the laws of property and theft do not impair their freedom. They refrain from stealing even where detection is impossible, and therefore not through fear. The answer I think is that they act from an inarticulate recognition of the admitted truth, that almost any system of law giving some security of possession is better than none; even bad laws secure more equal freedom than anarchy does, and so it is our duty to support any system of security unless the contrary behaviour will, with reasonable probability, contribute to substituting a better system, which pilfering and swindling cannot do. If people willingly conformed to a law forbidding access to mountains but gladly profited by its repeal, I think usage compels us to say it had inpaired their freedom. If, however, they actually voted or agitated against its repeal, I think we must say it did not. If by long custom people actually prefer and petition to remain slaves, or if they cease even to wish to enjoy what is in the occupation of others, then their slavery or exclusion does not diminish their freedom, unless they change their mind. We may call them free fools and blame somebody

---

he means actual restraint. And potential restraint only becomes actual when I begin to want to do what is forbidden. If freedom were power to do what I do not want, it would be worthless.

[1] Or forbidden under penalty. See below.

for their folly.[1] (b) Bribes and promises do not impair freedom. The man likes earning the bribe better than not earning it, whereas the man deterred by threats would have preferred to act otherwise could he have done so fearlessly.

(3) 'Other persons'. (a) We can be prevented from doing what we want by geographical conditions, weather, wild beasts or our own bodily state. A swollen stream, a wolf, a broken leg do not impair our freedom. If anybody thinks that usage is in favour of calling such impediments a lack of freedom I would ask him to read in this essay for 'freedom (or liberty)' 'social freedom'. The same I think applies to those who are prevented from doing what they like by belief about the supernatural. They may be unfree from superstition or the fear of God but not (socially or) *simpliciter* unfree. What influences their action is not persons but the supposed nature of the universe. (b) But *any* persons may impair my freedom: a neighbour, a dictator or a majority. The fact that I have voted for the restriction makes no difference if I should now like to break it. Ulysses' sailors impaired his freedom by his own orders when they prevented him from joining the Sirens. I can even limit my own freedom by locking myself in an upper storey and throwing the key out of the window; but not by vows or promises without enforceable penalty. I am free to break them.

(4) 'Interference': so far as our action is impeded not by other people's action but merely by their failure to act, I think we should not say our freedom was impaired. But the distinction here is clearly very difficult to draw. To block my path limits my freedom. Not to clear or repair it does not.

(5) 'Action'. (a) I mean action here to include the credible threat of action, since the most usual diminution of freedom is not by physical constraint or violence but by the fear of it. (b) But I mean it, though I am not sure I am right, to exclude deception. It seems clear that our freedom is not impaired by the withholding of useful inform-ation, and I am inclined to think not even by the giving of false information. That wrongs us in some other way. I should say that drugging a man, or (if that is possible) hypnotizing him against his

---

[1] Many women, e.g. resisted 'emancipation' from traditional domestic inferiority. Their *economic* inferiority, which had only become conspicuous with new conditions, was much more resented. Cf. Hume, *Essays*, II, xvi: 'The bulk of mankind being governed by authority, not reason, and never attributing authority to anything that has not the recommendation of antiquity.' How dangerous this innate conservatism is he shows two pages later: 'Exorbitant power proceeds not, in any government, from new laws, so much as from neglecting to remedy the abuses, which frequently rise from the old ones.' And cf. I, iv, 'Antiquity always begets the opinion of right'.

will, impaired his freedom, but am inclined to think that propaganda
and excitement by rhetoric, music and similar tricks do not. To
prevent or forbid his access to contrary propaganda of course would
impair his freedom to obtain it if he wanted to do so.

If our definition, so explained, is accepted as the nearest we can
get to consistency without much violating common usage, two points
become clear.

(1) The first is that there are other good things, or other things
to which a man has claims and which it may be our duty to secure him,
besides liberty; for instance education, food, society, a good water-
supply.[1] And it is possible that such claims might conflict with
the claim to liberty, and a compromise have to be struck. The writers
I have quoted seem to think equality is one of these things.

(2) The second point is that one man's liberty is apt to be inimical
to his neighbour's. I suppose the ideally free man outside a desert
island would be an irresponsible world-despot not even threatened
with assassination, but his freedom would almost certainly involve a
great deal of servitude for others. When therefore we say that men
have a right to freedom or that freedom is good (unless we mean
merely that each wants for himself all the freedom he can get) we can
only mean equal freedom. Indeed, if we use the language of natural
rights, the right to equality must be more fundamental than that to
liberty or life or anything else, since men cannot have absolute
rights to any of these things (for one man's possession of them may
be incompatible with another's) but only (*ceteris paribus*) *equal claims*.[2]
Aristotle indeed identified justice (other than legal) with equality,
though an equality taking account of 'desert'.[3] And justice (*Recht*)
is natural right. It is 'the treatment of every man as an end', 'counting

---

[1] Maitland points out that Alexander Selkirk was completely free and very miserable.
I may add that he might have a right to be rescued, but the moment he set foot on
ship his liberty would be diminished. He must obey the captain.

[2] Equal claims to what is divisible (as liberty is) imply rights to equal shares,
e.g. to ten shillings in the pound where the assets are half the liabilities.

'An equal admission to the means of improvement and pleasure is a law
vigorously enjoined upon mankind by the voice of justice. All other changes in
society are good only as they are fragments of this or steps to its attainment. Godwin,
Political Justice, VIII, iv. Here the utilitarian joins hands with the adherent of natural
rights.

[3] *Eth. Nic.* 129a 34, 130b 9, 131a 11, 158b 30, κατ ἀξίαν which I have rendered
'desert' might I think include 'need' and be paraphrased '*ceteris paribus*'. Need is so
hard to assess that perhaps law should only attempt to assess it in relation to efficient
work. Does one man 'need' a first-rate execution of Bach but only a country-inn
parlour, and another a 'luxury hotel' but only a cinema-organ?

every man for one', an equality numerical till reason is shown to the contrary. And, if for the moment we neglect other possibly conflicting claims, the amount of freedom a man has a right to, the amount we ought *prima facie* to secure him, is just so much as is compatible with an equal amount for others. The maximum of freedom would be obtained if men were never interfered with by others in doing anything they chose except when what they chose to do interfered with others, and if they then always were. One thing most people want to do which can hardly affect the liberty of others is to express their opinions and feelings. So, if we are merely considering maximum liberty, speech should be free, even, I think, arguments for slavery or censorship.

It remains then to ask how far equal liberty is favoured or impaired by equality in other respects.

(1) So far as 'political equality' goes, we have admitted that majority government does not infallibly guarantee liberty any more than any other form of government does. Empirically in most circumstances, certainly in modern civilization, it seems the most favourable to it. At any rate our allegiance to a democratic or any other form of government would seem to depend upon the degree in which it is likely (or more likely than anything we could substitute) to secure men their rights,[1] prominent among which would be the right to equal liberty.

(2) 'Equality before the law', if, as I suppose, that only means law effectively carried out and not arbitrarily perverted by caprice or partiality, is implied in the very nature of law. And any system of law giving some security of person and property is more favourable to liberty than the anarchic state of 'private war and scramble'.[2] If

---

[1] Cf. Maitland, Liberty (*Collected Papers*, I): 'It is not possible to decide who ought to govern until we know what a government ought to do.'

Cf. Hume, *Essays*, I, v: 'Government having ultimately no other object or purpose [i.e. justification?] but the distribution of justice ... obedience is a new duty which must be invented to support that of justice.' '*No other*' is an exaggeration unless justice is used in a very wide sense to include beneficence. A Sumerian king claims fame as having given his people 'equal justice *and canals*' (Woolley, Abraham).

[2] Known general laws, however bad, interfere less with freedom than decisions based on no previously known rule.' Maitland, op. cit. p. 81. In weighing the risks of insecurity from innovation and of injustice from obsolescence, we may remember the wise maxim of Hume that the breakdown of order would be the worse evil but the loss of liberty is the more probable. *Essays*, I, v, vii. The best reasoned defence of anarchy is perhaps Godwin, *Political Justice*, VII, viii, Of Law. Since 'every case is a rule to itself' it should be judged by pure equity, assessed by the unguided reason of the judges. Presumably laws of conformity in indifferent matters, like the rule of the road, would be allowed. Yet later (VIII, ii) Godwin says: 'It is not easy to say whether misery or absurdity would be most conspicuous in a plan which should invite every man to seize upon everything he conceived himself to want', and 'Unless I can foresee,

'Equality before the law' means not only that the rules are kept, but also that they are made for the equal advantage of all whose needs or deserts are equal (as it might be maintained most of our laws of murder and assault are) then the question is raised how far this is also true of our property laws. But I prefer to avoid the wider question whether our property laws are just and confine myself to the question whether the inequality which they protect and favour is, as has been suggested, favourable to liberty. To decide the wider question we should have to ascertain whether these now are (even if they once were) favourable to the securing of all men's other claims, such as those to improved opportunities for health, education, enjoyment, as well as to the equal distribution of the opportunities already available. And that might involve us in economic considerations.

(3) What distribution of property then should be promoted and protected by law if it is to secure men the maximum amount of doing as they choose without interference? It is clear that all laws and all taxes diminish, and are intended to diminish, somebody's liberty, frequently to the increase of general liberty, sometimes justifiably on other grounds.[1] A law which forbids me to appropriate what is in my brother's possession, if I want to do so, impairs my liberty as truly as a law compelling me to give him half what is in mine. We may not all covet our neighbour's husband or wife, his ox or his ass. But if we never covet his manservant or his maidservant, his leisure, job, education, something that his money can buy, we are lucky.

What sort of property-distribution would produce the general minimum of liberty as defined? Surely literal monopoly. Take an extreme and simple case. If the total water supply of an island were the legal property of one landlord and water-theft were a capital offence, the rest of the population would desire more passionately than anything else to do something which they were either prevented from doing or could only do in fear of their lives. They would be extremely unfree. No doubt the owner might be willing to sell at a 'reasonable' rate, but so far as he had a monopoly also of other goods he could not sell at a rate 'reasonable' to the purchasers. He would have either to watch them perish, to sell water for labour, or to stand drinks. Laws are not made good laws by being too absurd or inhuman for enforcement.

in a considerable degree, the treatment I shall receive from my species . . . I can engage in no valuable undertaking'.

[1]'No law can be made that does not take something from liberty.' Bentham; *Anarchical Fallacies*. Preamble.

Now just in proportion as the ownership of water were equalized, the prohibition of water-theft would become less burdensome, less obstructive of what each desired to do, even though still nobody had so much as he would have liked. The only loss of liberty would be in the original monopolist, and probably his loss would not be so great as the gain of any *one* of his neighbours, since he could hardly have desired to use his superfluity of water (say in watering orchids) so passionately as the other had desired to moisten his tongue. To be forcibly deprived of superabundance or even of conveniences impairs liberty less than to be forcibly prevented from appropriating necessities.[1]

If then we consider laws and institutions of property merely so far as they directly affect liberty I think we must conclude that those are most favourable to it which most favour equality in proportion to need. Against such equality there may of course be other reasons.

There remains to notice the obvious relation of economic equality with political equality and equality before the law. Clearly, without freedom of speech, discussion, and information, the bare possession of the vote is almost valueless, and great economic inequality gives influence and power of propaganda which are as destructive of any real equality of political power as a censorship itself. Even 'equality before the law', that is legal justice itself, is endangered by economic inequality in well-known ways. The expense of expert legal advice and of protracted legislation heavily handicaps the poor. From great economic inequalities rise class differences of education, speech, standard of life, which may make it very difficult for judges to sympathize with some of those who come before them.[2]

Those who contend that liberty and equality are incompatible inherit Burke's naïve conservatism, the belief that the present British social system is ideal and merely needs to be ideally administered:—the machine is perfect, if only we could eliminate friction, but to plan a machine with less friction is utopian. The liberty they praise is a liberty *within* that system, with just the present institutions of ownership, inheritance, taxation, combination, limited liability, banking, all compulsory. The equality they condemn is any alteration of that system which would secure a greater amount of liberty to a greater number of persons; within the sacred system *laisser-faire* is

---

[1] Hume, *Enquiry*, III: 'Whenever we depart from equality we rob the poor of more satisfaction [and liberty] than we add to the rich'; and *Essays*, I, vii: 'Property when united causes much greater dependence than the same property when dispersed.'

[2] And cf. Bentham, *Book of Fallacies*, 1; Appendix on 'Sinister interest of Lawyers'.

divinely guided; but if we do not enforce just that system, providence they think will lead us to ruin.

But 'economics' and 'politics' cannot be thus separated. We must follow the same principle in judging what administration of the law is just and in judging what laws are just. If men have a right to liberty and equality within the law, for the same reason they have a right to laws that promote liberty and equality. Harrington in his *Oceana* said that 'Equality of estates causes equality of power, and equality of power is liberty', and Maitland (Equality, *Collected Papers* II) adds the rider that equality of political power tends to produce equality of property. And that tends to produce liberty. Godwin[1] briefly stated a position sometimes attributed to later writers: 'It is only by means of accumulation that one man obtains an unresisted sway over multitudes of others. It is by means of a certain distribution of income that the present governments of the world are retained in existence. Nothing more easy than to plunge nations, so organized, into war.' Godwin really believed in both liberty and equality. His peculiarity is that he could also believe in *laisser-faire* because he believed in fraternity.

[1] *Political Justice*, VIII, iii (1793).

VIII

TWO CONCEPTS OF LIBERTY[1]

Sir Isaiah Berlin

I

To coerce a man is to deprive him of freedom—freedom from what? Almost every moralist in human history has praised freedom. Like happiness and goodness, like nature and reality, the meaning of this term is so porous that there is little interpretation that it seems able to resist. I do not propose to discuss either the history or the more than two hundred senses of this protean word, recorded by historians of ideas. I propose to examine no more than two of these senses—but those central ones, with a great deal of human history behind them, and, I dare say, still to come. The first of these political senses of freedom or liberty (I shall use both words to mean the same), which (following much precedent) I shall call the 'negative' sense, is involved in the answer to the question 'What is the area within which the subject—a person or group of persons—is or should be left to do or be what he is able to do or be, without interference by other persons?' The second, which I shall call the positive sense, is involved in the answer to the question 'What, or who, is the source of control or interference, that can determine someone to do, or be, one thing rather than another?' The two questions are clearly different, even though the answers to them may overlap.

The notion of 'negative' freedom

I am normally said to be free to the degree to which no human being interferes with my activity. Political liberty in this sense is simply the area within which a man can act unobstructed by others. If I am prevented by other persons from doing what I could otherwise do, I

From the revised version of his Inaugural Lecture 'Two Concepts of Liberty' (Clarendon Press, 1958, pp. 6–19) in *Four Essays on Liberty* by Sir Isaiah Berlin to be published as an Oxford University Press Paperback. Reprinted by permission of the author and the Clarendon Press.

[1] [Some pages of the beginning and end of the original text have here been omitted. Ed.]

am to that degree unfree; and if this area is contracted by other men beyond a certain minimum, I can be described as being coerced, or, it may be, enslaved. Coercion is not, however, a term that covers every form of inability. If I say that I am unable to jump more than 10 feet in the air, or cannot read because I am blind, or cannot understand the darker pages of Hegel, it would be eccentric to say that I am to that degree enslaved or coerced. Coercion implies the deliberate interference of other human beings within the area in which I could otherwise act. You lack political liberty or freedom only if you are prevented from attaining a goal by human beings.[1] Mere incapacity to attain a goal is not lack of political freedom.[2] This is brought out by the use of such modern expressions as 'economic freedom' and its counterpart, 'economic slavery'. It is argued, very plausibly, that if a man is too poor to afford something on which there is no legal ban—a loaf of bread, a journey round the world, recourse to the law courts—he is as little free to have it as he would be if it were forbidden him by law. If my poverty were a kind of disease, which prevented me from buying bread or paying for the journey round the world, or getting my case heard, as lameness prevents me from running, this inability would not naturally be described as a lack of freedom, least of all political freedom. It is only because I believe that my inability to get a given thing is due to the fact that other human beings have made arrangements whereby I am, whereas others are not, prevented from having enough money with which to pay for it, that I think myself a victim of coercion or slavery. In other words, this use of the term depends on a particular social and economic theory about the causes of my poverty or weakness. If my lack of material means is due to my lack of mental or physical capacity, then I begin to speak of being deprived of freedom (and not simply of poverty) only if I accept the theory.[3] If, in addition, I believe that I am being kept in want by a specific arrangement which I consider unjust or unfair, I speak of economic slavery or oppression. 'The nature of things does not madden us, only ill will does', said Rousseau. The criterion of oppression is the part that I believe to be played by other human beings, directly or

---

[1] I do not, of course, mean to imply the truth of the converse.

[2] Helvétius made this point very clearly: 'The free man is the man who is not in irons, nor imprisoned in a gaol, nor terrorized like a slave by the fear of punishment . . . it is not lack of freedom not to fly like an eagle or swim like a whale.'

[3] The Marxist conception of social laws is, of course, the best-known version of this theory, but it forms a large element in some Christian and utilitarian, and all socialist, doctrines.

indirectly, with or without the intention of doing so, in frustrating my wishes. By being free in this sense I mean not being interfered with by others. The wider the area of non-interference the wider my freedom.

This is what the classical English political philosophers meant when they used this word.[1] They disagreed about how wide the area could or should be. They supposed that it could not, as things were, be unlimited, because if it were, it would entail a state in which all men could boundlessly interfere with all other men; and this kind of 'natural' freedom would lead to social chaos in which men's minimum needs would not be satisfied; or else the liberties of the weak would be suppressed by the strong. Because they perceived that human purposes and activities do not automatically harmonize with one another; and, because (whatever their official doctrines) they put high value on other goals, such as justice, or happiness, or culture, or security, or varying degrees of equality, they were prepared to curtail freedom in the interests of other values and, indeed, of freedom itself. For, without this, it was impossible to create the kind of association that they thought desirable. Consequently, it is assumed by these thinkers that the area of men's free action must be limited by law. But equally it is assumed, especially by such libertarians as Locke and Mill in England, and Constant and Tocqueville in France, that there ought to exist a certain minimum area of personal freedom which must on no account be violated; for if it is overstepped, the individual will find himself in an area too narrow for even that minimum development of his natural faculties which alone makes it possible to pursue, and even to conceive, the various ends which men hold good or right or sacred. It follows that a frontier must be drawn between the area of private life and that of public authority. Where it is to be drawn is a matter of argument, indeed of haggling. Men are largely interdependent, and no man's activity is so completely private as never to obstruct the lives of others in any way. 'Freedom for the pike is death for the minnows'; the liberty of some must depend on the restraint of others.[2] Still, a practical compromise has to be found.

[1] 'A free man', said Hobbes, 'is he that ... is not hindered to do what he hath the will to do.' Law is always a 'fetter', even if it protects you from being bound in chains that are heavier than those of the law, say, arbitrary despotism or chaos. Bentham says much the same.

[2] 'Freedom for an Oxford don', others have been known to add, 'is a very different thing from freedom for an Egyptian peasant.'
This proposition derives its force from something that is both true and important, but the phrase itself remains a piece of political claptrap. It is true that to offer

Philosophers with an optimistic view of human nature, and a belief in the possibility of harmonizing human interests, such as Locke or Adam Smith and, in some moods, Mill, believed that social harmony and progress were compatible with reserving a large area for private life over which neither the state nor any other authority must be

political rights, or safeguards against intervention by the state, to men who are half-naked, illiterate, underfed, and diseased is to mock their condition; they need medical help or education before they can understand, or make use of, an increase in their freedom. What is freedom to those who cannot make use of it? Without adequate conditions of freedom what is the value of freedom? First things come first: there are situations, as a nineteenth-century Russian radical writer declared, in which boots are superior to the works of Shakespeare; individual freedom is not everyone's primary need. For freedom is not the mere absence of frustration of whatever kind; this would inflate the meaning of the word until it meant too much or too little. The Egyptian peasant needs clothes or medicine before, and more than, personal liberty, but the minimum freedom that he needs today, and the greater degree of freedom that he may need tomorrow, is not some species of freedom peculiar to him, but identical with that of professors, artists, and millionaires.

What troubles the consciences of Western liberals is not, I think, the belief that the freedom that men seek differs according to their social or economic conditions, but that the minority who possess it have gained it by exploiting or, at least, averting their gaze from the vast majority who do not. They believe, with good reason, that if individual liberty is an ultimate end for human beings, none should be deprived of it by others; least of all that some should enjoy it at the expense of others. Equality of liberty; not to treat others as I should not wish them to treat me; repayment of my debt to those who alone have made possible my liberty or prosperity or enlightenment; justice, in its simplest and most universal sense—these are the foundations of liberal morality. Liberty is not the only goal of men. I can, like the Russian critic Belinsky, say that if others are to be deprived of it—if my brothers are to remain in poverty, squalor, and chains—then I do not want it for myself, I reject it with both hands and infinitely prefer to share their fate. But nothing is gained by a confusion of terms. To avoid glaring inequality or widespread misery I am ready to sacrifice some, or all, of my freedom: I may do so willingly and freely: but it is freedom that I am giving up for the sake of justice or equality or the love of my fellow men. I should be guilt-stricken, and rightly so, if I were not, in some circumstances, ready to make this sacrifice. But a sacrifice is not an increase in what is being sacrificed, namely freedom, however great the moral need or the compensation for it. Everything is what it is: liberty is liberty, not equality or fairness or justice or culture or human happiness or a quiet conscience. If the liberty of myself or my class or nation depends on the misery of a number of other human beings, the system which promotes this is unjust and immoral. But if I curtail or lose my freedom, in order to lessen the shame of such inequality, and do not thereby materially increase the individual liberty of others, an absolute loss of liberty occurs. This may be compensated for by a gain in justice or in happiness or in peace, but the loss remains, and it is a confusion of values to say that although my 'liberal', individual freedom may go by the board, some other kind of freedom—'social' or 'economic'—is increased. Yet it remains true that the freedom of some must at times be curtailed to secure the freedom of others. Upon what principle should this be done? If freedom is a sacred, untouchable value, there can be no such principle. One or other of these conflicting principles must at any rate in practice yield: not always for reasons which can be clearly stated, let alone generalized into rules or universal maxims.

allowed to trespass, Hobbes, and those who agreed with him, especially conservative or reactionary thinkers, argued that if men were to be prevented from destroying one another, and making social life a jungle or a wilderness, greater safeguards must be instituted to keep them in their places, and wished correspondingly to increase the area of centralized control, and decrease that of the individual. But both sides agreed that some portion of human existence must remain independent of the sphere of social control. To invade that preserve, however small, would be despotism. The most eloquent of all defenders of freedom and privacy, Benjamin Constant, who had not forgotten the Jacobin dictatorship, declared that at the very least the liberty of religion, opinion, expression, property, must be guaranteed against arbitrary invasion. Jefferson, Burke, Paine, Mill, compiled different catalogues of individual liberties, but the argument for keeping authority at bay is always substantially the same. We must preserve a minimum area of personal freedom if we are not to 'degrade or deny our nature'. We cannot remain absolutely free, and must give up some of our liberty to preserve the rest. But total self-surrender is self-defeating. What then must the minimum be? That which a man cannot give up without offending against the essence of his human nature. What is this essence? What are the standards which it entails? This has been, and perhaps always will be, a matter of infinite debate. But whatever the principle in terms of which the area of non-interference is to be drawn, whether it is that of natural law or natural rights, or of utility or the pronouncements of a categorical imperative, or the sanctity of the social contract, or any other concept with which men have sought to clarify and justify their convictions, liberty in this sense means liberty *from*; absence of interference beyond the shifting, but always recognizable, frontier. 'The only freedom which deserves the name is that of pursuing our own good in our own way', said the most celebrated of its champions. If this is so, is compulsion ever justified? Mill had no doubt that it was. Since justice demands that all individuals be entitled to a minimum of freedom, all other individuals were of necessity to be restrained, if need be by force, from depriving anyone of it. Indeed, the whole function of law was the prevention of just such collisions: the state was reduced to what Lassalle contemptuously described as the functions of a nightwatchman or traffic policeman.

What made the protection of individual liberty so sacred to Mill? In his famous essay he declares that unless men are left to live as they wish 'in the path which merely concerns themselves', civilization cannot advance; the truth will not, for lack of a free market in ideas, come to light; there will be no scope for spontaneity, originality, genius, for mental energy, for moral courage. Society will be crushed by the weight of 'collective mediocrity'. Whatever is rich and diversified will be crushed by the weight of custom, by men's constant tendency to conformity, which breeds only 'withered capacities', 'pinched and hidebound', 'cramped and warped' human beings. 'Pagan self-assertion is as worthy as Christian self-denial.' 'All the errors which a man is likely to commit against advice and warning are far outweighed by the evil of allowing others to constrain him to what they deem is good.' The defence of liberty consists in the 'negative' goal of warding off interference. To threaten a man with persecution unless he submits to a life in which he exercises no choices of his goals; to block before him every door but one, no matter how noble the prospect upon which it opens, or how benevolent the motives of those who arrange this, is to sin against the truth that he is a man, a being with a life of his own to live. This is liberty as it has been conceived by liberals in the modern world from the days of Erasmus (some would say of Occam) to our own. Every plea for civil liberties and individual rights, every protest against exploitation and humiliation, against the encroachment of public authority, or the mass hypnosis of custom or organized propaganda, springs from this individualistic, and much disputed, conception of man.

Three facts about this position may be noted. In the first place Mill confuses two distinct notions. One is that all coercion is, in so far as it frustrates human desires, bad as such, although it may have to be applied to prevent other, greater evils; while non-interference, which is the opposite of coercion, is good as such, although it is not the only good. This is the 'negative' conception of liberty in its classical form. The other is that men should seek to discover the truth, or to develop a certain type of character of which Mill approved—fearless, original, imaginative, independent, non-conforming to the point of eccentricity, and so on—and that truth can be found, and such character can be bred, only in conditions of freedom. Both these are liberal views, but they are not identical, and the connexion between them is, at best, empirical. No one would argue that truth or freedom of self-expression could flourish where dogma crushes all thought. But the evidence of history tends to show (as, indeed, was argued by James Stephen in his formidable attack on Mill in his *Liberty*, *Equality*, *Fraternity*) that integrity, love of truth and fiery individualism grow at least as often in severely disciplined communities among, for example, the puritan Calvinists of Scotland or New England, or under military discipline, as in more tolerant or indifferent societies; and if this is so accepted, Mill's argument for liberty as a necessary condition for the growth of human genius falls to the ground. If his two goals proved incompatible, Mill would be faced with a cruel dilemma, quite apart from the further difficulties created by the inconsistency of his doctrines with strict utilitarianism, even in his own humane version of it.[1]

In the second place, the doctrine is comparatively modern. There seems to be scarcely any discussion of individual liberty as a conscious political ideal (as opposed to its actual existence) in the ancient world. Condorcet has already remarked that the notion of individual rights is absent from the legal conceptions of the Romans and Greeks; this seems to hold equally of the Jewish, Chinese, and all other ancient civilizations that have since come to light.[2] The domination of this ideal has been the exception rather than the rule, even in the recent history of the West. Nor has liberty in this sense often formed a rallying cry for the great masses of mankind. The desire not to be impinged upon, to be left to oneself, has been a mark of high civilization both on the part of individuals and communities. The sense of privacy itself, of the area of personal relationships as something sacred in its own right, derives from a conception of freedom which, for all its religious roots, is scarcely older, in its developed state, than the Renaissance or the Reformation.[3] Yet its decline would mark the death of a civilization, of an entire moral outlook.

The third characteristic of this notion of liberty is of greater importance. It is that liberty in this sense is not incompatible with some kinds of autocracy, or at any rate with the absence of self-government. Liberty in this sense is principally concerned with the area of control, not with its source. Just as a democracy may, in fact,

---

[1] This is but another illustration of the natural tendency of all but a very few thinkers to believe that all the things they hold good must be intimately connected, or at least compatible, with one another. The history of thought, like the history of nations, is strewn with examples of inconsistent, or at least disparate, elements artificially yoked together in a despotic system, or held together by the danger of some common enemy. In due course the danger passes, and conflicts between the allies arise, which often disrupt the system, sometimes to the great benefit of mankind.

[2] See the valuable discussion of this in Michel Villey, *Leçons d'Histoire de la Philosophie du Droit*, who traces the embryo of the notion of subjective rights to Occam.

[3] Christian (and Jewish or Moslem) belief in the absolute authority of divine or natural laws, or in the equality of all men in the sight of God, is very different from belief in freedom to live as one prefers.

deprive the individual citizen of a great many liberties which he might
have in some other form of society, so it is perfectly conceivable that
a liberal-minded despot would allow his subjects a large measure of
personal freedom. The despot who leaves his subjects a wide area of
liberty may be unjust, or encourage the wildest inequalities, care
little for order, or virtue, or knowledge; but provided he does not
curb their liberty, or at least curbs it less than many other régimes, he
meets with Mill's specification.[1] Freedom in this sense is not, at any
rate logically, connected with democracy or self-government. Self-
government may, on the whole, provide a better guarantee of the
preservation of civil liberties than other régimes, and has been
defended as such by libertarians. But there is no necessary connexion
between individual liberty and democratic rule. The answer to the
question 'Who governs me?' is logically distinct from the question
'How far does government interfere with me?' It is in this difference
that the great contrast between the two concepts of negative and
positive liberty, in the end, consists.[1] For the 'positive' sense of
liberty comes to light if we try to answer the question, not 'What am I
free to do or be?', but 'By whom am I ruled?' or 'Who is to say what I
am, and what I am not, to be or do?' The connexion between democracy and individual liberty is a good deal more tenuous than it seemed
to many advocates of both. The desire to be governed by myself, or at
any rate to participate in the process by which my life is to be control-
led, may be as deep a wish as that of a free area for action, and perhaps
historically older. But it is not a desire for the same thing. So different
is it, indeed, as to have led in the end to the great clash of ideologies
that dominates our world. For it is this—the 'positive' conception of
liberty: not freedom from, but freedom to—which the adherents of
the 'negative' notion represent as being, at times, no better than a
specious disguise for brutal tyranny.

[1] Indeed, it is arguable that in the Prussia of Frederick the Great or in the Austria
of Josef II, men of imagination, originality, and creative genius, and, indeed, minorities
of all kinds, were less persecuted and felt the pressure, both of institutions and
custom, less heavy upon them than in many an earlier or later democracy.

[2] 'Negative liberty' is something the extent of which, in a given case, it is difficult
to estimate. It might, prima facie, seem to depend simply on the power to choose
between at any rate two alternatives. Nevertheless, not all choices are equally free,
or free at all. If in a totalitarian state I betray my friend under threat of torture,
perhaps even if I act from fear of losing my job, I can reasonably say that I did not
act freely. Nevertheless, I did, of course, make a choice, and could, at any rate in
theory, have chosen to be killed or tortured or imprisoned. The mere existence of
alternatives is not, therefore, enough to make my action free (although it may be

II

The Notion of Positive Freedom

The 'positive' sense of the word 'liberty' derives from the wish on the part of the individual to be his own master. I wish my life and decisions to depend on myself, not on external forces of whatever kind. I wish to be the instrument of my own, not of other men's, acts of will. I wish to be a subject, not an object; to be moved by reasons, by conscious purposes which are my own, not by causes which affect me, as it were, from outside. I wish to be somebody, not nobody; a doer—deciding, not being decided for, self-directed and not acted upon by external nature or by other men as if I were a thing, or an animal, or a slave incapable of playing a human role, that is, of conceiving goals and policies of my own and realizing them. This is at least part of what I mean when I say that I am rational, and that it is my reason that distinguishes me as a human being from the rest of the world. I wish, above all, to be conscious of myself as a thinking, willing, active being, bearing responsibility for his choices and able to explain them by reference to his own ideas and purposes. I feel free to the degree that I believe this to be true, and enslaved to the degree that I am made to realize that it is not.

The freedom which consists in being one's own master, and the freedom which consists in not being prevented from choosing as I do

voluntary) in the normal sense of the word. The extent of my freedom seems to depend on (a) how many possibilities are open to me (although the method of counting these can never be more than impressionistic. Possibilities of action are not discrete entities like apples, which can be exhaustively enumerated); (b) how easy or difficult each of these possibilities is to actualize; (c) how important in my plan of life, given my character and circumstances, these possibilities are when compared with each other; (d) how far they are closed and opened by deliberate human acts; (e) what value not merely the agent, but the general sentiment of the society in which he lives, puts on the various possibilities. All these magnitudes must be 'integrated', and a conclusion, necessarily never precise, or indisputable, drawn from this process. It may well be that there are many incommensurable degrees of freedom, and that they cannot be drawn up on a single scale of magnitude, however conceived. Moreover, in the case of societies, we are faced by such (logically absurd) questions as 'Would arrangement X increase the liberty of Mr. A more than it would that of Messrs. B, C, and D between them, added together?' The same difficulties arise in applying utilitarian criteria. Nevertheless, provided we do not demand precise measurement, we can give valid reasons for saying that the average subject of the King of Sweden is, on the whole, a good deal freer today than the average citizen of the Republic of Rumania. Total patterns of life must be compared directly as wholes, although the method by which we make the comparison, and the truth of the conclusions, are difficult or impossible to demonstrate. But the vagueness of the concepts, and the multiplicity of the criteria involved, is an attribute of the subject-matter itself, not of our imperfect methods of measurement, or incapacity for precise thought.

by other men, may, on the face of it, seem concepts at no great logical distance from each other—no more than negative and positive ways of saying the same thing. Yet the 'positive' and 'negative' notions of freedom historically developed in divergent directions not always by logically reputable steps, until, in the end, they came into direct conflict with each other.

One way of making this clear is in terms of the independent momentum which the, initially perhaps quite harmless, metaphor of self-mastery acquired. 'I am my own master'; 'I am slave to no man'; but may I not (as, for instance, T. H. Green is always saying) be a slave to nature? Or to my own 'unbridled' passions? Are these not so many species of the identical genus 'slave'—some political or legal, others moral or spiritual? Have not men had the experience of liberating themselves from spiritual slavery, or slavery to nature, and do they not in the course of it become aware, on the one hand, of a self which dominates, and, on the other, of something in them which is brought to heel? This dominant self is then variously identified with reason, with my 'higher nature', with the self which calculates and aims at what will satisfy it in the long run, with my 'real', or 'ideal', or 'autonomous' self, or with my self 'at its best'; which is then contrasted with irrational impulse, uncontrolled desires, my 'lower' nature, the pursuit of immediate pleasures, my 'empirical' or 'heteronomous' self, swept by every gust of desire and passion, needing to be rigidly disciplined if it is ever to rise to the full height of its 'real' nature. Presently the two selves may be represented as divided by an even larger gap: the real self may be conceived as something wider than the individual (as the term is normally understood), as a social 'whole' of which the individual is an element or aspect: a tribe, a race, a church, a state, the great society of the living and the dead and the yet unborn. This entity is then identified as being the 'true' self which, by imposing its collective, or 'organic', single will upon its recalcitrant 'members', achieves its own, and, therefore, their, 'higher' freedom. The perils of using organic metaphors to justify the coercion of some men by others in order to raise them to a 'higher' level of freedom have often been pointed out. But what gives such plausibility as it has to this kind of language is that we recognize that it is possible, and at times justifiable, to coerce men in the name of some goal (let us say, justice or public health) which they would, if they were more enlightened, themselves pursue, but do not, because they are blind or ignorant or corrupt. This renders it easy for me to conceive of myself as coercing others for their own sake, in their, not my, interest. I am then claiming that I know what they truly need better than they know it themselves. What, at most, this entails is that they would not resist me if they were rational, and as wise as I, and understood their interests as I do. But I may go on to claim a good deal more than this. I may declare that they are actually aiming at what in their benighted state they consciously resist, because there exists within them an occult entity—their latent rational will, or their 'true' purpose—and that this entity, although it is belied by all that they overtly feel and do and say, is their 'real' self, of which the poor empirical self in space and time may know nothing or little; and that this inner spirit is the only self that deserves to have its wishes taken into account.[1] Once I take this view, I am in a position to ignore the actual wishes of men or societies, to bully, oppress, torture them in the name, and on behalf, of their 'real' selves, in the secure knowledge that whatever is the true goal of man (happiness, fulfilment of duty, wisdom, a just society, self-fulfilment) must be identical with his freedom—the free choice of his 'true', albeit submerged and inarticulate, self.

This paradox has been often exposed. It is one thing to say that I know what is good for X, while he himself does not; and even to ignore his wishes for its—and his—sake; and a very different one to say that he has *eo ipso* chosen it, not indeed consciously, not as he seems in everyday life, but in his role as a rational self which his empirical self may not know—the 'real' self which discerns the good, and cannot help choosing it once it is revealed. This monstrous impersonation, which consists in equating what X would choose if he were something he is not, or at least not yet, with what X actually seeks and chooses, is at the heart of all political theories of self-realization. It is one thing to say that I may be coerced for my own good which I am too blind to see: this may, on occasion, be for my benefit; indeed it may enlarge the scope of my liberty; it is another to say that if it is my good, then I am not being coerced, for I have willed it, whether I know this or not, and am free—or 'truly' free—even while my poor earthly body and foolish mind bitterly reject it, and struggle against those who seek however benevolently to impose it, with the greatest desperation.

This magical transformation, or sleight of hand (for which William

---

[1] 'The ideal of true freedom is the maximum of power for all the members of human society alive to make the best of themselves', said T. H. Green in 1881. Apart from the confusion of freedom with equality, this entails that if a man chose some immediate pleasure—which (in whose view?) would not enable him to make the best of himself (what self?) what he is exercising is not 'true' freedom: and, if deprived of it, he would not lose anything that mattered. Green was a genuine liberal: but many a tyrant could use this formula to justify his worst oppression.

James so justly mocked the Hegelians), can no doubt be perpetrated just as easily with the 'negative' concept of freedom, where the self that should not be interfered with is no longer the individual with his actual wishes and needs as they are normally conceived, but the 'real' man within, identified with the pursuit of some ideal purpose not dreamed of by his empirical self. And, as in the case of the 'positively' free self, this entity may be inflated into some super-personal entity—a state, a class, a nation, or the march of history itself, regarded as a more 'real' subject of attributes than the empirical self. But the 'positive' conception of freedom as self-mastery, with its suggestion of a man divided against himself, has, in fact, and as a matter of the history of doctrines and of practice, lent itself more easily to this splitting of personality into two: the transcendent, dominant controller, and the empirical bundle of desires and passions to be disciplined and brought to heel. This demonstrates (if demonstration of so obvious a truth is needed) that the conception of freedom directly derives from the view that is taken of what constitutes a self, a person, a man. Enough manipulation with the definition of man, and freedom can be made to mean whatever the manipulator wishes. Recent history has made it only too clear that the issue is not merely academic.

IX

TWO CONCEPTS OF DEMOCRACY

JOSEPH SCHUMPETER

1-THE CLASSICAL DOCTRINE OF DEMOCRACY

I. THE COMMON GOOD AND THE WILL OF THE PEOPLE

THE eighteenth-century philosophy of democracy may be couched in the following definition: the democratic method is that institutional arrangement for arriving at political decisions which realizes the common good by making the people itself decide issues through the election of individuals who are to assemble in order to carry out its will. Let us develop the implications of this.

It is held, then, that there exists a Common Good, the obvious beacon light of policy, which is always simple to define and which every normal person can be made to see by means of rational argument. There is hence no excuse for not seeing it and in fact no explanation for the presence of people who do not see it except ignorance—which can be removed—stupidity and anti-social interest. Moreover, this common good implies definite answers to all questions so that every social fact and every measure taken or to be taken can unequivocally be classed as 'good' or 'bad'. All people having therefore to agree, in principle at least, there is also a Common Will of the people (= will of all reasonable individuals) that is exactly coterminous with the common good or interest or welfare or happiness. The only thing, barring stupidity and sinister interests, that can possibly bring in disagreement and account for the presence of an opposition is a difference of opinion as to the speed with which the goal, itself common to nearly all, is to be approached. Thus every member of the community, conscious of that goal, knowing his or her mind, discerning what is good and what is bad, takes part, actively and responsibly, in furthering the former and fighting the latter and all the members taken together control their public affairs.

From *Capitalism, Socialism and Democracy* by Joseph Schumpeter (3rd edn., Allen & Unwin, 1950), pp. 250–83. Copyright 1942, 1947, by Joseph A. Schumpeter. Copyright 1950 by Harper and Brothers. Reprinted by permission of George Allen and Unwin and Harper and Row, Publishers.

It is true that the management of some of these affairs requires special aptitudes and techniques and will therefore have to be entrusted to specialists who have them. This does not affect the principle, however, because these specialists simply act in order to carry out the will of the people exactly as a doctor acts in order to carry out the will of the patient to get well. It is also true that in a community of any size, especially if it displays the phenomenon of division of labour, it would be highly inconvenient for every individual citizen to have to get into contact with all the other citizens on every issue in order to do his part in ruling or governing. It will be more convenient to reserve only the most important decisions for the individual citizens to pronounce upon—say by referendum—and to deal with the rest through a committee appointed by them—an assembly or parliament whose members will be elected by popular vote. This committee or body of delegates, as we have seen, will not represent the people in a legal sense but it will do so in a less technical one—it will voice, reflect or represent the will of the electorate. Again as a matter of convenience, this committee, being large, may resolve itself into smaller ones for the various departments of public affairs. Finally, among these smaller committees there will be a general-purpose committee, mainly for dealing with current administration, called cabinet or government, possibly with a general secretary or scapegoat at its head, a so-called prime minister.[1]

As soon as we accept all the assumptions that are being made by this theory of the polity—or implied by it—democracy indeed acquires a perfectly unambiguous meaning and there is no problem in connexion with it except how to bring it about. Moreover we need only forget a few logical qualms in order to be able to add that in this case the democratic arrangement would not only be the best of all conceivable ones, but that few people would care to consider any other. It is no less obvious however that these assumptions are so many statements of fact every one of which would have to be proved if we are to arrive at that conclusion. And it is much easier to disprove them.

There is, first, no such thing as a uniquely determined common good that all people could agree on or be made to agree on by the force of rational argument. This is due not primarily to the fact that some people may want things other than the common good but to the much more fundamental fact that to different individuals and groups

---

[1] The official theory of the functions of a cabinet minister holds in fact that he is appointed in order to see to it that in his department the will of the people prevails.

the common good is bound to mean different things. This fact, hidden from the utilitarian by the narrowness of his outlook on the world of human valuations, will introduce rifts on questions of principle which cannot be reconciled by rational argument because ultimate values—our conceptions of what life and what society should be—are beyond the range of mere logic. They may be bridged by compromise in some cases but not in others. Americans who say, 'We want this country to arm to its teeth and then to fight for what we conceive to be right all over the globe' and Americans who say, 'We want this country to work out its own problems which is the only way it can serve humanity' are facing irreducible differences of ultimate values which compromise could only maim and degrade.

Secondly, even if a sufficiently definite common good—such as for instance the utilitarian's maximum of economic satisfaction[1]—proved acceptable to all, this would not imply equally definite answers to individual issues. Opinions on these might differ to an extent important enough to produce most of the effects of 'fundamental' dissension about ends themselves. The problems centring in the evaluation of present versus future satisfactions, even the case of socialism versus capitalism, would be left still open, for instance, after the conversion of every individual citizen to utilitarianism. 'Health' might be desired by all, yet people would still disagree on vaccination and vasectomy. And so on.

The utilitarian fathers of democratic doctrine failed to see the full importance of this simply because none of them seriously considered any substantial change in the economic framework and the habits of bourgeois society. They saw little beyond the world of an eighteenth-century ironmonger.

But, third, as a consequence of both preceding propositions, the particular concept of the will of the people or the *volonté générale* that the utilitarians made their own vanishes into thin air. For that concept presupposes the existence of a uniquely determined common good discernible to all. Unlike the romanticists the utilitarians had no notion of that semi-mystic entity endowed with a will of its own—that 'soul of the people' which the historical school of jurisprudence made so much of. They frankly derived their will of the people from the

---

[1] The very meaning of 'greatest happiness' is open to serious doubt. But even if this doubt could be removed and definite meaning could be attached to the sum total of economic satisfaction of a group of people, that maximum would still be relative to geven situations and valuations which it may be impossible to alter, or compromise on, in a democratic way.

wills of individuals. And unless there is a centre, the common good, toward which, in the long run at least, *all* individual wills gravitate, we shall not get that particular type of 'natural' *volonté générale*. The utilitarian centre of gravity, on the one hand, unifies individual wills, tends to weld them by means of rational discussion into the will of the people and, on the other hand, confers upon the latter the exclusive ethical dignity claimed by the classic democratic creed. *This creed does not consist simply in worshipping the will of the people as such* but rests on certain assumptions about the 'natural' object of that will which object is sanctioned by utilitarian reason. Both the existence and the dignity of this kind of *volonté générale* are gone as soon as the idea of the common good fails us. And both the pillars of the classical doctrine inevitably crumble into dust.

II. THE WILL OF THE PEOPLE AND INDIVIDUAL VOLITION

Of course, however conclusively those arguments may tell against this particular conception of the will of the people, they do not debar us from trying to build up another and more realistic one. I do not intend to question either the reality or the importance of the socio-psychological facts we think of when speaking of the will of a nation. Their analysis is certainly the prerequisite for making headway with the problems of democracy. It would however be better not to retain the term because this tends to obscure the fact that as soon as we have severed the will of the people from its utilitarian connotation we are building not merely a different theory of the same thing, but a theory of a completely different thing. We have every reason to be on our guard against the pitfalls that lie on the path of those defenders of democracy who while accepting, under pressure of accumulating evidence, more and more of the facts of the democratic process, yet try to anoint the results that process turns out with oil taken from eighteenth-century jars.

But though a common will or public opinion of some sort may still be said to emerge from the infinitely complex jumble of individual and group-wise situations, volitions, influences, actions and reactions of the 'democratic process', the result lacks not only rational unity but also rational sanction. The former means that, though from the stand-point of analysis, the democratic process is not simply chaotic—for the analyst nothing is chaotic that can be brought within the reach of explanatory principles—yet the results would not, except by chance, be meaningful in themselves—as for instance the realization of any definite end or ideal would be. The latter means, since *that* will is no longer congruent with any 'good', that in order to claim ethical dignity for the result it will now be necessary to fall back upon an unqualified confidence in democratic forms of government as such— a belief that in principle would have to be independent of the desirability of results. As we have seen, it is not easy to place oneself on that standpoint. But even if we do so, the dropping of the utilitarian common good still leaves us with plenty of difficulties on our hands.

In particular, we still remain under the practical necessity of attributing to the will of the *individual* an independence and a rational quality that are altogether unrealistic. If we are to argue that the will of the citizens *per se* is a political factor entitled to respect, it must first exist. That is to say, it must be something more than an indeterminate bundle of vague impulses loosely playing about given slogans and mistaken impressions. Everyone would have to know definitely what he wants to stand for. This definite will would have to be implemented by the ability to observe and interpret correctly the facts that are directly accessible to everyone and to sift critically the information about the facts that are not. Finally, from that definite will and from these ascertained facts a clear *and prompt* conclusion as to particular issues would have to be derived according to the rules of logical inference—with so high a degree of general efficiency moreover that one man's opinion could be held, without glaring absurdity, to be roughly as good as every other man's.[1] And all this the modal citizen would have to perform for himself and independently of pressure groups and propaganda,[2] for volitions and

[1]This accounts for the strongly equalitarian character both of the classical doctrine of democracy and of popular democratic beliefs. It will be pointed out later on how Equality may acquire the status of an ethical postulate. As a factual statement about human nature it cannot be true in any conceivable sense. In recognition of this the postulate itself has often been reformulated so as to mean 'equality of opportunity'. But, disregarding even the difficulties inherent in the word opportunity, this reformulation does not help us much because it is actual and not potential equality of performance in matters of political behaviour that is required if each man's vote is to carry the same weight in the decision of issues.

It should be noted in passing that democratic phraseology has been instrumental in fostering the association of inequality of any kind with 'injustice' which is so important an element in the psychic pattern of the unsuccessful and in the arsenal of the politician who uses him. One of the most curious symptoms of this was the Athenian institution of ostracism or rather the use to which it was sometimes put. Ostracism consisted in banishing an individual by popular vote, not necessarily for any particular reason: it sometimes served as a method of eliminating an uncomfortably prominent citizen who was felt to 'count for more than one'.

[2]This term is here being used in its original sense and not in the sense which it is rapidly acquiring at present and which suggests the definition: propaganda is any

inferences that are imposed upon the electorate obviously do not qualify for ultimate data of the democratic process. The question whether these conditions are fulfilled to the extent required in order to make democracy work should not be answered by reckless assertion or equally reckless denial. It can be answered only by a laborious appraisal of a maze of conflicting evidence.

Before embarking upon this, however, I want to make quite sure that the reader fully appreciates another point that has been made already. I will therefore repeat that even if the opinions and desires of individual citizens were perfectly definite and independent data for the democratic process to work with, and if everyone acted on them with ideal rationality and promptitude, it would not necessarily follow that the political decisions produced by that process from the raw material of those individual volitions would represent anything that could in any convincing sense be called the will of the people. It is not only conceivable but, whenever individual wills are much divided, very likely that the political decisions produced will not conform to 'what people really want'. Nor can it be replied that, if not exactly what they want, they will get a 'fair compromise'. This may be so. The chances for this to happen are greatest with those issues which are quantitative in nature or admit of gradation, such as the question how much is to be spent on unemployment relief provided everybody favours some expenditure for that purpose. But with qualitative issues, such as the question whether to persecute heretics or to enter upon a war, the result attained may well, though for different reasons, be equally distasteful to all the people whereas the decision imposed by a non-democratic agency might prove much more acceptable to them.

An example will illustrate. I may, I take it, describe the rule of Napoleon, when First Consul, as a military dictatorship. One of the most pressing political needs of the moment was a religious settlement that would clear the chaos left by the revolution and the directorate and bring peace to millions of hearts. This he achieved by a number of master strokes, culminating in a concordat with the Pope (1801) and the 'organic articles' (1802) that, reconciling the irreconcilable, gave just the right amount of freedom to religious worship while strongly

statement emanating from a source that we do not like. I suppose that the term derives from the name of the committee of cardinals which deals with matters concerning the spreading of the Catholic faith, the *congregatio de propaganda fide*. In itself therefore it does not carry any derogatory meaning and in particular it does not imply distortion of facts. One can make propaganda, for instance, for a scientific method. It simply means the presentation of facts and arguments with a view to influencing people's actions or opinions in a definite direction.

upholding the authority of the state. He also reorganized and refinanced the French Catholic church, solved the delicate question of the 'constitutional' clergy, and most successfully launched the new establishment with a minimum of friction. If ever there was any justification at all for holding that the people actually want something definite, this arrangement affords one of the best instances in history. This must be obvious to anyone who looks at the French class structure of that time and it is amply borne out by the fact that this ecclesiastical policy greatly contributed to the almost universal popularity which the consular regime enjoyed. But it is difficult to see how this result could have been achieved in a democratic way. Anti-church sentiment had not died out and was by no means confined to the vanquished Jacobins. People of that persuasion, or their leaders, could not possibly have compromised to that extent.[1] On the other end of the scale, a strong wave of wrathful Catholic sentiment was steadily gaining momentum. People who shared that sentiment, or leaders dependent on their good will, could not possibly have stopped at the Napoleonic limit; in particular, they could not have dealt so firmly with the Holy See for which moreover there would have been no motive to give in, seeing which way things were moving. And the will of the peasants who more than anything else wanted their priests, their churches and processions would have been paralyzed by the very natural fear that the revolutionary settlement of the land question might be endangered once the clergy—the bishops especially—were in the saddle again. Deadlock or interminable struggle, engendering increasing irritation, would have been the most probable outcome of any attempt to settle the question democratically. But Napoleon was able to settle it reasonably, precisely because all those groups which could not yield their points of their own accord were at the same time able and willing to accept the arrangement if imposed.

This instance of course is not an isolated one.[2] If results that prove in the long run satisfactory to the people at large are made the test of government *for* the people, than government *by* the people, as conceived by the classical doctrine of democracy, would often fail to meet it.

[1] The legislative bodies, cowed though they were, completely failed in fact to support Napoleon in this policy. And some of his most trusted paladins opposed it.

[2] Other instances could in fact be adduced from Napoleon's practice. He was an autocrat who, whenever his dynastic interests and his foreign policy were not concerned, simply strove to do what he conceived the people wanted or needed. This is what the advice amounted to which he gave to Eugène Beauharnais concerning the latter's administration of northern Italy.

III. HUMAN NATURE IN POLITICS

It remains to answer our question about the definiteness and independence of the voter's will, his powers of observation and interpretation of facts, and his ability to draw, clearly and promptly, rational inferences from both. This subject belongs to a chapter of social psychology that might be entitled Human Nature in Politics.[1]

During the second half of the last century, the idea of the human personality that is a homogeneous unit and the idea of a definite will that is the prime mover of action have been steadily fading—even before the times of Théodule Ribot and of Sigmund Freud. In particular, these ideas have been increasingly discounted in the field of social sciences where the importance of the extra-rational and irrational element in our behaviour has been receiving more and more attention, witness Pareto's *Mind and Society*. Of the many sources of the evidence that accumulated against the hypothesis of rationality, I shall mention only two.

The one—in spite of much more careful later work—may still be associated with the name of Gustave Le Bon, the founder or, at any rate, the first effective exponent of the psychology of crowds (*psychologie des foules*).[2] By showing up, though overstressing, the realities of human behaviour when under the influence of agglomeration—in particular the sudden disappearance, in a state of excitement, of moral restraints and civilized modes of thinking and feeling, the sudden eruption of primitive impulses, infantilisms and criminal propensities—he made us face gruesome facts that everybody knew but nobody wished to see and he thereby dealt a serious blow to the

---

[1] This is the title of the frank and charming book by one of the most lovable English radicals who ever lived, Graham Wallas. In spite of all that has since been written on the subject and especially in spite of all the detailed case studies that now make it possible to see so much more clearly, that book may still be recommended as the best introduction to political psychology. Yet, after having stated with admirable honesty the case against the uncritical acceptance of the classical doctrine, the author fails to draw the obvious conclusion. This is all the more remarkable because he rightly insists on the necessity of a scientific attitude of mind and because he does not fail to take Lord Bryce to task for having, in his book on the American commonwealth, professed himself 'grimly' resolved to see some blue sky in the midst of clouds of disillusioning facts. Why, so Graham Wallas seems to exclaim, what should we say of a meteorologist who insisted from the outset that he saw some blue sky? Nevertheless in the constructive part of his book he takes much the same ground.

[2] The German term, *Massenpsychologie*, suggests a warning: the psychology of crowds must not be confused with the psychology of the masses. The former does not necessarily carry any class connotation and in itself has nothing to do with a study of the ways of thinking and feeling of, say, the working class.

picture of man's nature which underlies the classical doctrine of democracy and democratic folklore about revolutions. No doubt there is much to be said about the narrowness of the factual basis of Le Bon's inferences which, for instance, do not fit at all well the normal behaviour of an English or Anglo-American crowd. Critics, especially those to whom the implications of this branch of social psychology were uncongenial, did not fail to make the most of its vulnerable points. But on the other hand it must not be forgotten that the phenomena of crowd psychology are by no means confined to mobs rioting in the narrow streets of a Latin town. Every parliament, every committee, every council of war composed of a dozen generals in their sixties, displays, in however mild a form, some of those features that stand out so glaringly in the case of the rabble, in particular a reduced sense of responsibility, a lower level of energy of thought and greater sensitiveness to non-logical influences. Moreover, those phenomena are not confined to a crowd in the sense of a physical agglomeration of many people. Newspaper readers, radio audiences, members of a party even if not physically gathered together are terribly easy to work up into a psychological crowd and into a state of frenzy in which attempt at rational argument only spurs the animal spirits.

The other source of disillusioning evidence that I am going to mention is a much humbler one—no blood flows from it, only nonsense. Economists, learning to observe their facts more closely, have begun to discover that, even in the most ordinary currents of daily life, their consumers do not quite live up to the idea that the economic text-book used to convey. On the one hand their wants are nothing like as definite and their actions upon those wants nothing like as rational and prompt. On the other hand they are so amenable to the influence of advertising and other methods of persuasion that producers often seem to dictate to them instead of being directed by them. The technique of successful advertising is particularly instructive. There is indeed nearly always some appeal to reason. But mere assertion, often repeated, counts more than rational argument and so does the direct attack upon the subconscious which takes the form of attempts to evoke and crystallize pleasant associations of an entirely extra-rational, very frequently of a sexual, nature.

The conclusion, while obvious, must be drawn with care. In the ordinary run of often repeated decisions the individual is subject to the salutary and rationalizing influence of favourable and unfavourable experience. He is also under the influence of relatively simple and unproblematical motives and interests which are but occasionally interfered with by excitement. Historically, the consumers' desire for shoes may, at least in part, have been shaped by the action of producers offering attractive footgear and campaigning for it; yet at any given time it is a genuine want, the definiteness of which extends beyond 'shoes in general' and which prolonged experimenting clears of much of the irrationalities that may originally have surrounded it.[1] Moreover, under the stimulus of those simple motives consumers learn to act upon unbiased expert advice about some things (houses, motor-cars) and themselves become experts in others. It is simply not true that housewives are easily fooled in the matter of foods, *familiar* household articles, wearing apparel. And, as every salesman knows to his cost, most of them have a way of insisting on the exact article they want.

This of course holds true still more obviously on the producers' side of the picture. No doubt, a manufacturer may be indolent, a bad judge of opportunities or otherwise incompetent; but there is an effective mechanism that will reform or eliminate him. Again Taylorism rests on the fact that man may perform simple handicraft operations for thousands of years and yet perform them inefficiently. But neither the intention to act as rationally as possible nor a steady pressure toward rationality can seriously be called into question at whatever level of industrial or commercial activity we choose to look.[2]

And so it is with most of the decisions of daily life that lie within the little field which the individual citizen's mind encompasses with a full sense of its reality. Roughly, it consists of the things that directly concern himself, his family, his business dealings, his hobbies, his friends and enemies, his township or ward, his class, church, trade union or any other social group of which he is an active member— the things under his personal observation, the things which are familiar to him independently of what his newspaper tells him, which he can directly influence or manage and for which he develops the kind

[1] In the above passage irrationality means failure to act rationally upon a given wish. It does not refer to the reasonableness of the wish itself in the opinion of the observer. This is important to note because economists in appraising the extent of consumers' irrationality sometimes exaggerate it by confusing the two things. Thus, a factory girl's finery may seem to a professor an indication of irrational behaviour for which there is no other explanation but the advertiser's arts. Actually, it may be all she craves for. If so her expenditure on it may be ideally rational in the above sense.

[2] This level differs of course not only as between epochs and places but also, at a given time and place, as between different industrial sectors and classes. There is no such thing as a universal pattern of rationality.

of responsibility that is induced by a direct relation to the favourable or unfavourable effects of a course of action.

Once more: definiteness and rationality in thought and action[1] are not guaranteed by this familiarity with men and things or by that sense of reality or responsibility. Quite a few other conditions which often fail to be fulfilled would be necessary for that. For instance, generation after generation may suffer from irrational behaviour in matters of hygiene and yet fail to link their sufferings with their noxious habits. As long as this is not done, objective consequences, however regular, of course do not produce subjective experience. Thus it proved unbelievably hard for humanity to realize the relation between infection and epidemics: the facts pointed to it with what to us seems unmistakable clearness; yet to the end of the eighteenth century doctors did next to nothing to keep people afflicted with infectious disease, such as measles or smallpox, from mixing with other people. And things must be expected to be still worse whenever there is not only inability but reluctance to recognize causal relations or when some interest fights against recognizing them.

Nevertheless and in spite of all the qualifications that impose themselves, there is for everyone, within a much wider horizon, a narrower field—widely differing in extent as between different groups and individuals and bounded by a broad zone rather than a sharp line—which is distinguished by a sense of reality or familiarity or responsibility. And this field harbours relatively definite individual volitions. These may often strike us as unintelligent, narrow, egotistical; and it may not be obvious to everyone why, when it comes to political decisions, we should worship at their shrine, still less why we should feel bound to count each of them for one and none of them for more than one. If, however, we do choose to worship we shall at least not find the shrine empty.[2]

[1]Rationality of thought and rationality of action are two different things. Rationality of thought does not always guarantee rationality of action. And the latter may be present without any conscious deliberation and irrespective of any ability to formulate the rationale of one's action correctly. The observer, particularly the observer who uses interview and questionnaire methods, often overlooks this and hence acquires an exaggerated idea of the importance of irrationality in behaviour. This is another source of those overstatements which we meet so often.

[2]It should be observed that in speaking of definite and genuine volitions I do not mean to exalt them into ultimate data for all kinds of social analysis. Of course they are themselves the product of the social process and the social environment. All I mean is that they may serve as data for the kind of special-purpose analysis which the economist has in mind when he derives prices from tastes or wants that are 'given' at any moment and need not be further analysed each time. Similarly we may for our pur-

Now this comparative definiteness of volition and rationality of behaviour does not suddenly vanish as we move away from those concerns of daily life in the home and in business which educate and discipline us. In the realm of public affairs there are sectors that are more within the reach of the citizen's mind than others. This is true, first, of local affairs. Even there we find a reduced power of discerning facts, a reduced preparedness to act upon them, a reduced sense of responsibility. We all know the man—and a very good specimen he frequently is—who says that the local administration is not his business and callously shrugs his shoulders at practices which he would rather die than suffer in his own office. High-minded citizens in a hortatory mood who preach the responsibility of the individual voter or taxpayer invariably discover the fact that this voter does not feel responsible for what the local politicians do. Still, especially in communities not too big for personal contacts, local patriotism may be a very important factor in 'making democracy work'. Also, the problems of a town are in many respects akin to the problems of a manufacturing concern. The man who understands the latter also understands, to some extent, the former. The manufacturer, grocer or workman need not step out of his world to have a rationally defensible view (that may of course be right or wrong) on street cleaning or town halls.

Second, there are many national issues that concern individuals and groups so directly and unmistakably as to evoke volitions that are genuine and definite enough. The most important instance is afforded by issues involving immediate and personal pecuniary profit to individual voters and groups of voters, such as direct payments, protective duties, silver policies and so on. Experience that goes back to antiquity shows that by and large voters react promptly and rationally to any such chance. But the classical doctrine of democracy evidently stands to gain little from displays of rationality of this kind. Voters thereby prove themselves bad and indeed corrupt judges of such issues,[1] and often they even prove themselves bad judges of their own

pose speak of genuine and definite volitions that at any moment are given independently of attempts to manufacture them, although we recognize that these genuine volitions themselves are the result of environmental influences in the past, propagandist influences included. This distinction between genuine and manufactured will (see below) is a difficult one and cannot be applied in all cases and for all purposes. For our purpose however it is sufficient to point to the obvious common-sense case which can be made for it.

[1]The reason why the Benthamites so completely overlooked this is that they did not consider the possibilities of mass corruption in modern capitalism. Committing in their political theory the same error which they committed in their economic theory,

long-run interests, for it is only the short-run promise that tells politically and only short-run rationality that asserts itself effectively.

However, when we move still farther away from the private concerns of the family and the business office into those regions of national and international affairs that lack a direct and unmistakable link with those private concerns, individual volition, command of facts and method of inference soon cease to fulfil the requirements of the classical doctrine. What strikes me most of all and seems to me to be the core of the trouble is the fact that the sense of reality[1] is so completely lost. Normally, the great political questions take their place in the psychic economy of the typical citizen with those leisure-hour interests that have not attained the rank of hobbies, and with the subjects of irresponsible conversation. These things seem so far off; they are not at all like a business proposition; dangers may not materialize at all and if they should they may not prove so very serious; one feels oneself to be moving in a fictitious world.

This reduced sense of reality accounts not only for a reduced sense of responsibility but also for the absence of effective volition. One has one's phrases, of course, and one's wishes and daydreams and grumbles; especially, one has one's likes and dislikes. But ordinarily they do not amount to what we call a will—the psychic counterpart of purposeful responsible action. In fact, for the private citizen musing over national affairs there is no scope for such a will and no task at which it could develop. He is a member of an unworkable committee, the committee of the whole nation, and this is why he expends less disciplined effort on mastering a political problem than he expends on a game of bridge.[2]

---

they felt no compunction about postulating that 'the people' were the best judges of their own individual interests and that these must necessarily coincide with the interests of all the people taken together. Of course this was made easier for them because actually though not intentionally they philosophized in terms of bourgeois interests which had more to gain from a parsimonious state than from any direct bribes.

[1] William James' 'pungent sense of reality'. The relevance of this point has been particularly emphasized by Graham Wallas.

[2] It will help to clarify the point if we ask ourselves why so much more intelligence and clear-headedness show up at a bridge table than in, say, political discussion among non-politicians. At the bridge table we have a definite task; we have rules that discipline us; success and failure are clearly defined; and we are prevented from behaving irresponsibly because every mistake we make will not only immediately tell but also be immediately allocated to us. These conditions, by their failure to be fulfilled for the political behaviour of the ordinary citizen, show why it is that in politics he lacks all the alertness and the judgement he may display in his profession.

The reduced sense of responsibility and the absence of effective volition in turn explain the ordinary citizen's ignorance and lack of judgement in matters of domestic and foreign policy which are if anything more shocking in the case of educated people and of people who are successfully active in non-political walks of life than it is with uneducated people in humble stations. Information is plentiful and readily available. But this does not seem to make any difference. Nor should we wonder at it. We need only compare a lawyer's attitude to his brief and the same lawyer's attitude to the statements of political fact presented in his newspaper in order to see what is the matter. In the one case the lawyer has qualified for appreciating the relevance of his facts by years of purposeful labour done under the definite stimulus of interest in his professional competence; and under a stimulus that is no less powerful he then bends his acquirements, his intellect, his will to the contents of the brief. In the other case, he has not taken the trouble to qualify; he does not care to absorb the information or to apply to it the canons of criticism he knows so well how to handle; and he is impatient of long or complicated argument. All of this goes to show that without the initiative that comes from immediate responsibility, ignorance will persist in the face of masses of information however complete and correct. It persists even in the face of the meritorious efforts that are being made to go beyond presenting information and to teach the use of it by means of lectures, classes, discussion groups. Results are not zero. But they are small. People cannot be carried up the ladder.

Thus the typical citizen drops down to a lower level of mental performance as soon as he enters the political field. He argues and analyses in a way which he would readily recognize as infantile within the sphere of his real interests. He becomes a primitive again. His thinking becomes associative and affective.[1] And this entails two further consequences of ominous significance.

First, even if there were no political groups trying to influence him, the typical citizen would in political matters tend to yield to extra-rational or irrational prejudice and impulse. The weakness of the rational processes he applies to politics and the absence of effective logical control over the results he arrives at would in themselves suffice to account for that. Moreover, simply because he is not 'all there', he will relax his usual moral standards as well and occasionally give in to dark urges which the conditions of private

[1]See ch. xii.

life help him to repress. But as to the wisdom or rationality of his inferences and conclusions, it may be just as bad if he gives in to a burst of generous indignation. This will make it still more difficult for him to see things in their correct proportions or even to see more than one aspect of one thing at a time. Hence, if for once he does emerge from his usual vagueness and does display the definite will postulated by the classical doctrine of democracy, he is as likely as not to become still more unintelligent and irresponsible than he usually is. At certain junctures, this may prove fatal to his nation.[1]

Second, however, the weaker the logical element in the processes of the public mind and the more complete the absence of rational criticism and of the rationalizing influence of personal experience and responsibility, the greater are the opportunities for groups with an axe to grind. These groups may consist of professional politicians or of exponents of an economic interest or of idealists of one kind or another or of people simply interested in staging and managing political shows. The sociology of such groups is immaterial to the argument in hand. The only point that matters here is that, Human Nature in Politics being what it is, they are able to fashion and, within very wide limits, even to create the will of the people. What we are confronted with in the analysis of political processes is largely not a genuine but a manufactured will. And often this artefact is all that in reality corresponds to the *volonté générale* of the classical doctrine. So far as this is so, the will of the people is the product and not the motive power of the political process.

The ways in which issues and the popular will on any issue are being manufactured is exactly analogous to the ways of commercial advertising. We find the same attempts to contact the subconscious. We find the same technique of creating favourable and unfavourable associations which are the more effective the less rational they are. We find the same evasions and reticences and the same trick of producing opinion by reiterated assertion that is successful precisely to the extent to which it avoids rational argument and the danger of awakening the critical faculties of the people. And so on. Only, all

---

[1] The importance of such bursts cannot be doubted. But it is possible to doubt their genuineness. Analysis will show in many instances that they are induced by the action of some group and do not spontaneously arise from the people. In this case they enter into a (second) class of phenomena which we are about to deal with. Personally, I do believe that genuine instances exist. But I cannot be sure that more thorough analysis would not reveal some psycho-technical effort at the bottom of them.

these arts have infinitely more scope in the sphere of public affairs than they have in the sphere of private and professional life. The picture of the prettiest girl that ever lived will in the long run prove powerless to maintain the sales of a bad cigarette. There is no equally effective safeguard in the case of political decisions. Many decisions of fateful importance are of a nature that makes it impossible for the public to experiment with them at its leisure and at moderate cost. Even if that is possible, however, judgement is as a rule not so easy to arrive at as it is in the case of the cigarette, because effects are less easy to interpret.

But such arts also vitiate, to an extent quite unknown in the field of commercial advertising, those forms of political advertising that profess to address themselves to reason. To the observer, the antirational or, at all events, the extra-rational appeal and the defencelessness of the victim stand out more and not less clearly when cloaked in facts and arguments. We have seen above why it is so difficult to impart to the public unbiased information about political problems and logically correct inferences from it and why it is that information and arguments in political matters will 'register' only if they link up with the citizen's preconceived ideas. As a rule, however, these ideas are not definite enough to determine particular conclusions. Since they can themselves be manufactured, effective political argument almost inevitably implies the attempt to twist existing volitional premises into a particular shape and not merely the attempt to implement them or to help the citizen to make up his mind.

Thus information and arguments that are really driven home are likely to be the servants of political intent. Since the first thing man will do for his ideal or interest is to lie, we shall expect, and as a matter of fact we find, that effective information is almost always adulterated or selective[1] and that effective reasoning in politics consists mainly in trying to exalt certain propositions into axioms and to put others out of court; it thus reduces to the psycho-technics mentioned before. The reader who thinks me unduly pessimistic need only ask himself whether he has never heard—or said himself—that this or that awkward fact must not be told publicly, or that a certain line of reasoning, though valid, is undesirable. If men who according to any current standard are perfectly honourable or even high-minded reconcile themselves to the implications of this, do they not thereby show what they think about the merits or even the existence of the will of the people?

[1] Selective information, if in itself correct, is an attempt to lie by speaking the truth.

There are of course limits to all this.[1] And there is truth in Jefferson's dictum that in the end the people are wiser than any single individual can be, or in Lincoln's about the impossibility of 'fooling all the people all the time'. But both dicta stress the long-run aspect in a highly significant way. It is no doubt possible to argue that given time the collective psyche will evolve opinions that not infrequently strike us as highly reasonable and even shrewd. History however consists of a succession of short-run situations that may alter the course of events for good. If all the people can in the short run be 'fooled' step by step into something they do not really want, and if this is not an exceptional case which we could afford to neglect, then no amount of retrospective common sense will alter the fact that in reality they neither raise nor decide issues but that the issues that shape their fate are normally raised and decided for them. More than anyone else the lover of democracy has every reason to accept this fact and to clear his creed from the aspersion that it rests upon make-believe.

IV. REASONS FOR THE SURVIVAL OF THE CLASSICAL DOCTRINE

But how is it possible that a doctrine so patently contrary to fact should have survived to this day and continued to hold its place in the hearts of the people and in the official language of governments? The refuting facts are known to all; everybody admits them with perfect, frequently with cynical, frankness. The theoretical basis, utilitarian rationalism, is dead; nobody accepts it as a correct theory of the body politic. Nevertheless that question is not difficult to answer.

First of all, though the classical doctrine of collective action may not be supported by the results of empirical analysis, it is powerfully supported by that association with religious belief to which I have adverted already. This may not be obvious at first sight. The utilitarian leaders were anything but religious in the ordinary sense of the term. In fact they believed themselves to be anti-religious and they were so considered almost universally. They took pride in what they thought was precisely an unmetaphysical attitude and they were quite out of sympathy with the religious institutions and the religious movements of their time. But we need only cast another glance at the picture they drew of the social process in order to discover that it embodied essential features of the faith of protestant Christianity and was in

[1] Possibly they might show more clearly if issues were more frequently decided by referendum. Politicians presumably know why they are almost invariably hostile to that institution.

fact derived from that faith. For the intellectual who had cast off his religion the utilitarian creed provided a substitute for it. For many of those who had retained their religious belief the classical doctrine became the political complement of it.[1]

Thus transposed into the categories of religion, this doctrine—and in consequence the kind of democratic persuasion which is based upon it—changes its very nature. There is no longer any need for logical scruples about the Common Good and Ultimate Values. All this is settled for us by the plan of the Creator whose purpose defines and sanctions everything. What seemed indefinite or unmotivated before is suddenly quite definite and convincing. The voice of the people that is the voice of God for instance. Or take Equality. Its very meaning is in doubt, and there is hardly any rational warrant for exalting it into a postulate, so long as we move in the sphere of empirical analysis. But Christianity harbours a strong equalitarian element. The Redeemer died for all: He did not differentiate between individuals of different social status. In doing so, He testified to the intrinsic value of the individual soul, a value that admits of no gradations. Is not this a sanction—and, as it seems to me, the only possible sanction[2]—of 'everyone to count for one, no one to count for more than one'—a sanction that pours super-mundane meaning into articles of the democratic creed for which it is not easy to find any other? To be sure this interpretation does not cover the whole ground. However, so far as it goes, it seems to explain many things that otherwise would be unexplainable and in fact meaningless. In particular, it explains the believer's attitude toward criticism: again, as in the case of socialism, fundamental dissent is looked upon not merely as error but as sin; it elicits not merely logical counterargument but also moral indignation.

We may put our problem differently and say that democracy, when motivated in this way, ceases to be a mere method that can be dis-

[1] Observe the analogy with socialist belief which also is a substitute for Christian belief to some and a complement of it to others.

[2] It might be objected that, however difficult it may be to attach a *general* meaning to the word Equality, such meaning can be unravelled from its context in most if not all cases. For instance, it may be permissible to infer from the circumstances in which the Gettysburg address was delivered that by the 'proposition that all men are created free and equal', Lincoln simply meant equality of legal status versus the kind of inequality that is implied in the recognition of slavery. This meaning would be definite enough. But if we ask why that proposition should be morally and politically binding and if we refuse to answer 'Because every man is by nature exactly like every other man', then we can only fall back upon the divine sanction supplied by Christian belief. This solution is conceivably implied in the word 'created'.

cussed rationally like a steam engine or a disinfectant. It actually becomes what from another standpoint I have held it incapable of becoming, viz., an ideal or rather a part of an ideal schema of things. The very word may become a flag, a symbol of all a man holds dear, of everything that he loves about his nation whether rationally contingent to it or not. On the one hand, the question how the various propositions implied in the democratic belief are related to the facts of politics will then become as irrelevant to him as is, to the believing Catholic, the question how the doings of Alexander VI tally with the supernatural halo surrounding the papal office. On the other hand, the democrat of this type, while accepting postulates carrying large implications about equality and brotherliness, will be in a position also to accept, in all sincerity, almost any amount of deviations from them that his own behaviour or position may involve. That is not even illogical. Mere distance from fact is no argument against an ethical maxim or a mystical hope.

Second, there is the fact that the forms and phrases of classical democracy are for many nations associated with events and developments in their history which are enthusiastically approved by large majorities. Any opposition to an established regime is likely to use these forms and phrases whatever its meaning and social roots may be.[1] If it prevails and if subsequent developments prove satisfactory, then these forms will take root in the national ideology.

The United States is the outstanding example. Its very existence as a sovereign state is associated with a struggle against a monarchial and aristocratic England. A minority of loyalists excepted, Americans had, at the time of the Grenville administration, probably ceased to look upon the English monarch as *their* king and the English aristocracy as *their* aristocracy. In the War of Independence they fought what in fact as well as in their feeling had become a foreign monarch and a foreign aristocracy who interfered with their political and economic interests. Yet from an early stage of the troubles they presented their case, which really was a national one, as a case of the 'people' versus its 'ruler', in terms of inalienable Rights of Man and in the light of the general principles of classical democracy. The wording of the Declaration of Independence and of the Constitution

[1] It might seem that an exception should be made for oppositions that issue into frankly autocratic regimes. But even most of these rose, as a matter of history, in democratic ways and based their rule on the approval of the people. Caesar was not killed by plebeians. But the aristocratic oligarchs who did kill him also used democratic phrases.

adopted these principles. A prodigious development followed that absorbed and satisfied most people and thereby seemed to verify the doctrine embalmed in the sacred documents of the nation.

Oppositions rarely conquer when the groups in possession are in the prime of their power and success. In the first half of the nineteenth century, the oppositions that professed the classical creed of democracy rose and eventually prevailed against governments some of which—especially in Italy—were obviously in a state of decay and had become bywords of incompetence, brutality and corruption. Naturally though not quite logically, this redounded to the credit of that creed which moreover showed up to advantage when compared with the benighted superstitions sponsored by those governments. Under these circumstances, democratic revolution meant the advent of freedom and decency, and the democratic creed meant a gospel of reason and betterment. To be sure, this advantage was bound to be lost and the gulf between the doctrine and the practice of democracy was bound to be discovered. But the glamour of the dawn was slow to fade.

Third, it must not be forgotten that there are social patterns in which the classical doctrine will actually fit facts with a sufficient degree of approximation. As has been pointed out, this is the case with many small and primitive societies which as a matter of fact served as a prototype to the authors of that doctrine. It may be the case also with societies that are not primitive provided they are not too differentiated and do not harbour any serious problems. Switzerland is the best example. There is so little to quarrel about in a world of peasants which, excepting hotels and banks, contains no great capitalist industry, and the problems of public policy are so simple and so stable that an overwhelming majority can be expected to understand them and to agree about them. But if we can conclude that in such cases the classical doctrine approximates reality we have to add immediately that it does so not because it describes an effective mechanism of political decision but only because there are no great decisions to be made. Finally, the case of the United States may again be invoked in order to show that the classical doctrine sometimes appears to fit facts even in a society that is big and highly differentiated and in which there are great issues to decide provided the sting is taken out of them by favourable conditions. Until this country's entry into the First World War, the public mind was concerned mainly with the business of exploiting the economic possibilities of the environment. So long as this business was not seriously interfered with nothing mattered fundamentally to the average citizen who looked on the antics of politicians with good-natured contempt. Sections might get excited over the tariff, over silver, over local misgovernment, or over an occasional squabble with England. The people at large did not care much, except in the one case of serious disagreement which in fact produced national disaster, the Civil War.

And fourth, of course, politicians appreciate a phraseology that flatters the masses and offers an excellent opportunity not only for evading responsibility but also for crushing opponents in the name of the people.

2–ANOTHER THEORY OF DEMOCRACY

I. COMPETITION FOR POLITICAL LEADERSHIP

I THINK that most students of politics have by now come to accept the criticisms levelled at the classical doctrine of democracy in the preceding chapter. I also think that most of them agree, or will agree before long, in accepting another theory which is much truer to life and at the same time salvages much of what sponsors of the democratic method really mean by this term. Like the classical theory, it may be put into the nutshell of a definition.

It will be remembered that our chief troubles about the classical theory centred in the proposition that 'the people' hold a definite and rational opinion about every individual question and that they give effect to this opinion—in a democracy—by choosing 'representatives' who will see to it that that opinion is carried out. Thus the selection of the representatives is made secondary to the primary purpose of the democratic arrangement which is to vest the power of deciding political issues in the electorate. Suppose we reverse the roles of these two elements and make the deciding of issues by the electorate secondary to the election of the men who are to do the deciding. To put it differently, we now take the view that the role of the people is to produce a government, or else an intermediate body which in turn will produce a national executive[1] or government. And we define: the democratic method is that institutional arrangement for arriving at political decisions in which individuals acquire the

[1] The insincere word 'executive' really points in the wrong direction. It ceases however to do so if we use it in the sense in which we speak of the 'executives' of a business corporation who also do a great deal more than 'execute' the will of stockholders.

power to decide by means of a competitive struggle for the people's vote.

Defence and explanation of this idea will speedily show that, as to both plausibility of assumptions and tenability of propositions, it greatly improves the theory of the democratic process.

First of all, we are provided with a reasonably efficient criterion by which to distinguish democratic governments from others. We have seen that the classical theory meets with difficulties on that score because both the will and the good of the people may be, and in many historical instances have been, served just as well or better by governments that cannot be described as democratic according to any accepted usage of the term. Now we are in a somewhat better position partly because we are resolved to stress a *modus procedendi* the presence or absence of which it is in most cases easy to verify.[1]

For instance, a parliamentary monarchy like the English one fulfils the requirements of the democratic method because the monarch is practically constrained to appoint to cabinet office the same people as parliament would elect. A 'constitutional' monarchy does not qualify to be called democratic because electorates and parliaments, while having all the other rights that electorates and parliaments have in parliamentary monarchies, lack the power to impose their choice as to the governing committee: the cabinet ministers are in this case servants of the monarch, in substance as well as in name, and can in principle be dismissed as well as appointed by him. Such an arrangement may satisfy the people. The electorate may reaffirm this fact by voting against any proposal for change. The monarch may be so popular as to be able to defeat any competition for the supreme office. But since no machinery is provided for making this competition effective the case does not come within our definition.

Second, the theory embodied in this definition leaves all the room we may wish to have for a proper recognition of the vital fact of leadership. The classical theory did not do this but, as we have seen, attributed to the electorate an altogether unrealistic degree of initiative which practically amounted to ignoring leadership. But collectives act almost exclusively by accepting leadership—this is the dominant mechanism of practically any collective action which is more than a reflex. Propositions about the working and the results of the democratic method that take account of this are bound to be infinitely more realistic than propositions which do not. They will not

[1]See however the fourth point below.

stop at the execution of a *volonté générale* but will go some way toward showing how it emerges or how it is substituted or faked. What we have termed Manufactured Will is no longer outside the theory, an aberration for the absence of which we piously pray; it enters on the ground floor as it should.

Third, however, so far as there are genuine group-wise volitions at all—for instance the will of the unemployed to receive unemployment benefit or the will of other groups to help—our theory does not neglect them. On the contrary we are now able to insert them in exactly the role they actually play. Such volitions do not as a rule assert themselves directly. Even if strong and definite they remain latent, often for decades, until they are called to life by some political leader who turns them into political factors. This he does, or else his agents do it for him, by organizing these volitions, by working them up and by including eventually appropriate items in his competitive offering. The interaction between sectional interests and public opinion and the way in which they produce the pattern we call the political situation appear from this angle in a new and much clearer light.

Fourth, our theory is of course no more definite than is the concept of competition for leadership. This concept presents similar difficulties as the concept of competition in the economic sphere, with which it may be usefully compared. In economic life competition is never completely lacking, but hardly ever is it perfect.[1] Similarly, in political life there is always some competition, though perhaps only a potential one, for the allegiance of the people. To simplify matters we have restricted the kind of competition for leadership which is to define democracy, to free competition for a free vote. The justification for this is that democracy seems to imply a recognized method by which to conduct the competitive struggle, and that the electoral method is practically the only one available for communities of any size. But though this excludes many ways of securing leadership which should be excluded,[2] such as competition by military insurrection, it does not exclude the cases that are strikingly analogous to the economic

---

[1] In Part II we had examples of the problems which arise out of this.

[2] It also excludes methods which should not be excluded, for instance, the acquisition of political leadership by the people's tacit acceptance of it or by election *quasi per inspirationem*. The latter differs from election by voting only by a technicality. But the former is not quite without importance even in modern politics; the sway held by a party boss *within his party* is often based on nothing but tacit acceptance of his leadership. Comparatively speaking however these are details which may, I think, be neglected in a sketch like this.

phenomena we label 'unfair' or 'fraudulent' competition or restraint of competition. And we cannot exclude them because if we did we should be left with a completely unrealistic ideal.[1] Between this ideal case which does not exist and the cases in which all competition with the established leader is prevented by force, there is a continuous range of variation within which the democratic method of government shades off into the autocratic one by imperceptible steps. But if we wish to understand and not to philosophize, this is as it should be. The value of our criterion is not seriously impaired thereby.

Fifth, our theory seems to clarify the relation that subsists between democracy and individual freedom. If by the latter we mean the existence of a sphere of individual self-government the boundaries of which are historically variable—*no* society tolerates absolute freedom even of conscience and of speech, *no* society reduces that sphere to zero—the question clearly becomes a matter of degree. We have seen that the democratic method does not necessarily guarantee a greater amount of individual freedom than another political method would permit in similar circumstances. It may well be the other way round. But there is still a relation between the two. If, on principle at least, everyone is free to compete for political leadership[2] by presenting himself to the electorate, this will in most cases though not in all mean a considerable amount of freedom of discussion *for all*. In particular it will normally mean a considerable amount of freedom of the press. This relation between democracy and freedom is not absolutely stringent and can be tampered with. But, from the standpoint of the intellectual, it is nevertheless very important. At the same time, it is all there is to that relation.

Sixth, it should be observed that in making it the primary function of the electorate to produce a government (directly or through an intermediate body) I intended to include in this phrase also the function of evicting it. The one means simply the acceptance of a leader or a group of leaders, the other means simply the withdrawal of this acceptance. This takes care of an element the reader may have missed. He may have thought that the electorate controls as well as installs. But since electorates normally do not control their political leaders in any way except by refusing to reelect them or the parliamentary majorities that support them, it seems well to reduce our ideas about this control in the way indicated by our definition. Occasionally,

[1] As in the economic field, *some* restrictions are implicit in the legal and moral principles of the community.

[2] Free, that is, in the same sense in which everyone is free to start another textile mill.

spontaneous revulsions occur which upset a government or an individual minister directly or else enforce a certain course of action. But they are not only exceptional, they are, as we shall see, contrary to the spirit of the democratic method.

Seventh, our theory sheds much-needed light on an old controversy. Whoever accepts the classical doctrine of democracy and in consequence believes that the democratic method is to guarantee that issues be decided and policies framed according to the will of the people must be struck by the fact that, even if that will were undeniably real and definite, decision by simple majorities would in many cases distort it rather than give effect to it. Evidently the will of the majority is the will of the majority and not the will of 'the people'. The latter is a mosaic that the former completely fails to 'represent'. To equate both by definition is not to solve the problem. Attempts at real solutions have however been made by the authors of the various plans for Proportional Representation.

These plans have met with adverse criticism on practical grounds. It is in fact obvious not only that proportional representation will offer opportunities for all sorts of idiosyncrasies to assert themselves but also that it may prevent democracy from producing efficient governments and thus prove a danger in times of stress.[1] But before concluding that democracy becomes unworkable if its principle is carried out consistently, it is just as well to ask ourselves whether this principle really implies proportional representation. As a matter of fact it does not. If acceptance of leadership is the true function of the electorate's vote, the case for proportional representation collapses because its premises are no longer binding. The principle of democracy then merely means that the reins of government should be handed to those who command more support than do any of the competing individuals or teams. And this in turn seems to assure the standing of the majority system within the logic of the democratic method, although we might still condemn it on grounds that lie outside of that logic.

II. The Principle Applied

The theory outlined in the preceding section we are now going to try out on some of the more important features of the structure and working of the political engine in democratic countries.

[1] The argument against proportional representation has been ably stated by Professor F. A. Hermens in 'The Trojan Horse of Democracy', *Social Research*, November 1938.

1. In a democracy, as I have said, the primary function of the elector's vote is to produce government. This may mean the election of a complete set of individual officers. This practice however is in the main a feature of local government and will be neglected henceforth.[1] Considering national government only, we may say that producing government practically amounts to deciding who the leading man shall be.[2] As before, we shall call him Prime Minister.

There is only one democracy in which the electorate's vote does this directly, viz., the United States.[3] In all other cases the electorate's

[1]This we shall do for simplicity's sake only. The phenomenon fits perfectly into our schema.

[2]This is only approximately true. The elector's vote does indeed put into power a group that in all normal cases acknowledges an individual leader but there are as a rule leaders of second and third rank who carry political guns in their own right and whom the leader has no choice but to put into appropriate offices. This fact will be recognized presently.

Another point must be kept in mind. Although there is reason to expect that a man who rises to a position of supreme command will in general be a man of considerable personal force, whatever else he may be—to this we shall return later on—it does not follow that this will always be the case. Therefore the term 'leader' or 'leading man' is not to imply that the individuals thus designated are necessarily endowed with qualities of leadership or that they always do give any personal leads. There are political situations favourable to the rise of men deficient in leadership (and other qualities) and unfavourable to the establishment of strong individual positions. A party or a combination of parties hence may occasionally be acephalous. But everyone recognizes that this is a pathological state and one of the typical causes of defeat.

[3]We may, I take it, disregard the electoral college. In calling the President of the United States a prime minister I wish to stress the fundamental similarity of his position to that of prime ministers in other democracies. But I do not wish to minimize the differences, although some of them are more formal than real. The least important of them is that the President also fulfils those largely ceremonial functions of, say, the French presidents. Much more important is it that he cannot dissolve Congress— but neither could the French Prime Minister do so. On the other hand, his position is stronger than that of the English Prime Minister by virtue of the fact that his leadership is independent of his having a majority in Congress—at least legally; for as a matter of fact he is checkmated if he has none. Also, he can appoint and dismiss cabinet officers (almost) at will. The latter can hardly be called ministers in the English sense of the word and are really no more than the word 'secretary' conveys in common parlance. We might say, therefore, that in a sense the President is not only prime minister but sole minister, unless we find an analogy between the functions of an English Cabinet minister and the functions of the managers of the administration's forces in Congress.

There is no difficulty about interpreting and explaining these and many other peculiarities in this or any other country that uses the democratic method. But in order to save space we shall mainly think of the English pattern and consider all other cases as more or less important 'deviations' on the theory that thus far the logic of democratic government has worked itself out most completely in the English practice though not in its legal forms.

vote does not directly produce government but an intermediate organ, henceforth called parliament,[1] upon which the government-producing function devolves. It might seem to account for the adoption or rather the evolution of this arrangement, both on historical grounds and on grounds of expediency, and for the various forms it took in different social patterns. But it is not a logical construct; it is a natural growth the subtle meanings and results of which completely escape the official, let alone legal, doctrines.

How does a parliament produce government? The most obvious method is to elect it or, more realistically, to elect the prime minister and then to vote the list of ministers he presents. This method is rarely used.[2] But it brings out the nature of the procedure better than any of the others. Moreover, these can all be reduced to it, because the man who becomes prime minister is in all normal cases the one whom parliament would elect. The way in which he is actually appointed to office, by a monarch as in England, by a President as in France or by a special agency or committee as in the Prussian Free State of the Weimar period, is merely a matter of form.

The classical English practice is this. After a general election the victorious party normally commands a majority of seats in Parliament and thus is in a position to carry a vote of want of confidence against everyone except its own leader who in this negative way is designated 'by Parliament' for national leadership. He receives his commission from the monarch—'kisses hands'—and presents to him his list of ministers of which the list of cabinet ministers is a part. In this he includes, first, some party veterans who receive what might be called complimentary office; secondly, the leaders of the second rank, those men on whom he counts for the current fighting in Parliament and who owe their preferment partly to their positive political value and partly to their value as potential nuisances; third, the rising men whom he invites to the charmed circle of office in order to 'extract the brains from below the gangway'; and sometimes, fourth, a few men whom he thinks particularly well qualified to fill certain offices.[3]

---

[1] It will be recalled that I have defined parliament as an organ of the state. Although that was done simply for reasons of formal (legal) logic, this definition fits in particularly well with our conception of the democratic method. Membership in parliament is hence an office.

[2] For example, it was adopted in Austria after the breakdown in 1918.

[3] To lament, as some people do, how little fitness for office counts in these arrangements is beside the point where description is concerned; it is of the essence of democratic government that political values should count primarily and fitness only incidentally.

But again, in all normal cases this practice will tend to produce the same result as election by Parliament would. The reader will also see that where, as in England, the prime minister has the actual power to dissolve ('to go to the country'), the result will to some extent approximate the result we should expect from direct election of the cabinet by the electorate so long as the latter supports him.[1] This may be illustrated by a famous instance.

2. In 1879, when the Beaconsfield (Disraeli) government, after almost six years of prosperous tenure of power culminating in the spectacular success of the Congress of Berlin,[2] was on all ordinary counts entitled to expect a success at the polls, Gladstone suddenly roused the country by a series of addresses of unsurpassable force (Midlothian campaign) which played up Turkish atrocities so successfully as to place him on the crest of a wave of popular enthusiasm *for him personally*. The official party had nothing to do with it. Several of its leaders in fact disapproved. Gladstone had resigned the leadership years before and tackled the country single-handed. But when the liberal party under this impetus had won a smashing victory, it was obvious to everyone that he had to be again accepted as the party leader—nay, that he had become the party leader by virtue of his national leadership and that there simply was no room for any other. He came into power in a halo of glory.

[1] If, as was the case in France, the prime minister has no such power, parliamentary *coteries* acquire so much independence that this parallelism between acceptance of a man by parliament and acceptance of the same man by the electorate is weakened or destroyed. This is the situation in which the parlour game of parliamentary politics runs riot. From our standpoint this is a deviation from the design of the machine. Raymond Poincaré was of the same opinion.

Of course, such situations also occur in England. For the Prime Minister's power to dissolve—strictly, his power to 'advise' the monarch to dissolve the House of Commons—is inoperative either if his party's inner circle sets its face against it or if there is no chance that elections will strengthen his hold upon Parliament. That is to say, he may be stronger (though possibly still weak) in Parliament than he is in the country. Such a state of things tends to develop with some regularity after a government has been in power for some years. But under the English system this deviation from design cannot last very long.

[2] I do not mean that the temporary settlement of the questions raised by the Russo-Turkish War and the acquisition of the perfectly useless island of Cyprus were in themselves such masterpieces of statesmanship. But I do mean that from the standpoint of domestic politics they were just the kind of showy success that would normally flatter the average citizen's vanity and would greatly enhance the government's prospects in an atmosphere of jingo patriotism. In fact it was the general opinion that Disraeli would have won if he had dissolved immediately on returning from Berlin.

Now this instance teaches us a lot about the working of the democratic method. To begin with, it must be realized that it is unique only in its dramatic quality, but in nothing else. It is the oversized specimen of a normal genus. The cases of both Pitts, Peel, Palmerston, Disraeli, Campbell Bannerman and others differ from it only in degree.

First, as to the Prime Minister's political leadership.[1] Our example shows that it is composed of three different elements which must not be confused and which in every case mix in different proportions, the mixture then determining the nature of every individual Prime Minister's rule. On the face of it, he comes into office as the leading man of his party *in Parliament*. As soon as installed however, he becomes in a sense the leader *of Parliament*, directly of the house of which he is a member, indirectly also of the other. This is more than an official euphemism, more also than is implied in his hold upon his own party. He acquires influence on, or excites the antipathy of,

[1] It is characteristic of the English way of doing things that official recognition of the existence of the Prime Minister's office was deferred until 1907, when it was allowed to appear in the official order of precedence at court. But it is as old as democratic government. However, since democratic government was never introduced by a distinct act but slowly evolved as part of a comprehensive social process, it is not easy to indicate even an approximate birthday or birth period. There is a long stretch that presents embryonic cases. It is tempting to date the institution from the reign of William III, whose position, so much weaker than that of the native rulers had been, seems to give colour to the idea. The objection to this however is not so much that England was no 'democracy' then—the reader will recall that we do not define democracy by the extent of the franchise—as that, on the one hand, the embryonic case of Danby had occurred under Charles II and that, on the other hand, William III never reconciled himself to the arrangement and kept certain matters successfully in his own hands. We must not of course confuse prime ministers with mere advisers, however powerful with their sovereign and however firmly entrenched in the very centre of the public power plant they may be—such men as Richelieu, Mazarin or Strafford for instance. Godolphin and Harley under Queen Anne were clearly transitional cases. The first man to be universally recognized at the time and by political historians was Sir Robert Walpole. But he as well as the Duke of Newcastle (or his brother Henry Pelham or both jointly) and in fact all the leading men down to Lord Shelburne (including the elder Pitt who even as foreign secretary came very near to fulfilling our requirements *in substance*) lack one or another of the characteristics. The first full-fledged specimen was the younger Pitt.

It is interesting to note that what his own time recognized in the case of Sir Robert Walpole (and later in that of Lord Carteret [Earl of Granville]) was not that here was an organ essential to democratic government that was breaking through atrophic tissues. On the contrary, public opinion felt it to be a most vicious cancer the growth of which was a menace to the national welfare and to democracy—'sole minister' or 'first minister' was a term of opprobrium hurled at Walpole by his enemies. This fact is significant. It not only indicates the resistance new institutions usually meet with. It also indicates that this institution was felt to be incompatible with the classic doctrine of democracy which in fact has no place for political leadership in our sense, hence no place for the realities of the position of a prime minister.

the other parties and individual members of the other parties as well, and this makes a lot of difference in his chances of success. In the limiting case, best exemplified by the practice of Sir Robert Peel, he may coerce his own party by means of another. Finally, though in all normal cases he will also be the head of his party in *the country*, the well-developed specimen of the prime ministerial genus will have a position in the country distinct from what he automatically acquires by heading the party organization. He will lead party opinion creatively—shape it—and eventually rise toward a formative leadership of public opinion beyond the lines of party, toward national leadership that may to some extent become independent of mere party opinion. It is needless to say how very personal such an achievement is and how great the importance of such a foothold outside of both party and Parliament. It puts a whip into the hand of the leader the crack of which may bring unwilling and conspiring followers to heel, though its thong will sharply hit the hand that uses it unsuccessfully.

This suggests an important qualification to our proposition that in a parliamentary system the function of producing a government devolves upon parliament. Parliament does normally decide who will be Prime Minister, but in doing so it is not completely free. It decides by acceptance rather than by initiative. Excepting pathological cases like the French *chambre*, the wishes of members are not as a rule the ultimate data of the process from which government emerges. Members are not only handcuffed by party obligations. They also are driven by the man whom they 'elect'—driven to the act of the 'election' itself exactly as they are driven by him once they have 'elected' him. Every horse is of course free to kick over the traces and it does not always run up to its bit. But revolt or passive resistance against the leader's lead only shows up the normal relation. And this normal relation is of the essence of the democratic method. Gladstone's personal victory in 1880 is the answer to the official theory that Parliament creates and cashiers government.[1]

[1] Gladstone himself upheld that theory strongly. In 1874, when defeated at the polls, he still argued for meeting Parliament because it was up to Parliament to pass the sentence of dismissal. This of course means nothing at all. In the same way he studiously professed unbounded deference to the crown. One biographer after another has marvelled at this courtly attitude of the great democratic leader. But surely Queen Victoria showed better discernment than did those biographers if we may judge from the strong dislike which she displayed for Gladstone from 1879 on and which the biographers attribute simply to the baleful influence of Disraeli. Is it really necessary to point out that professions of deference may mean two different things? The man who treats his wife with elaborate courtliness is not as a rule the one to accept comradeship between the sexes on terms of equality. As a matter of fact, the courtly attitude is precisely a method to evade this.

3. Next, as to the nature and role of the cabinet.[1] It is a curiously double-faced thing, the joint product of Parliament and Prime Minister. The latter designates its members for appointment, as we have seen, and the former accepts but also influences his choice. Looked at from the party's standpoint it is an assemblage of subleaders more or less reflecting its own structure. Looked at from the Prime Minister's standpoint it is an assemblage not only of comrades in arms but of party men who have their own interests and prospects to consider—a miniature Parliament. For the combination to come about and to work it is necessary for prospective cabinet ministers to make up their minds—not necessarily from enthusiastic love—to serve under Mr. X and for Mr. X to shape his programme so that his colleagues in the cabinet will not too often feel like 'reconsidering their position', as official phraseology has it, or like going on a sit-down strike. Thus the cabinet—and the same applies to the wider ministry that comprises also the political officers not in the cabinet—has a distinct function in the democratic process as against Prime Minister, party, Parliament and electorate. This function of intermediate leadership is associated with, but by no means based upon, the current business transacted by the individual cabinet officers in the several departments to which they are appointed in order to keep the leading group's hands on the bureaucratic engine. And it has only a distant relation, if any, with 'seeing to it that the will of the people is carried out in each of them'. Precisely in the best instances, the people are presented with results they never thought of and would not have approved of in advance.

4. Again, as to Parliament. I have both defined what seems to me to be its primary function and qualified that definition. But it might be objected that my definition fails to do justice to its other functions. Parliament obviously does a lot of other things besides setting up and pulling down governments. It legislates. And it even administers. For although every act of a parliament, except resolutions and

---

[1] Still more than the evolution of the prime minister's office, that of the cabinet is blurred by the historical continuity that covers changes in the nature of an institution. To this day the English cabinet is legally the operative part of the Privy Council, which of course was an instrument of government in decidedly predemocratic times. But below this surface an entirely different organ has evolved. As soon as we realize this we find the task of dating its emergence somewhat easier than we found the analogous task in the case of the prime minister. Though embryonic cabinets existed in the time of Charles II (the 'cabal' ministry was one, and the committee of four that was formed in connexion with Temple's experiment was another), the Whig 'junto' under William III is a fair candidate for first place. From the reign of Anne on only minor points of membership or functioning remain to disagree on.

declarations of policy, makes 'law' in a formal sense, there are many acts which must be considered as administrative measures. The budget is the most important instance. To make it is an administrative function. Yet in this country it is drawn up by Congress. Even where it is drawn up by the minister of finance with the approval of the cabinet, as it is in England, Parliament has to vote on it and by this vote it becomes an act of Parliament. Does not this refute our theory?

When two armies operate against each other, their individual moves are always centred upon particular objects that are determined by their strategical or tactical situations. They may contend for a particular stretch of country or for a particular hill. But the desirability of conquering that stretch or hill must be derived from the strategical or tactical purpose, which is to beat the enemy. It would be obviously absurd to attempt to derive it from any extra-military properties the stretch or hill may have. Similarly, the first and foremost aim of each political party is to prevail over the others in order to get into power or to stay in it. Like the conquest of the stretch of country or the hill, the decision of the political issues is, from the standpoint of the politician, not the end but only the material of parliamentary activity. Since politicians fire off words instead of bullets and since those words are unavoidably supplied by the issues under debate, this may not always be as clear as it is in the military case. But victory over the opponent is nevertheless the essence of both games.[1]

Fundamentally, then, the current production of parliamentary decisions on national questions is the very method by which Parliament keeps or refuses to keep a government in power or by which Parliament accepts or refuses to accept the Prime Minister's leadership.[2] With the exceptions to be noticed presently, *every* vote is a vote

[1] Sometimes politicians do emerge from phraseological mists. To cite an example to which no objection can be raised on the score of frivolity: no lesser politician than Sir Robert Peel characterized the nature of his craft when he said after his parliamentary victory over the Whig government on the issue of the latter's policy in Jamaica: 'Jamaica was a good horse to start'. The reader should ponder over this.

[2] This of course applies to the pre-Vichy French and pre-Fascist Italian practice just as much as to the English practice. It may however be called in question in the case of the United States where defeat of the administration on a major issue does not entail resignation of the President. But this is merely due to the fact that the Constitution, which embodies a different political theory, did not permit parliamentary practice to develop according to its logic. In actual fact this logic did not entirely fail to assert itself. Defeats on major issues, though they cannot displace the President, will in general so weaken his prestige as to oust him from a position of leadership. For the time being this creates an abnormal situation. But whether he wins or loses the subsequent presidential election, the conflict is then settled in a way that does not fundamentally differ from the way in which an English Prime Minister deals with a similar situation when he dissolves Parliament.

of confidence or want of confidence, and the votes that are technically so called merely bring out *in abstracto* the essential element that is common to all. Of this we can satisfy ourselves by observing that the initiative in bringing up matters for parliamentary decision as a rule lies with the government or else with the opposition's shadow cabinet and not with private members.

It is the Prime Minister who selects from the incessant stream of current problems those which he is going to make parliamentary issues, that is to say, those on which his government proposes to introduce bills or, if he is not sure of his ground, at least resolutions. Of course every government receives from its predecessor a legacy of open questions which it may be unable to shelve; others are taken up as a matter of routine politics; it is only in the case of the most brilliant achievement that a Prime Minister is in a position to impose measures about a political issue which he has created himself. In any case however the government's choice or lead, whether free or not, is the factor that dominates parliamentary activity. If a bill is brought in by the opposition, this means that it is offering battle: such a move is an attack which the government must either thwart by purloining the issue or else defeat. If a major bill that is not on the governmental menu is brought in by a group of the governmental party, this spells revolt and it is from this angle and not from the extra-tactical merits of the case that it is looked upon by the ministers. This even extends to the raising of a debate. Unless suggested or sanctioned by the government, these are symptoms of the government forces' getting out of hand. Finally, if a measure is carried by inter-party agreement, this means a drawn battle or a battle avoided on strategical grounds.[1]

5. The exceptions to this principle of governmental leadership in 'representative' assemblies only serve to show how realistic it is. They are of two kinds.

[1] Another highly significant piece of English technique may be mentioned in this connexion. A major bill is or was usually not proceeded with if the majority for it fell to a very low figure on the second reading. This practice first of all recognized an important limitation of the majority principle as actually applied in well-managed democracies: it would not be correct to say that in a democracy the minority is always compelled to surrender. But there is a second point. While the minority is not always compelled to yield to the majority on the particular issue under debate, it is practically always—there were exceptions even to this—compelled to yield to it on the question whether the cabinet is to stay in power. Such a vote on the second reading of a major government measure may be said to combine a vote of confidence with a vote for shelving a bill. If the contents of the bill were all that mattered there would hardly be any sense in voting for it if it is not to make the statute book. But if Parliament is primarily concerned with keeping the cabinet in office, then such tactics become at once understandable.

First, no leadership is absolute. Political leadership exerted according to the democratic method is even less so than are others because of that competitive element which is of the essence of democracy. Since theoretically every follower has the right of displacing his leader and since there are nearly always some followers who have a real chance of doing so, the private member and—if he feels that he could do with a bigger hat—the minister within and without the inner circle steers a middle course between an unconditional allegiance to the leader's standard and an unconditional raising of a standard of his own, balancing risks and chances with a nicety that is sometimes truly admirable.[1] The leader in turn responds by steering a middle course between insisting on discipline and allowing himself to be thwarted. He tempers pressure with more or less judicious concessions, frowns with compliments, punishments with benefits. This game results, according to the relative strength of individuals and their positions, in a very variable but in most cases considerable amount of freedom. In particular, groups that are strong enough to make their resentment felt yet not strong enough to make it profitable to include their protagonists and their programmes in the governmental arrangement will in general be allowed to have their way in minor questions or, at any rate, in questions which the Prime Minister can be induced to consider as of minor or only sectional importance. Thus, groups of followers or even individual members may occasionally have the opportunity of carrying bills of their own and still more indulgence will of course be extended to mere criticism or to failure to vote mechanically for every government measure. But we need only look at this in a practical spirit in order to realize, from the limits that are set to the use of this freedom, that it embodies not the principle of the working of a parliament but deviations from it.

Second, there are cases in which the political engine fails to absorb certain issues either because the high commands of the government's and the opposition's forces do not appreciate their political values or because these values are in fact doubtful.[2] Such issues may then

[1] One of the most instructive examples by which the above can be illustrated is afforded by the course taken by Joseph Chamberlain with respect to the Irish question in the 1880's. He finally outmanoeuvered Gladstone, but he started the campaign while officially an ardent adherent. And the case is exceptional only in the force and brilliance of the man. As every political captain knows, only mediocrities can be counted on for loyalty. That is why some of the greatest of those captains, Disraeli for instance, surrounded themselves by thoroughly second-rate men.

[2] An issue that has never been tried out is the typical instance of the first class. The typical reasons why a government and the shadow cabinet of the opposition may tacitly agree to leave an issue alone in spite of their realizing its potentialities are technical difficulty of handling it and the fear that it will cause sectional difficulties.

be taken up by outsiders who prefer making an independent bid for power to serving in the ranks of one of the existing parties. This of course is perfectly normal politics. But there is another possibility. A man may feel so strongly about a particular question that he may enter the political arena merely in order to have it solved in his way and without harbouring any wish to start in on a normal political career. This however is so unusual that it is difficult to find instances of first-rank importance of it. Perhaps Richard Cobden was one. It is true that instances of second-rank importance are more frequent, especially instances of the crusader type. But nobody will hold that they are anything but deviations from standard practice.

We may sum up as follows. In observing human societies we do not as a rule find it difficult to specify, as least in a rough common-sense manner, the various ends that the societies under study struggle to attain. These ends may be said to provide the rationale or meaning of corresponding individual activities. But it does not follow that the social meaning of a type of activity will necessarily provide the motive power, hence the explanation of the latter. If it does not, a theory that contents itself with an analysis of the social end or need to be served cannot be accepted as an adequate account of the activities that serve it. For instance, the reason why there is such a thing as economic activity is of course that people want to eat, to clothe themselves and so on. To provide the means to satisfy those wants is the social end or meaning of production. Nevertheless we all agree that this proposition would make a most unrealistic starting point for a theory of economic activity in commercial society and that we shall do much better if we start from propositions about profits. Similarly, the social meaning or function of parliamentary activity is no doubt to turn out legislation and, in part, administrative measures. But in order to understand how democratic politics serve this social end, we must start from the competitive struggle for power and office and realize that the social function is fulfilled, as it were, incidentally—in the same sense as production is incidental to the making of profits.

6. Finally, as to the role of the electorate, only one additional point need be mentioned. We have seen that the wishes of the members of a parliament are not the ultimate data of the process that produces government. A similar statement must be made concerning the electorate. Its choice—ideologically glorified into the Call from the People—does not flow from its initiative but is being shaped, and the shaping of it is an essential part of the democratic process. Voters do not decide issues. But neither do they pick their members of parliament from the eligible population with a perfectly

open mind. In all normal cases the initiative lies with the candidate who makes a bid for the office of member of parliament and such local leadership as that may imply. Voters confine themselves to accepting this bid in preference to others or refusing to accept it. Even most of those exceptional cases in which a man is *genuinely* drafted by the electors come into the same category for either of two reasons: naturally a man need not bid for leadership if he has acquired leadership already; or it may happen that a local leader who can control or influence the vote but is unable or unwilling to compete for election himself designates another man who then may seem to have been sought out by the voters acting on their own initiative.

But even as much of electoral initiative as acceptance of one of the competing candidates would in itself imply is further restricted by the existence of parties. A party is not, as classical doctrine (or Edmund Burke) would have us believe, a group of men who intend to promote public welfare 'upon some principle on which they are all agreed'. This rationalization is so dangerous because it is so tempting. For all parties will of course, at any given time, provide themselves with a stock of principles or planks and these principles or planks may be as characteristic of the party that adopts them and as important for its success as the brands of goods a department store sells are characteristic of it and important for its success. But the department store cannot be defined in terms of its brands and a party cannot be defined in terms of its principles. A party is a group whose members propose to act in concert in the competitive struggle for political power. If that were not so it would be impossible for different parties to adopt exactly or almost exactly the same programme. Yet this happens as everyone knows. Party and machine politicians are simply the response to the fact that the electoral mass is incapable of action other than a stampede, and they constitute an attempt to regulate political competition exactly similar to the corresponding practices of a trade association. The psycho-technics of party management and party advertising, slogans and marching tunes, are not accessories. They are of the essence of politics. So is the political boss.

X

JUSTICE AND THE COMMON GOOD

Brian Barry

I

Social Principles and the Democratic State, by S. I. Benn and R. S. Peters (George Allen & Unwin, London, 1959) is far more than a textbook; for the authors' object is not merely to say, 'Justice means this, equality means that, freedom means the other. Where they conflict you take your pick'. Their thesis is the daring one that all political arguments fit into a single pattern and that this pattern is identical with morality.

The authors reject any sociological definition of 'moral rule'. According to them, a rule is moral if and only if it is:

critically accepted by the individual in the light of certain criteria. The criteria can be summarized by saying that a rule should be considered in the light of the needs and interests of people likely to be affected by it with no partiality towards the claims of any of those whose needs and interests are at stake. (p. 56)

People have interests and needs which they put forward as claims. The criteria of impersonality and respect for persons are satisfied when claims are assessed on relevant grounds, and privileges excluded as a basis for allowing a claim. (p. 51)

I think the *inconvenience* of this definition is fairly clear: it follows from it, for example, that one can never talk about the moral rules of a group unless one has first ascertained whether everyone who acts on the rules and expects others to act on them has accepted them after an impartial consideration of their effects. The theoretical disadvantages of making stipulative restrictions on the expression 'moral rules' are very similar to the disadvantages (which the authors recognize) of calling only good laws 'laws'.

My main objection, however, is that no single scheme can be sufficient to cover all the arguments which even in liberal-democratic

From *Analysis*, Vol. 21 (Blackwell, 1960–61), pp. 86–90. Reprinted by permission of the author, *Analysis*, and Basil Blackwell.

communities would ordinarily be thought 'moral'. If Benn and Peters do succeed in interpreting their schema so as to fit any argument presented into it, this is at a cost of both misrepresenting most arguments and making the schema vacuous.

II

This must be so, I suggest, because when we are dealing with interests there are two conflicting principles at work: aggregative and distributive. They are both, it seems to me, independently operative in most men's minds; and where they give conflicting answers there is no higher principle to which the conflict can be referred.

Suppose, for example, that one can see no reason in terms of desert or need why science teachers should be paid more than others; but that one also believes that unless all the money available for raising pay goes to them the standard of science teaching will decline with grave results. Or again, suppose that one believes on the one hand that dropping two atomic bombs on Japan will cause less suffering than continuing the war with 'conventional' weapons, but that it is unjust to use weapons which rely on devastating civilian populations rather than military targets. In both cases we have a conflict between an aggregative result and a distributive principle. If these were all the relevant considerations (which in fact they are not) then how one decided would depend on how highly one ranked the two kinds of principle (moral philosophers can be divided according to which side they exaggerate at the expense of the other).

The point I wish to make is that 'impartiality' is no help here in providing a schema for decision. If it means 'everyone to count for one and nobody for more than one', this is satisfied by the result of aggregation, which may still be morally unacceptable to many people. If on the other hand one is to say, 'The arts teachers aren't given *enough* consideration by straight aggregation; they must be given some more', my objection is that the formula is now useless as a guide to decision. It merely gives us a thoroughly misleading way of justifying *ex post facto* whatever decision we may in fact reach.

III

There is still, however, one possible escape route for the authors' formula. This lies in emphasizing the bit about 'relevant grounds for treating people differently'. But this manoeuvre fails in one of two ways, depending on the construction of 'relevant'. If you say that what subject someone teaches is not a relevant criterion in determining his pay, you certainly get the answer that scientists ought not to be paid more. But this is too good a demonstration, for according to the authors, anyone who admits this and still says that science teachers ought to be paid more is not arguing morally; yet such a position seems to me perfectly reasonable. Some one who takes this view has chosen in favour of the education of children and against professional equity—surely a perfectly reputable thing to do. If on the other hand you say that what subject someone teaches is made relevant simply by the fact that science teachers are in shorter supply than others and paying them more will keep up educational standards, you are right back at a simple aggregationist position.

In fact the authors give some support to each interpretation. Thus, on p. 112, they say ' . . . it is up to whoever should make distinctions to justify the criteria in terms . . . ultimately of a balance of advantage to all concerned'. Phrases such as 'beneficent consequences' and 'beneficial results' occur in a similar context on pp. 169 and 170. This sounds like a straight aggregationist position: you show that something is just, or for the common good, by showing that it makes relevant distinctions, and these distinctions are relevant if they provide 'a balance of advantage to all concerned'. This form of argument is certainly used by the authors and I shall discuss an example in section IV.

Against this, they say on pp. 272–3:

> Two politicians may each say, with perfect sincerity, that he is seeking the public interest, or the common good, though one proposes to ex-propriate private capital and the other to defend it for the death. Does one of them have to be wrong . . . ? Is the disagreement about fact at all? It may be . . . but the probability is that this is less important than a disagreement on moral principle. One holds private capital to be an immoral thing in itself, the other that it represents the legitimate fruits of thrift, industry, and other economic virtues . . . . What then have the two politicians in common that enables them to appeal, with equal sincerity to 'the common good'? . . . (Each) is saying, in effect, that having considered the claims of *all* sections in a spirit of impartiality, the balance of advantage lies in the course he recommends.

Here it is quite clear that 'the balance of advantage' is not something obtainable by aggregation; it is simply a repetition of the procedural point that one must have considered all claims impartially. To say on this analysis that relevant distinctions are those based on a balance of advantage is to add nothing. 'We have to *decide* what is relevant' (p. 113).

My object in pointing out this inconsistency is not to score a cheap debating point but to substantiate my view that it is impossible to fit into one theory questions of distributive principle (the sort of thing the two politicians in the argument are disagreeing about) and aggregative ones (which phrases such as 'balance of advantage' would naturally be thought to refer to).

IV

In this section I shall apply the above analysis to two of the discussions of particular questions in the book to illustrate how the authors' insistence on trying to show all concepts as aspects of a single criterion leads them to distort characteristic forms of argument. In the first example, we see a straight question of distribution obscured by reference to an aggregative concept. On p. 272, the authors say:

... the government would have resented being told in 1957 that decontrolling rents was not for the common good. But the government clearly had to choose between the interests of the landlords and the interest of the tenants. Whether or not it chose rightly, it did little good to the tenants.

Now if it is correct that the issue is one where one side's losses are the other side's gains, I would suggest that the 'common good' is out of place. *Of course* the government would resent being told its action was *not* for the common good; but neither would it justify the measure by saying it was *for* the common good. The concept is out of place. If the government is willing to admit that it is simply transferring money from one set of pockets to another, it will say, for example, that control was unfair between owners of different forms of property, or between owner-occupiers and tenants, or that it was unjust between landlords and tenants; i.e., it would support a distributive change by distributive arguments. (More likely, of course, it would deny that only one side would be benefited, pointing to the benefits of a free market in producing a rational allocation of resources, and then it *could* talk about the common good; but I follow the authors' assumption for the sake of the argument.)

What I am trying to show is that it is not an *accident* that we have different concepts; they really do have different jobs. We have one set which point out various distributive comparisons, such as justice, fairness, equity, equality (that these all differ is not hard to show but it would take me out of my way here. One example: a lottery is fair if honestly run, but a lottery which distributed prizes *justly*, i.e., according to desert or need, would no longer be fair). And we have another set which point out the results of various methods of aggregation, such as 'public interest', 'common good' and 'general welfare' ('good' and 'interest' for example require one to include different ways in which people are affected). To say, as Benn and Peters do, that 'to seek the common good' means 'to try to act justly', is to make nonsense of the subtle and complex way in which we go about criticizing political programmes, in the pursuit of a tidy but barren theory.

My second example shows the same error operating in reverse. In chapters 4 and 5, the authors have an excellent study of the grounds on which one might justify various claims to income. Unfortunately, however, they are again hampered by their theoretical apparatus, for all claims, according to their general theory, must be established by being shown to be just. This works excellently for claims based on personal desert and need; but it does not work at all for arguments for property based on the advantage of having a group of politically independent or cultured citizens (pp. 167–70):

> If it were true that fortunes based on inheritable property were indispensable for an elite of this sort, and if such an elite were really so valuable, the property system would be justified by its beneficient consequences. (p. 169)

Now, this is fine; and the situation should in my view be summed up by saying that in this case justice would have to be qualified by utilitarian considerations.

But this course is not open to Benn and Peters. They have to say that the general advantage of property makes the amount of money your father had a relevant and therefore just ground for differences in income (pp. 169–70). This seems to me highly misleading. Although Hume used the expression 'rules of justice' to cover precisely such things as property rules, 'justice' is nowadays analytically tied to 'desert' and 'need', so that one could quite properly say that some of what Hume called 'rules of justice' were unjust. Again, we see how the attempt to reduce all arguments to one pattern forces Benn and Peters to assimilate quite different kinds of arguments to one another.

NOTES ON THE CONTRIBUTORS

JOHN PLAMENATZ is Chichele Professor of Social and Political Theory at Oxford and a Fellow of All Souls College. He was formerly a Fellow of Nuffield College. His *German Marxism and Russian Communism* was published in 1961, and *Man and Society*, in two volumes, in 1963.

P. H. PARTRIDGE teaches at the Australian National University, Canberra.

H. L. A. HART has been Professor of Jurisprudence in Oxford since 1952. Among his publications are *Causation in the Law* (1961), and *Law, Liberty, and Morality*, (1963).

STANLEY I. BENN, until recently Lecturer in Government at the University of Southampton, is now at the Australian National University, Canberra. He is the author, with R. S. Peters, of *Social Principles and the Democratic State* (1959).

R. S. PETERS is Professor of the Philosophy of Education in the University of London Institute of Education. Among his publications are *The Concept of Motivation* (1958), *Social Principles and the Democratic State* (with S. I. Benn, 1959), and *Ethics and Education* (1966).

PETER WINCH, formerly of the University College of Swansea, is now Professor of Philosophy at King's College, London; his *The Idea of a Social Science* was published in 1958.

BRIAN BARRY has been a Fellow of Nuffield College, Oxford, since 1966. His book *Political Argument* was published in 1965.

E. F. CARRITT, who died in 1963, was for many years a Fellow of University College, Oxford. His book *Ethical and Political Thinking* was published in 1947, and he wrote also on the philosophical problems of aesthetics.

SIR ISAIAH BERLIN is President of Wolton College, Oxford. He was Chichele Professor of Social and Political Theory at Oxford from 1957 to 1967. Among his publications are *The Hedgehog and the Fox* (1953), a study of Tolstoy, and *Karl Marx* (2nd. edn., 1956).

JOSEPH A. SCHUMPETER went to Harvard from his native Austria in 1932, and taught there for many years before his death in 1950. He published a number of widely influential works in the field of economics.

BIBLIOGRAPHY

(*not including material in this volume*)

I. General and Methodological

The best elementary introduction to political theory is J. D. Mabbott's *The State and the Citizen* (Hutchinson, London, 1948). Charles Vereker's *The Development of Political Theory* (Hutchinson, London, 1957) gives an overall survey of the historical development of the subject. S. I. Benn and R. S. Peters, in *Social Principles and the Democratic State* (Allen and Unwin, London, 1959), cover the main topics of political theory from the point of view of analytic philosophy. Arnold Brecht's massive *Political Theory* (Princeton U.P., Princeton, 1959) does the same thing in a more Teutonic and elaborately scholarly way.

G. H. Sabine's *History of Political Theory* (Harrap, London, 1937) deserves its reputation as a model text-book, being lucid, thorough and reliable to a very high degree. J. P. Plamenatz's *Man and Society* (Longmans, London, 1963) is confined to the major figures in the history of political thought but subjects their ideas to a full critical examination. Sheldon Wolin's *Politics and Vision* (Allen and Unwin, London, 1961) is more interpretative again and is as much concerned with the historical setting as with the logical cogency of political theories; a most impressively intelligent and original book.

A useful, if somewhat mechanically written, survey of methodological issues is *The Study of Political Theory* by Thomas P. Jenkin (Random House, New York, 1955). The relations between political philosophy and political science are thoroughly and penetratingly examined with a wealth of references in David Easton's *The Political System* (Knopf, New York, 1953). T. D. Weldon's *The Vocabulary of Politics* (Penguin Books, London, 1953) expresses the hostility of some analytic philosophers to political theory with the artless enthusiasm of a convert. At the opposite extreme is the defence of the traditional attitude, which takes political theory to be concerned to demonstrate the timeless, essential nature of the state, in Leo Strauss's *What is Political Philosophy* (Free Press, Glencoe, 1959). G. H. Sabine's 'What is political theory?' in the *Journal of Politics* (1939), and Isaiah Berlin's 'Does political theory still exist?', in *Philosophy, Politics and Society*, second series, ed. Laslett and Runciman (Blackwell, Oxford, 1962) are noteworthy brief general statements. Cf. also J. D. Mabbott, 'Political Concepts' in *Philosophy*, (1938); J. M. Cameron and T. D. Weldon, 'The Justification of Political Attitudes' in the *Proceedings of the Aristotelian Society*, Supplementary Volume (1955); H. B. Action 'Political Justification' in *Contemporary British Philosophy*, Third Series, ed. H. D. Lewis (Allen and Unwin, London, 1956).

R. M. MacIver's *The Web of Government* (Macmillan, New York, 1947) is a large, reflective survey of the field of political science. Robert A. Dahl's *Modern Political Analysis* (Prentice-Hall, New Jersey, 1963) is an elementary introduction to political science with a strong methodological emphasis. S. M. Lipset's *Political Man* (Doubleday, New York, 1960) is a notable example of political sociology.

II. State, law and morality

A definition of the political is developed in chapter 2 of Robert A. Dahl's *Modern Political Analysis* (Prentice-Hall, New Jersey, 1963). For sovereignty and related issues see S. I. Benn and R. S. Peters, *Social Principles and the Democratic State* (Allen and Unwin, London, 1959), chapters 11, 12 and 13; A. D. Lindsay's 'Sovereignty' in *Proceedings of the Aristotelian Society* (1923-4); W. J. Rees's 'The Theory of Sovereignty Restated' in *Mind* (1950) and in *Philosophy, Politics and Society*, first series, ed. Laslett (Blackwell, Oxford, 1956).

A classical and much-discussed definition of law is to be found in H. Kelsen's *General Theory of Law and the State* (Harvard 1945). There is a most delicate and penetrating discussion of the subject in H. L. A. Hart's *The Concept of Law* (Clarendon Press, Oxford, 1961). See also Benn and Peters, op. cit., chapter 3.

On rights in general and natural rights in particular see E. F. Carritt, *Morals and Politics* (Clarendon Press, Oxford, 1935), chapter 13, and also his *Ethical and Political Thinking* (Clarendon Press, Oxford, 1947); J. P. Plamenatz, *Consent, Freedom and Political Obligation* (Clarendon Press, Oxford, 1938); A. C. Ewing, 'The Rights of the Individual against the State' in *Revue Internationale de Philosophie* (1948), and in chapter 2 of his *Individual, State and World Government* (Macmillan, New York, 1947); M. Macdonald, 'Natural Rights', in *Proceedings of the Aristotelian Society* (1946-7), and in *Philosophy, Politics and Society*, first series, ed. Laslett (Blackwell, Oxford, 1956); J. D. Mabbott *The State and the Citizen* (Hutchinson, London, 1948), part B; A. P. d'Entrèves *Natural Law* (Hutchinson, London, 1951); J. P. Plamenatz and H. B. Acton, 'Rights', in *Proceedings of the Aristotelian Society*, Supplementary Volume (1950); A. I. Melden and W. K. Frankena,

'Human Rights', in *Proceedings of the American Philosophical Association, Eastern Division*, volume 1 (1952); S. M. Brown and W. K. Frankena, in *Philosophical Review* (1955) (commenting on chapter 3 of this anthology, Hart's 'Are There Any Natural Rights?'); Benn and Peters, op. cit., chapter 4; R. B. Brandt, *Ethical Theory* (Prentice-Hall, New Jersey, 1959) chapter 17; J. Hospers, *Human Conduct* (Harcourt Brace, New York, 1961), chapter 19.

III. Political Obligation

The first chapter of J. P. Plamenatz's *Consent, Freedom and Political Obligation* (Clarendon Press, Oxford, 1938) on consent is an excellent example of the clarificatory power of philosphical analysis in the field of political ideas. Chapter 7 of the same book deals with political obligation. Theories of obligation are discussed in E. F. Carritt's *Morals and Politics* (Clarendon Press, Oxford, 1935), chapter 14, and in his *Ethical and Political Thinking* (Clarendon Press, Oxford, 1947), part II, chapter 14. Benn and Peters, op. cit., chapter 14, give a brief and convenient survey of different grounds of political obligation.

The social contract theory is reinterpreted in a somewhat far-fetched way in H. D. Lewis's 'Is there a Social Contract?' in *Philosophy* (1940). A survey of the history of the contract theory from its first beginnings in Greek thought is given in J. W. Gough, *The Social Contract* (Clarendon Press, Oxford, 1936).

Discussions of the general will theory are more numerous. See H. D. Lewis 'Natural Rights and the General Will' in *Mind* (1937); J. P. Plamenatz, *Constant, Freedom and Political Obligation* (Clarendon Press, Oxford, 1938) chapters 2 and 3; J. D. Mabbott, *The State and The Citizen* (Hutchinson, London, 1948), part D; G. R. G. Mure, 'The Organic State' in *Philosophy* (1949); B. Mayo, 'Is there a case for the general will?', in *Philosophy* (1951), and in *Philosophy, Politics and Society*, first series, ed. Laslett (Blackwell, Oxford, 1956); B. Blanshard, *Reason and Goodness* (Allen and Unwin, London, 1961), chapter 14.

Traditionalism is examined in H. B. Action, 'Tradition and some other forms of order', in *Proceedings of the Aristotelian Society* (1952–3), and supported in M. Oakeshott, *Rationalism in Politics* (Methuen, London, 1962).

IV. The ends of government

J. R. Pennock's *Liberal Democracy* (Rinehart, New York, 1950) is a good general survey of liberal ideals, from the point of view of both meaning and justification, and contains a most valuable bibliography.

As a counterpoise mention may be made of a piece of writing much older than any other included here, J. F. Stephen's *Liberty, Equality, Fraternity* (Smith Elder, London, 1873), both on account of its analytic clarity and the trenchancy of its opinions. B. M. Barry, *Political Argument* (Routledge, London, 1965) is a recent work of comparable scope, much greater philosophical technicality and utterly different opinions.

Liberty is defined in chapter 5 and justified in chapter 6 of J. P. Plamenatz, *Consent, Freedom and Political Obligation* (Clarendon Press, Oxford, 1938) with the author's characteristic clarity and definiteness. C. I. Lewis's 'The Meaning of Liberty', in *Revue Internationale de Philosophie* (1948), is brief but all-embracing. See also Benn and Peters, op. cit., chapter 10.

On democracy see R. A. Dahl, *Preface to Democratic Theory* (Chicago U. P., 1961); Benn and Peters, op. cit., chapter 15; J. Hospers, *Human Conduct* (Harcourt Brace, New York, 1961) chapter 18; R. Wollheim, 'A Paradox in the Theory of Democracy', in *Philosophy, Politics and Society*, second series, ed. Laslett and Runciman (Blackwell, Oxford, 1962); C. B. Macpherson, *The Real World of Democracy* (Clarendon Press, Oxford, 1966).

On justice and equality see H. Spiegelberg in *Philosophical Review* (1944); D. D. Raphael, 'Equality and Equity', in *Philosophy* (1946), and his 'Justice and Liberty' in *Proceedings of the Aristotelian Society* (1950–51). I. Berlin and R. Wollheim, 'Equality', in *Proceedings of the Aristotelian Society*, Supplementary Volume, (1955); R. B. Brandt, *Ethical Theory* (Prentice-Hall, New Jersey, 1959), chapter 16; J. Rawls, 'Justice as fairness', in *Philosophical Review* (1958); J. Hospers, *Human Conduct* (Harcourt Brace, New York, 1961), chapters 20–22; Benn and Peters, op. cit., chapters 5 and 6; B. A. O. Williams, 'The idea of equality' in *Philosophy, Politics and Society*, second series, ed. Laslett and Runciman (Blackwell, Oxford, 1962).

INDEX OF NAMES

(not including authors mentioned only in the Bibliography)